Teaching Writing

A Developmental, Systematic, Cooperative Approach for Learning to Write and Writing to Learn

Fifth Edition
Revised and Expanded
K-12

by

Dr. Evelyn Rothstein
Dr. Diane Gess

Editorial Consultant
Charles Nix

THE WRITE TRACK™
Educational Consultants and Publishers

16 Charnwood Drive   P.O. Box 875   Suffern, N.Y. 10901
Tel. 914-368-2795   FAX 914-357-5327
Toll-Free 800-845-8402 (Outside of New York State)

ERA/CCR Corp.
The Write Track™ Company
P.O. Box 875
Suffern, New York 10901
(914) 368-2795
800-845-8402
(outside New York State)

Fifth Edition 1992
Reprinted 1995

Printed in the United States of America
ISBN 0-9-913935-39-5

LIBRARY OF CONGRESS # 91-75991

CONTENTS

TEACHING WRITING

Writing/Editing - A Merged Process Using WRITE TRACK™ Strategies

Questions and Procedures

Starters and Improvers

A Process to Product Model

The Writer's Questions

1. To whom am I writing?
2. How long will it be?
3. What do I want to say?
4. How do I want to say it?
5. What is my plan for writing?
6. Can I say it in a better way?
7. Can I add anything to my writing?
8. Does my writing make sense?
9. Is my writing product ready for my audience?

The Starters

Words
Sentences
WH-Questions
Frames
Blueprints, outlines, plans

The Improvers

Additions
Deletions
Substitutions
Rearrangements

The Writer's Procedures

1. Identifying the purpose of writing or audience to be addressed

2. Gathering pertinent material or experiences

3. Planning and organizing the material or experiences

4. Composing - or writing a draft

5. Improving the draft through revisions

6. Rewriting the final product or "publishing"

The Levels of Editing

Drafting
Proofreading
Editing
Revising
Publishing

The Levels of Editors

Self
Peer
"Top"

A NOTE ABOUT OUR FIFTH EDITION ON TEACHING WRITING

In 1987 we wrote our fourth edition of *TEACHING WRITING*. At that time we felt we had already learned much about writing. We knew about pre-writing and drafting and about revising and sharing and about editing and publishing. We firmly believed (and still do) that writing must be taught systematically and developmentally from kindergarten through grade twelve and then some. We advocated (and still do) the teaching of specific strategies and urged that students practice these strategies in much the way musicians practice scales and notes and small pieces in preparation for playing concertos and symphonies.

By 1987 we had traveled across the country to hundreds of school districts, talking with coordinators and administrators and training teachers at every level and in every discipline. We felt confident about what we had learned about writing, and we were fully committed to making writing an essential component of the total curriculum. What we didn't know was how much more we would continue to learn — not just about the teaching of writing, but about how teaching writing changes the way teachers teach and students learn. What we really found out is that teaching writing is a way of teaching and that learning to write is a way of learning.

Since 1987, as we expanded our repertory of strategies and continued to work in more schools and with more teachers, we watched "small miracles." Students once considered poor readers or underachievers began to seem "smart" through their writings. Students with poor self-images, because of low grades and repeated failures, began to think of themselves as writers and authors and communicators and started to recognize their own self-worth. Teachers who were afraid to teach writing and guiltily gave their students daily doses of ditto sheets emerged as confident teachers of writing, converted to the belief that, if they knew **HOW** to teach writing, they could indeed teach writing.

We have become totally convinced that writing is a powerful magnet for learning. By learning to write — and writing to learn — students start to

. think deeply and critically
. express ideas, values, beliefs, feelings
. develop high-level literacy skills
. value themselves as academically capable

Furthermore, by teaching writing, teachers

- help students actively participate in learning
- engage their students in cooperative and collaborative activities
- help students to narrate, persuade, and explain through organized, sequential, and elaborated responses rather than through simplistic, rote, one-word answers
- communicate personally with each student who has found "something to say" through the written word

We have greatly expanded our manual as a result of our own new insights. We've added more about writing and thinking; we've included activities for cooperative learning; we've put in many more suggestions for writing in every subject; we've coordinated writing with reading to reflect a true whole language perspective. If you've found our fourth edition helpful, we're sure you will be delighted with this new edition. If you're using our manual for the first time, we believe it will add a valuable dimension to your school or classroom. We are convinced that **TEACHING WRITING** is **EXEMPLARY TEACHING,** and we hope our fifth edition provides you with the ideas, suggestions, strategies, and techniques to make your students good writers and good learners, capable of functioning successfully in a literate society.

A PERSONAL NOTE ABOUT THIS MANUAL
by Evelyn Rothstein

For many years I considered myself a teacher of reading. I found this to be a most comfortable teaching situation because it meant I never had to teach writing. Teaching writing was, from my perspective, the job of other teachers — those who taught in the classroom or those who taught English. Of course, from time to time, I assigned writing activities to my students; that is, I asked them or told them to write. Then I corrected their papers. I told them, in red ink, that they had "awkward sentences," "run-ons," "fragments," and "lack of organization." When I found myself completely overwhelmed by their errors, I resorted to the comment which has terrified students for generations. In the upper left-hand corner I wrote:

SEE ME!

A number of years ago, when universities and colleges began to complain about their students' inability to write and when boards of education began to speak of the need for teaching writing, I knew that I could no longer be just a reading teacher. The struggle to write for most students was often greater than the struggle to read. I knew the panic when I told my students to "write a composition about . . . ." First, they bombarded me with questions:

How long should it be?

Does spelling count?

What should I write about?

Will I have to write it over again?

Then there was my own panic:

Will I stifle their creativity if I correct their papers?

What do I mark? Grammar or content?

Do I really want to give up my weekend correcting reluctantly written, unedited pieces of writing?

I knew I had to learn how to teach my students to write and I knew that I had to teach them how to edit their own writing. I also had to be able to answer their questions. They needed to know from me, their teacher/editor, how long I wanted their compositions to be. They needed to know when spelling counts and when, or if, a piece of writing gets rewritten.

They needed to know how to start and how to continue. And above all, they needed my teaching expertise because writing requires deep thinking, language proficiency, and patience.

Fortunately, teachers everywhere have been concerned about the problem of teaching students to write. Almost magically, workshops and programs have emerged. Teachers have attended programs in the San Francisco Bay Area where they have practiced their own writing so that they, in turn, could teach their students. Other teachers have heard about the Individual Language Arts Program (Weehawken) which stresses sequential skills. Donald Graves, Lucy Calkins, and Nancie Atwell have observed children writing in the classroom and have offered new and exciting insights on the writing process.

This manual is the result of my teaching writing for a relatively short time out of my thirty years of teaching. I have come to love teaching students to write, not because writing has become easy or magical, but because I think I have learned how to answer my students' questions and ease their anxieties. From the Bay Area and Weehawken Programs, from Donald Graves and other authorities, and out of my own childhood fear of writing, I have found out that:

. I can start with a "plain" sentence if I don't have an "interesting" sentence.
. I know something about something and can write about that something.
. I start with a list of words about what I know and can write from that list of words.
. I will make mistakes when I write — lots of mistakes.
. But I will get help because I know that all writers need help.
. I can be a creative writer because all writing involves creativity. From my words I am creating sentences, ideas, concepts, communication.

I hope this manual helps you help your students to write. Teach them slowly, step-by-step. Let them know that writing takes time and practice. Answer their questions and listen to what they have written. Show them how. Enjoy!

TEACHING WRITING — AN IDEA WHOSE TIME HAS COME

School districts across the country are finally recognizing the need to TEACH their students to write. For over two decades we have heard representatives of colleges and universities complain about the abysmal writing of their entering freshmen. We have seen corporations of all sizes institute costly programs to "retrain" or even "train" both management and secretarial staff to write clear, concise, and understandable English. Why do so many people — students and professionals — not know how to write?

The Decline of Teaching Writing

We believe that the absence or the avoidance of the teaching of writing has its roots in the educational changes which occurred over a period of time: the introduction of the workbook as an appendage to the basal reader; the college methods courses which vaguely referred to "creative" writing, possibly in contrast to "non-creative" writing; and the commonly accepted belief that the teaching of grammar and spelling, by itself, turns students into good writers.

Writing — A Victim of the Workbook and the Short Answer

When we began teaching some thirty years ago, our students were provided with the latest innovation — two books for learning to read: a reader and a workbook. The reader, obviously, was for reading stories, while the workbook was its companion for teaching students the "skills" of reading. In the workbook were the activities that would ask children to find "the main idea." The students would read a brief selection in this soft covered book and then be directed to find one main idea, marked either a, b, c, or d. Two of the answers were clearly ridiculous; one was almost right; and one, of course, was "absolutely" right.

Students who may have thought that there were several main ideas or who had formulated their own concepts of the story were clearly wrong. And, of course, no child ever had to write out the main idea, since the workbook already contained the answer; it was only a matter of circling or underlining the best, and often the only, choice.

Similarly, students using the workbook could easily put a story into sequence. Instead of retelling the story from understanding or memory, the child would merely reorder a set of numbers so that 4, 8, 5, 3, 7, 6, 2, 1 became 1, 2, 3, 4, and so forth. Even expressing opinions about the story could be stated as a, b, c, d, as in the following example:

I liked the clown when he

    a) jumped in the pool

    b) rode his bike

    c) ate an apple

    d) got out of the car

So as beginning teachers, and for many years after, we participated in the "conspiracy of the workbook" which unequivocally stated to students that written responses can be reduced to circles, X's, and underlining. Why, indeed, should anyone have to write an opinion or full-length answer when everything was contained in the workbook?

We hadn't fully grasped how unimportant writing had become in our classrooms until we visited several British infant schools in 1969. For the first time we observed young children — 6, 7, 8 years old — writing lengthy stories, articles, and reports on sheets of newsprint. Children were writing, in their own words, the stories of *Hansel and Gretel* and *Cinderella;* they were describing a Viking ship; they were keeping journals on the life and habits of a gerbil.

When we admired the brilliance and precocity of these British "infants," as they're called, a modest headmaster told us that this brilliance came about because Britain was poorer than the United States. "What does being poor have to do with writing ability?" we naively asked. And Peter Smith, the astute headmaster, explained that poverty (of the schools) resulted in the absence of workbooks and ditto masters. British children, therefore, had to write out their responses. If the British schools, he said, could afford duplicating machines, then the writing skills of British children would decline as they had among American children.

Writing — A Victim of Creativity

Of course, there is never one simple cause for the decline or lack of development of a major subject area. So while the introduction of the workbook was one nail in the coffin of writing, a second nail was the use of the modifier "creative" that preceded the word "writing." When we took our teaching methods courses, and again through the ensuing years, education faculty referred to creative writing as if there were an opposite type called "non-creative."

In creative writing, we were told, children would be free to express themselves without the constraints of rules or structure. Their imaginations would not be inhibited and they could write as they pleased. Structure should be imposed only for the creation of the haiku or the diamante or for comparing Mazzini with Garibaldi or for contrasting the French Revolution with the American Revolution. Students merely had to use their "creative, imaginary skills" — which indeed they did, much to the shock and dismay of their social studies teachers.

Furthermore, because "creative writing" suggested a somewhat *lassez-faire* approach, writing became a casual subject, taught only casually — and often during that part of the day when children had completed their more "substantial" language arts subjects, such as reading, spelling, and grammar. In our own classrooms, we remember trying to fit in creative writing on Thursday afternoon from one to one-thirty, just before gym and dismissal.

Writing — A Victim of Spelling and Grammar

As students, and later as teachers, we were taught to believe that those who could spell perfectly and underline correctly the subject once and the predicate twice would automatically know how to write. Obedient children diligently studied their spelling words and memorized the grammar rules and possibly got a 100 percent on the Friday test. Then Tuesday would be composition time. Yet, somehow nothing about spelling and grammar seemed to work for the assignment that said, "Write 250 words about the Pilgrims' search for religious freedom in Massachusetts Bay Colony."

What was wrong? The answer is that no other school subject is as misunderstood as writing. No math teacher, for example, would ask students to study physics in order to learn multiplication. No physical education teacher would tell students to know all the parts of the muscle, but never practice using the muscles themselves for developing strength. Yet we as teachers of reading, language arts, and English were falsely led to believe that knowing some of the ingredients of writing, such as spelling and grammar, were sufficient for knowing how to analyze, interpret, explain, compare, narrate, and describe. Worse yet, we often asked students to "dash off" these written forms in forty minutes or less!

Further deceptions were practiced upon both teacher and student. Teachers were led to believe that we were the "co-authors" of our students' writing. A "good, conscientious teacher" was expected to read and correct and alter every student's piece of writing — in essence, to be in partnership with each student and contribute to the writing. Unfortunately, one teacher with thirty, or ninety, students would eventually suffer both eyestrain and mental fatigue and usually ended up writing meaningless abbreviations like *awk., punc., org.,* or *sp.* which rarely helped the student improve his paper.

We were led to believe that we needn't give a student too much information about the assignment itself. For example, when a student asked, "How long should this writing be?" we too often replied, "As long as you want it to be," as if any student wanted the paper to be long. Or we said, "Till you've covered the subject," as if any of us wanted a student to write everything about the Panama Canal. Students who asked, "Pen or pencil?" "Script or cursive?" and "Will this count?" were dismissed as procrastinators and interrupters. As teachers we were rarely told that unless the student knows what the editor or assigner wants and expects, he or she cannot successfully write.

We believe that we as teachers and teacher trainers were led astray. We thought if we teach reading skills from a workbook, if we teach spelling and grammar, and if we say "use your imagination," our students would figure out how to write stories and essays. We thought that they, our students, would write and we, their teachers, would edit, only to find that we became excellent editors and they, the students, rarely became good writers.

Writer

Writer whose occupation or profession is writing.
Reads only good literature.
Inventive with story characters and story plots.
Thoroughly researches the subject she writes about.
Enthusiasm motivates a writer's imagination.
Rewrites boring materials and makes them exciting to read.

Leticia   - Gr. 4

Writing, according to the eminent linguist Dr. Robert Allen, is our speech written down and heavily edited. It is, in fact, our most fluent speech, organized and edited so that our readers or audience can follow what we are saying and know exactly what we want to say. These three concepts — fluent, organized, and edited — are the foundations of writing. To teach writing means to teach students systems for becoming fluent and for using the organizing schemes which are inherent in every written piece from haiku to personal expression to research. We define writing, therefore, as the formula:

$$W = F + O$$

WRITING = FLUENCY + ORGANIZATION

Fluency refers to:

. producing a variety of ideas, responses, solutions, or questions

. using varied and precise words for expressing ideas

. being able to express the many possibilities and alternative solutions to a problem

Organization refers to:

. planning strategies for gathering information

. arranging ideas so that "someone else" can follow the "arrangement"

. supporting generalizations with clearly stated details

. keeping track of what has gone before and what is to come next

We also recognize that all good writing is creative. It is the synthesis of raw words in creating related structures that unite a writer with a reader. These structural formats make every piece of writing genre-based, whether it be a business letter or a novel. We cannot merely say to students, "Write about a pet," and expect anything worthwhile to emerge. The student who is given such an assignment can only guess as to what we want — a personal statement, a description, a short story, a poem. What does "write about" mean?

Furthermore, we must accept that writing, at least in school, generally emanates from assignments and less frequently from personal desire. The purpose of these assignments is (or should be) to help students express feelings, beliefs, humor, or fantasy, or to explain what they know or have learned. No writing should be desultory since no one purposely writes without concern for the reader. Somewhat facetiously we have asked teachers in our workshops to raise their hands if they relax on the weekend by "just writing." Few hands go up.

What Should Students Know About Writing?

At a very early age — in nursery school or kindergarten — children know or believe they can write. The preschool child makes a series of scribbles, goes to a parent, and asks, "Mommy, what does this say?" The young child in a literate environment learns that writing is different from speaking. Writing goes to a specific person (audience), it tells about a specific event or events, and it begins and ends. As children hear stories, they also begin to realize that stories sound different from speech. Stories have words such as *once upon a time* and *many years ago*. They have special words such as *monsters, witches, dragons, princesses,* and *happily ever after*.

Around age six, most children have observed that a story is an organized way of relating a series of events. Yet we make children almost unlearn this idea when we withhold structures or schemes for writing or give them the impression that how we speak is how we write. We must begin teaching writing by showing our students the structures of writing and having them practice these structures. Good writing emerges when the creator learns the craft, thoroughly and deeply, and gradually hones that craft until there is a work of art.

The purpose of this book is to help you add some new approaches to teaching your students to write — approaches that we, Diane and Evelyn, have found outstandingly successful in classrooms all across the country both in overcrowded inner city schools and in sparse rural places. We think we have been successful because we have provided students with explanation, modeling, guided practice, feedback, and constant empathy and encouragement. Writing is not easy; it takes a lot of energy, motivation, and determination, but the results are magnificent. They are magnificent because you will have, in your hands and for all to see, the charm, the humor, the emotions, and the message in the voices of your students.

> 9-13-   Lorne ·
> President Bush's Message.
> There's a lot of people who like to
> take drugs and President Bush told
> everyone, Do not take drugs. I repeat
> Do not take drugs because it can
> kill you. If somebody cames up to
> you and asks do you want some drugs—just
> say no to drugs and say no I do
> not take drugs.

WRITING — AN ALTERNATIVE TO SPEAKING

WRITING AS COMMUNICATION

Writing can be defined as a communication system which requires finding the words to express our thoughts, putting those words on paper, and then revising, editing, or improving what we have written so that it "sounds like writing." Writing, of course, springs from the spoken language and derives its nuturing from the oral traditions which are universal among all people. There are, however, several factors that distinguish speech from writing. Writing requires deliberation and planning, while speech is generally spontaneous in nature, stimulated by the events of the moment. The writer imagines the audience; the speaker knows who is listening.

And while the child learns to speak at a very early age and with virtually little effort, the writer must learn very specific skills in order to transfer what he or she wants to say into what he or she wants to write. Furthermore, the writer must think ahead or plan, which means having a defined organizational theme or framework that marks a beginning and an end.

The writer gathers, combines, organizes, and reorganizes. She begins by drawing from experiences or knowledge and thinks about what she would like to say about these experiences. Then she must find the vocabulary and grammatical structures which are appropriate for saying what she wants to say in writing. She must organize the writing so that one idea follows another and must make it conform to conversational structures. This means the words have to be spelled without error, the sentences must be punctuated, and the ideas must be grouped into paragraphs.

Writing is an alternative to speaking. It is the alternative used when we want to make or preserve a record of what we are saying. We use it when we want to communicate to an audience larger than one we could reach by speaking, or when (as in school) we have to "prove" our knowledge or understanding of particular subject matter or material. Writing permits us to express ourselves in modes or language styles which differ from speech. We search for just the right word or phrase, the most descriptive adjectives, the precise term. We feel intuitively that if we commit our words to writing they should be our "better" words or the words of the writer.

As a form of communication, writing becomes shared, and the student learning to write must have the experience of sharing. It is an experience which can begin with only one person, someone whom the writer trusts, and who will not be too harsh or judgemental of early awkwardness or clumsiness in committing words to print. Moving beyond the one-person audience, the writer may seek a group of peers who merely listen and comment. Or the writer may need a mentor or teacher who can suggest what is needed and assist in the process of improvement — adding, deleting, substituting, and moving words, phrases, sentences.

Finally, the writing is ready for a wider audience. It is produced or reproduced for others to read in a newsletter or newspaper, on a bulletin board, or in other "published" form. The writing no longer belongs only to the writer; it reaches out to others. Through this process the student writer follows in the footsteps of all those who have already learned how a writer writes. He or she gathers ideas, writes a draft, shares it, improves it, rewrites it, and shares it again.

WRITING: A CREATIVE ACT

We want to emphasize that there is no distinction between "creative" writing, for example, and "other" writing. All writing is creative because it involves the generating of ideas, which are expressed through words. A student can write a creative biography, a creative essay, and a creative short story. What the writer must deal with is not creativity, but the variations in style which each written form requires and the differences between spoken and written language.

With all written expression viewed as creative, each form or genre has its own value. Each student, therefore, must have the opportunity, through instruction, to write a variety of genres that include the following:

lists	stories
labels and captions	directions
messages	information
dialogues	opinions
diaries or logs	suggestions
letters	advertisements

Short, varied, genre-based pieces, which are shared, revised, and shared again, will develop the students' skills of fluency and organization.

WRITING AS THINKING

To write is to imagine, decide, compare, classify, sequence, organize, analyze, synthesize, and evaluate — all of which are defined as thinking skills or processes and which cause writing to be the most difficult aspect of communication. Certainly, writing requires great mental energy, especially when compared with speaking.

What is thinking and how does it relate to writing? Thinking is a deliberate act that requires decision-making and output. We can get a better understanding of thinking by comparing reading with writing. In reading, the reader must mainly interpret someone else's output, a somewhat passive thinking skill, while writing requires the writer to produce or "put out" words in an arrangement that makes sense to the reader. From the moment the writer begins to write, she/he must keep producing until the product is completed. But merely "outputting" words is not sufficient. As words tumble through the writer's mind, she must continuously make decisions — which words do I keep? which do I discard? which belong with which?

These two aspects of writing — decision-making and output — while covering only two aspects of thinking, tap into other thinking processes. Output requires knowledge of subject or knowing what you want to say. But this knowledge cannot simply be reported out as in a short-answer test. It must be selected or narrowed. Output requires the writer to hold a two-way conversation — the writer with the listener or reader. Thus the writer's output is determined by the writer's ability to imagine what the reader expects to hear or wants to know.

Output in writing also demands that the writer shift language codes. As we write this segment to you, our unknown audience, we must think of the appropriate words, sentence structure, and writing conventions that will make our message clear. Output, therefore, comes about through imagining, selecting, categorizing, and organizing.

These last two actions — categorizing and organizing — comprise the decision-making aspect of writing, illustrated in the following example. Suppose you have to rewrite *Little Red Riding Hood* in your own words. To fulfill this task, you must actively decide:

. how much you recall of the story

. how you should begin — "once upon a time," "long ago"

. whether to be serious or humorous

. whether to "give the facts" or elaborate upon the meaning of the story

Until you decide, you cannot produce.

By conceiving of thinking as output and decision-making, and by developing your students' skills in these areas, you can enhance your students' writing ability. A student's output occurs when she develops the skills of brainstorming, expansion, and substitution. Decision-making skills develop through categorizing, classifying, rearranging, outlining, analyzing, synthesizing, and evaluating.

We believe that the writing strategies emphasized in subsequent chapters will integrate thinking and writing processes so that your students will learn how to make appropriate decisions about length, style, language, clarity, and organization — the requisites for every piece of writing.

WRITING AS INTELLIGENT BEHAVIOR

In a literate society we expect everyone to know how to read; but we expect only those who are "intelligent" to known how to write. That is, we think of "writers" as the intellectual elite of our society, and take for granted that a much wider range of the population will read. Perhaps there is truth in this perception, but of greater importance to those of us who teach is to understand why this perception exists.

We might begin by looking at ten of Arthur L. Costa's "Dozen Characteristics of Intelligent Human Behavior"(1985). By listing these characteristics and relating them to what a writer must do or know, we can quickly see why those who write are intelligent and why those who are intelligent are likely to write. Let's examine the list below:

CHARACTERISTICS OF INTELLIGENT BEHAVIOR	CHARACTERISTICS OF WRITING
Persistence and Perseverance	Seeing a piece through from inception through publication
Deliberation and Patience	Planning, reflecting, revising, editing
Listening to Others/Showing Empathy	Sharing ideas; building on ideas of others; expressing alternate points of view; collaborating
Flexibility	Expressing more than a single answer; using words in a variety of ways; accepting editorial criticism and changes
Metacognition/Self-Awareness	Conscious knowledge of one's sources of information; awareness of problem-solving approaches

Accuracy/Precision	Concern with exactness and clarity; alertness to grammatical and mechanical conventions
Questioning and Problem Posing	Raising issues; identifying problems; seeking solutions
Drawing Upon Past Knowledge	Using what is known to expand to new ideas; relating past experiences to new experiences
Using the Senses	Using a variety of modalities to express ideas; considering both the common and the uncommon; observing and recording
Inquisitiveness/Wonderment/Curiosity	Playing with language; saying the outrageous; searching for the new, the old, the different

CENTER FOR LEARNING THROUGH WRITING
CRESTVIEW ELEMENTARY SCHOOL

NAME: Nichole

If I had been in the earthquake in San Francisco, I would have been very scared. Many lives were affected, and many homes were destroyed. Also many loved ones were lost with out a trace. The people that survived have to live in tents for the time being. There also was a survivor who was found under a bridge, but he was lucky to be alive.

EARTH-QUAKE
10/17/89
SAN FRANCISCO
BAY AREA

THINKING AND WRITING
A WRITE TRACK PARTNERSHIP

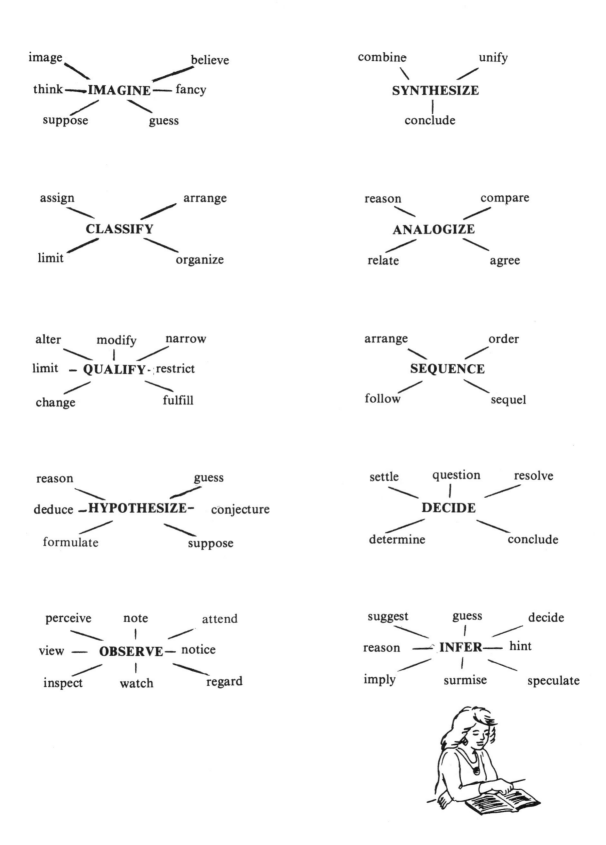

image   believe
think —**IMAGINE**— fancy
    suppose   guess

combine   unify
    SYNTHESIZE
    conclude

assign   arrange
    CLASSIFY
limit   organize

reason   compare
    ANALOGIZE
    relate   agree

alter   modify   narrow
limit – **QUALIFY** - restrict
    change   fulfill

arrange   order
    SEQUENCE
follow   sequel

reason   guess
deduce –**HYPOTHESIZE**–   conjecture
    formulate   suppose

settle   question   resolve
    DECIDE
    determine   conclude

perceive   note   attend
view — **OBSERVE** - notice
    inspect   watch   regard

suggest   guess   decide
reason — **INFER** — hint
    imply   surmise   speculate

WRITING/EDITING — A MERGED PROCESS

Young children are often told by their parents that the stories in books are "talk written down." Yet when children dictate or write their own stories, they are often disappointed to find that their own "talk written down" is different from the stories they have heard in books. Indeed, the stories in books rarely sound like "talk." In fact, any teacher who has attempted to record a student's story from dictation finds that she is often compelled to edit or to resist editing. Writing is not so much talk written down as it is an approximate representation of talk (speech) or, as stated before, edited speech.

In order to write, therefore, we must not only have something to say, but we must be able to "re-say" it. In other words (to borrow a phrase from speech), we frequently restate and replace words that are different from those which were first on our tongues. Rarely, if ever, does the writer have the privilege or ease of retaining the original words of the "first copy." Because writing is edited speech, and because the student needs to be aware of this concept, the teaching of writing has to become a joint enterprise with the teaching of editing. This does not mean that the child cannot ever write freely without constraints of grammar, punctuation, or spelling, but it does mean that such "free writing" will eventually be subject to the conventions of written language or the "sharp pencil" of some editor/teacher.

Consequently, from the beginning of instruction, the student must view herself as wearing two hats — the writer's and the editor's. This view of oneself as writer/editor emerges with the teacher's use and development of four key concepts relating to the writing/editing process:

DRAFT
REVISE
EDIT
PUBLISH

DRAFTING — Drafting is the first working copy and any subsequent copies which precede the final copy. Most writing, with the possible exception of informal letters and messages, begins with a draft. By beginning with a draft, the student realizes that there will be revising and possible changes. There may even be a second draft. Second drafts are often necessary before a piece of writing is ready for final editing and publication.

REVISING — This stage implies changes in ideas and organization. Changes or revisions may be made by adding or deleting words or phrases, moving sentences, changing paragraphs, or reorganizing the overall structure. The term "revise" can be used interchangeably with "improve," although "improve" may also refer to a general upgrading of vocabulary and style. In the revising stage, emphasis is upon strengthening the message or the ideas.

EDITING — The distinction between revising and editing is that editing generally refers to all phases of correction and change made before final copy. It can include changes in sentence structure, content, grammar, punctuation, and organization. In the editing stage, emphasis shifts to using the accepted conventions of writing.

PUBLISHING — For the student, publishing means going to "final copy." It is the culmination of the writing process. In the classroom, publication involves the author and the editor in reviewing the second draft (or an excellent first draft) for future improvement or revision and the development of an esthetic format. Not all writing needs to go to publication. The decision can be made by the student and teacher based on a set of criteria such as whether the writing will be displayed, reproduced for the class or school, or given to a parent, friend, or others.

WRITING THE DRAFT

After there has been motivation and planning for writing (gathering and tentatively organizing ideas), the student writes the draft, using DRAFT FORMAT. This means that the student writes a "draft copy," which is identifiably different from the final copy. The student always uses double space or skips lines on the draft copy. Skipping lines leaves room and permits the student, and other editors, to make changes and to write in the changes with greater ease.

LEVELS OF EDITING — Since all writing requires editing, editors must be provided and trained to edit. Within a classroom there are three levels of editors: self-editor, peer editor, and "top" editor.

First, each writer is his or her own editor. The student is directed to take responsibility for doing a first-level editing job before giving the draft to an "outside" editor. A second editor may be a peer, someone who is close to the ideas of the writer and who can read the draft with the perspective of the writer in mind. A peer may notice small inconsistencies or mechanical problems. A peer can also serve as a trial audience and can respond to the writer's question, "Does it sound all right?" Third is the "top" editor, who, in a classroom, is the teacher. The teacher is the editor who can suggest final touches — change of a word, inclusion of an idea, suggestions on organization, correction of spelling and punctuation, and so forth.

Students can be expected to edit only what they have been taught to edit. A checklist of editing procedures must always be provided, and continuously revised, to remind the student of what to look for when proofreading. It should include the following reminders:

. Did you read your writing aloud?

. Did you say what you wanted to say?

. Did you say it the way you wanted to say it?

. Do you need to add, take away, substitute, or move words?

. Did you begin each sentence with a capital letter?

. Did you end sentences with punctuation — period, exclamation or question mark?

. Did you check your spelling?

. Did you check for paragraph indentation?

Self-Editing — The student, as proofreader or self-editor, needs to learn and use basic proofreading symbols. The following symbols are essential for indicating the main aspects of improvement or revision:

. the caret mark — to add words

colorful

The ∧ *bird sang.*

. the cross-out line — to delete or substitute words

agriculture.

The student took a course in ~~farming.~~

. the circle-with-arrow — to indicate moving or rearranging

↲ We lost our boat ⟨*last week.*⟩

As students become more skilled in proofreading, they can use the paragraph symbol

Encourage students to cross out and not erase on their draft copies. Crossing out permits the continuation of writing without interrupting the flow of thought. In addition, the writer retains the original words which he may want to retrieve for later use, or which can be matched against words in the second version in order to decide which "sounds better."

Peer-Editing — Peer editing is a process in which a classmate serves as the intermediary between the writer and the final "top" editor. A peer editor is like a good friend who can tell you what you need to do, but doesn't hurt your feelings. Peer editors can be the whole class, a small group, or an individual student. It is also possible to have a peer read the selection and then discuss it with the writer. Most important to the success of peer editing is the student's understanding of the rules and procedures. Several guidlines should be followed:

. Peer editors make positive statements.

. They listen to a selection for one specific purpose at a time: for example, variety of vocabulary or variety of sentence starters.

. At the upper grades, they learn how to take notes on another student's composition.

. The writer (student) has the right to accept or reject advice regarding style or ideas.

Teacher or "Top" Editor — The teacher's role is to indicate where the student can improve the writing. The areas of improvement should be based only on techniques which have been taught in the classroom.

. The teacher encourages or rewards students for submitting pieces of writing which show self-editing.

. The teacher asks questions which refer specifically to techniques taught:
   Can you begin your sentences with different words?
   Can you add more describing words?
   Can you include your new vocabulary words?
   Can you substitute more precise words?

Students are willing to proofread their own work when they receive positive feedback on their efforts and if the comments relate to the task, such as

"You have written about dinosaurs in an interesting way. I'm glad you used some of the vocabulary from our brainstorming."

or

"I'm pleased that you crossed out the word 'man' and substituted 'carpenter'."

Your goal is to guide each student through a piece of writing so that you can set simple, easy-to-follow criteria that allow the writing to be VERY GOOD or "V.G." V.G. means that the student has followed the basic specifications of length, organization, inclusion of key vocabulary, and whatever else you have taught to eventually bring the writing to the publication stage.

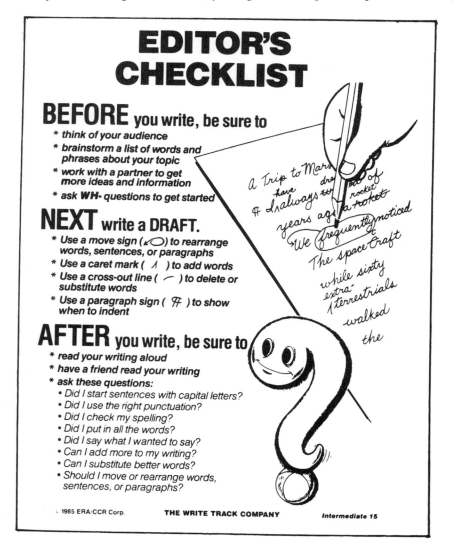

EDITOR'S CHECKLIST

BEFORE you write, be sure to
* *think of your audience*
* *brainstorm a list of words and phrases about your topic*
* *work with a partner to get more ideas and information*
* *ask* **WH-** *questions to get started*

NEXT write a DRAFT.
* *Use a move sign (◠◯) to rearrange words, sentences, or paragraphs*
* *Use a caret mark (⋀) to add words*
* *Use a cross-out line (⌒) to delete or substitute words*
* *Use a paragraph sign (¶) to show when to indent*

AFTER you write, be sure to
* *read your writing aloud*
* *have a friend read your writing*
* *ask these questions:*
  * *Did I start sentences with capital letters?*
  * *Did I use the right punctuation?*
  * *Did I check my spelling?*
  * *Did I put in all the words?*
  * *Did I say what I wanted to say?*
  * *Can I add more to my writing?*
  * *Can I substitute better words?*
  * *Should I move or rearrange words, sentences, or paragraphs?*

Rules for Writing Your Draft Copy

Review these rules before you get ready to write.

- Write your DRAFT COPY on 8-1/2 x11 lined paper.

- Write the words DRAFT COPY on the top of your paper.

- Write your name only if you have to hand it in to your teacher or show it to a classmate.

- Always SKIP LINES on the DRAFT COPY.

- Use the following symbols to make changes or revisions:

  * To add words, use the caret mark. ∧

  * To delete or substitute words, use the cross-out line.
    ~~cross out~~

  * To move or rearrange words, use the oval and arrow.

    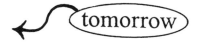

- Do not erase or use white-out on your draft copy.

INSTRUCTIONAL BEGINNINGS

A MODEL FOR TEACHING WRITING FROM
FROM PROCESS TO PRODUCT

THE WRITER ASKS QUESTIONS	THE WRITER RESPONDS
To whom am I writing?	Identifies purpose and audience
How long should it be?	Gathers material/information
What should I say?	Plans and organizes the material
How should I say it?	Selects a "voice" — friendly, humorous, formal, satirical, etc.
How do I begin?	Brainstorm? List? Cluster? Use a starter sentence? Use a framed outline? Ask WH- questions? Do research? Interview?
How should I improve?	Rereads aloud, shares with peers, gives to editor, revises
Is it ready for my audience?	Goes to final copy, publishes

CREATING A WRITING CENTER

PROCESS OBSERVATION

Is writing instruction provided on a regular and frequent basis?

Are the students composing frequently and regularly?

- generating original sentences
- planning or outlining in preparation for writing
- recording information
- proofreading written material
- composing writing pieces (narrative, letter, story, poem)
- practicing improvement and revision tasks (rewriting material using expansion, reduction, substitution, moving or rearranging)

ENVIRONMENTAL OBSERVATION

What evidence of writing appears in the classroom?

- variety of pieces written by each student
  - narrative
  - poetry
  - expository
  - labels
  - charts
  - logs
  - responses to text
- "published" work
  - "super" sentences
  - short paragraphs
  - outlines
  - fictional stories
  - group compositions

- writing area
  - table
  - draft paper
  - final copy paper
  - construction paper
  - appropriate writing implements
  - thesaurus
  - dictionaries
  - word banks
  - checklists

THE WRITING CENTER — ESSENTIAL CREATIVE HUB

THIS IS OUR WRITING CENTER

CHARTS FOR WORDS, FORMS, & IDEAS

REFERENCE DICTIONARIES SPELLERS THESAURUSES ETC.

PAPER & BOOKMAKING SUPPLIES

PUBLICATION SUPPLIES

TABLE FOR WRITING PENCILS CRAYONS MARKERS

TABLE FOR BOOKS WE HAVE WRITTEN

BULLETIN BOARD • READ OUR PUBLISHED WORKS •

FILE POETRY WRITING FRAMES BOOK OF LISTS STORY STARTERS

This is our Writing Center

We come here to get:
Paper for writing
            lined or unlined
Paper for making books
Dictionaries to find words
Charts with words
Pictures for ideas.

We can print.
We can make labels.
We can send letters.
We can send birthday cards and get-well wishes.
We can write a good sentence.
            or a short story.
            or a message.

We are authors and editors.
We write about ourselves.
We write about friends.
We write about things we like and things we don't like.

In our Writing Center
We have a book of favorite jokes.
            a book of favorite pictures
            a book of favorite songs
            a book of favorite T.V. programs
            a book of our hobbies
            a scrapbook of our families

So far this year
            We have written many things:

            We have written thank-you letters.
            We have written about the weather.
            We have written about Martin Luther King.
            We have written about Abraham Lincoln.
            We have written about our new plants in the room.
            We have written sentences for
                        our favorite T.V. shows.
                        our favorite pictures
                        our favorite toys

We have made and bound books.

THE CONCEPT OF A DEVELOPMENTAL, SYSTEMATIC, COOPERATIVE APPROACH

Unlike other subjects such as math, social studies, or reading, writing has often been taught on a somewhat haphazard basis. Some teachers **ASK** their children to do a lot of writing; other teachers shy away from it. And very few teachers, until recently, were trained or required to consistently *teach* writing on a regular basis, with specific emphasis on developmental strategies. A systematic approach to writing, in our opinion, includes teaching students from kindergarten through grade twelve how to:

. choose or develop topics

. gather words, phrases, jottings, notes

. combine those words into various sentence combinations

. utilize appropriate organizational and genre schemes

. employ the revision skills of adding, deleting, substituting, combining/rearranging

. edit and make final copy for publication

In a systematic approach, each teacher must ask the question: **WHAT AM I UP TO IN TEACHING WRITING?** This question implies that the teacher has a starting point in September and will be giving the students specific instruction. From this instruction there will be an accrual of knowledge relating to the writing process and the development of a wide variety of writing products. We believe that the following strategies, explained in the following chapters and taught both sequentially and recursively year after year, can make all of your students "writing literate."

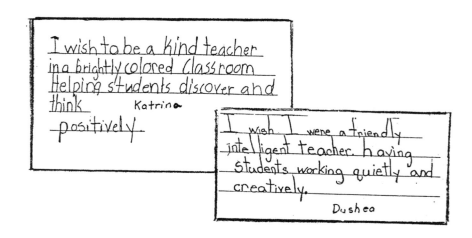

BRAINSTORMING, LISTING, CLUSTERING AND WRITING FROM KEY WORDS

Gathering words on a given topic through a variety of approaches and then writing with those words is a basic technique for starting almost any piece of writing.

SENTENCE COMPOSING OR SENTENCE SYNTHESIS

Because written sentences vary from spoken ones, the student practices composing varieties of sentences by using words from both spoken vocabulary and content areas.

SENTENCE EXPANDING

To a writer the sentence is a "carrier of information" that can be expanded at the writer's option — to clarify ideas. Students practice adding appropriate words to their original composings. Sentences can be expanded by adding words or phrases that answer the **WH-questions** of **who, what, where, when, why,** and **how.**

SUBSTITUTING WORDS AND PHRASES

Words carry ideas, but precise words carry ideas more clearly. Through varied activities students practice improving their sentences by substituting precise and varied vocabulary for vague or repetitive words.

MOVING AND REARRANGING

There are many times when the shift of a word, phrase, or clause gives greater coherence to a piece of writing. Many students are unaware that such shifts are necessary and they must be guided in moving or shifting words from one part of a sentence or paragraph to another.

SENTENCE COMBINING

Writing has its own "sound" which comes from the organization and structure of the written sentence. It also has its own cadences which result from variety of length and embeddings. Combining involves deleting repetitive material, coordinating and subordinating clauses, and incorporating (embedding) parts of one sentence into another.

FRAMES AND PARAGRAPH STRUCTURES

Ideas are best understood by the reader when grouped or organized in logical, recognizable sequences. The student practices organizing and planning a variety of framed paragraphs in all subject or content areas.

PLANS, BLUEPRINTS, AND OUTLINES

Full-length writings — stories, descriptions, narratives, comparisons — require planning. The student is given instruction and practice in planning and writing a variety of pieces which incorporate the complete writing process — gathering information, questioning, planning, composing a draft, sharing, revising, sharing again, editing and publishing.

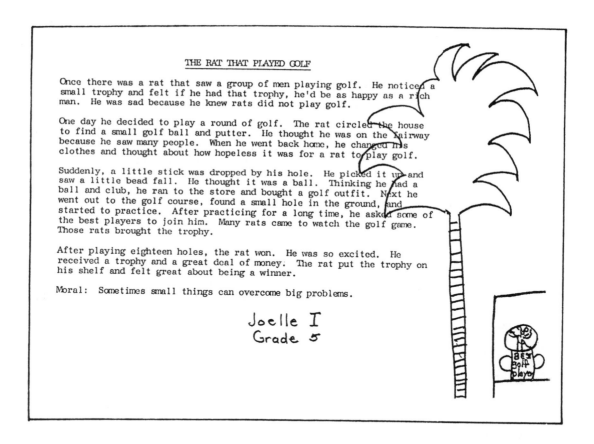

THE RAT THAT PLAYED GOLF

Once there was a rat that saw a group of men playing golf. He noticed a small trophy and felt if he had that trophy, he'd be as happy as a rich man. He was sad because he knew rats did not play golf.

One day he decided to play a round of golf. The rat circled the house to find a small golf ball and putter. He thought he was on the fairway because he saw many people. When he went back home, he changed his clothes and thought about how hopeless it was for a rat to play golf.

Suddenly, a little stick was dropped by his hole. He picked it up and saw a little bead fall. He thought it was a ball. Thinking he had a ball and club, he ran to the store and bought a golf outfit. Next he went out to the golf course, found a small hole in the ground, and started to practice. After practicing for a long time, he asked some of the best players to join him. Many rats came to watch the golf game. Those rats brought the trophy.

After playing eighteen holes, the rat won. He was so excited. He received a trophy and a great deal of money. The rat put the trophy on his shelf and felt great about being a winner.

Moral: Sometimes small things can overcome big problems.

Joelle I
Grade 5

ANSWERING THE WRITER'S QUESTIONS

You probably remember being asked to write, first in elementary and later in secondary school. As your teacher announced, "All right students, go home and write about ....," some student's hand would shoot up and that student would ask the question that was on everyone else's mind:

How long should it be?

Most likely you remember receiving all or several of these answers to this constantly repeated question:

. "250 (or 350 or 150) words."

. "As long as it needs to be."

   (Some students felt a sentence was all that it needed to be.)

. "Till you've covered the subject."

   (The subject is the Panama Canal!)

. "As long as a woman's skirt."

   (Mini? Maxi? Above the knee? Below the knee?)

And then, before the teacher even stated the assignment, three more questions popped out from the students:

What do you want me to say?

How do I start?

Does spelling count?

If these questions sound familiar and if, perhaps, your own students are asking them, we believe it's time to answer them. In fact, we begin teaching writing with these "writer's questions":

HOW LONG SHOULD IT BE?

WHAT SHOULD I SAY?

HOW DO I START?

WHAT COUNTS?

HOW LONG SHOULD IT BE? means the student realizes that all writing has length and that the genre identifies the length. A haiku cannot be twelve pages long, nor can a novel be only three pages. Business letters that go beyond two pages scare away the client, and a fable needs to tell its moral in one or two pages.

The student's desire to know the length should not be treated as a "dumb question," but as part of the teaching process. As you introduce different genres (letter, myth, report, essay), you need to discuss the options of length, telling the students that you will be giving them clear, precise instructions for every piece of assigned writing. You and their peers will serve as their "editors" throughout the draft stages, commenting on whether or not the piece is meeting the criteria of the genre.

WHAT SHOULD I SAY? means, "Tell me precisely what YOU have in mind for this piece of writing." A good editor clarifies the assignment:

"Write as if you're the child in the story. Use the words from your thesaurus that express fear. Remember you're writing to your grandmother, so keep your writing friendly."

The question **HOW DO I START?** is the pivotal point of teaching writing because we begin by showing the students **"STARTERS."** These starters (listed below) are taught systematically and are described in detail in subsequent chapters.

"STARTERS" OR WAYS TO GET STARTED WRITING:

- listing key words related to the topic
- composing a starting sentence or question using key words
- organizing key words by categories
- asking **WH-questions**
- using a **FRAMED OUTLINE**
- setting up a **DEFINITION MODE** outline
- organizing a **Q.A.D.** (Question/Answer/Detail)

The fourth question, **WHAT COUNTS?** is the student's request to know exactly how you will grade the writing. Are you counting length, organization, spelling, punctuation, vocabulary, neatness? What exactly do you want so that **YOU** will approve of the writing? But before we answer this question, we must be sure that we teach the student the **"IMPROVERS"** that change a draft copy paper to a revised paper.

"IMPROVERS" FOR MAKING WRITING BETTER:

- **ADDING** or **EXPANDING** to provide more information
- **DELETING** or **REMOVING** unnecessary words
- **SUBSTITUTING** imprecise or repetitive words
- **MOVING, REARRANGING,** or **COMBINING** for improved organization or style

BEGINNING STAGES IN LEARNING TO WRITE

Most young children come to school believing they know how to write. They know they cannot read, but they are sure they can write. Any child who has been fortunate enough to have a pencil or crayons and some large sheets of paper has already written. That child has written "letters," "stories," "messages," "grocery lists," and much more. That child knows that certain "marks" on the page can be read by any "intelligent" adult who understands children's writing. Because of children's belief in their ability to write, writing activities in kindergarten and first grade can be an exciting and essential aspect of literary development.

Why Should Young Children Write?

We believe that the child who writes learns not only to write, but also to read and love reading. Do you know of any writer who isn't a prolific reader? People who read widely may or may not write, but people who write always read. The writer is someone who wants to know and needs to know. To write about dinosaurs, the writer must read about dinosaurs. To write a fairy tale, the writer must read fairy tales. As children write, they learn the skills of both writing and reading in a developmental and meaningful way.

In addition, the child who writes begins to think about letters, words, illustrations, and the whole construct of literacy. Children begin to use high-level thinking processes when they formulate such questions as "How should I write to grandpa?" "Where do I put the word 'dear'?" "How do you write the letter K?" "How can I write 'sh' like in 'shh'?" "Can I use an 'R' to start the name 'Arnie'?" The child who is writing is thinking and uncovering and discovering.

The child who writes finds an audience — a parent, a grandparent, a sibling, a friend, a classmate — and through this audience develops self-esteem. "You're so smart to know how to write." "What a beautiful story you've written." "Your story made me laugh." "Your story made me cry." However, encouragement to write is not enough. Children soon want some guidance and help in knowing how to write and what to write about. So we can begin, early in the school year and every day after that, with these suggested procedures:

. First, ask the children if they know how to write. Almost all the children will raise their hands. Ask what they know about writing. Some children will mention "making pictures." Others will let you know that you have to use letters. Guide the children in thinking about writing as "saying something with letters."

. Then over the next few weeks, take an informal survey of the developmental stages of your students' writing. In a kindergarten class you are likely to see the following stages at the beginning of the school year (Fields, 1988):

. The scribble stage where the child makes "linear designs" on the page and may or may not distinguish between drawing and writing.

. The linear/repetitive stage in which the child makes a series of lines across or up and down the page that the child believes looks like adult writing. At this stage the child is likely to separate drawing from writing.

. The stage of letter-like forms and circles that begin to approximate several of the letters of the alphabet, especially X, T, S, and O. By this stage most children will clearly know that they are writing and expect adults to "read" their writing.

. The invented spelling stage where children may use a combination of letters as words (I C U), some sound-symbol relationships (RNEE for Arnie), and visual memory (MOMMY, STOP).

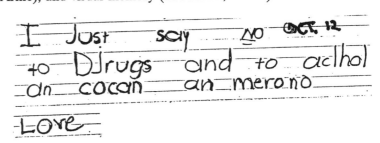

An understanding of these stages will help you track and guide the progress of your children through the school year. Marie Clay, the distinguished New Zealand educator, suggests using the scale below for guiding the writing development of young children (1975). Record the number of the highest level used by the child:

1. Alphabetic (letters only)
2. Word (any recognizable word)
3. Word group (any two-word phrase)
4. Sentence (any simple sentence)
5. Punctuated story (two or more sentences)
6. Paragraphed story (two themes)

In addition, either during the middle of kindergarten or at the beginning of first grade, you can simply ask the children to write whatever words they think they know. You can take a simple inventory every two or three months and you will begin to have an informal, but fairly accurate, measure of your children's writing progress. After you have taken these inventories, use the following procedures as the beginning stages of writing instruction:

. Place a permanent copy of the upper and lower case letters on each child's desk. In addition, have these letters displayed in full view of the class.

. Make the children comfortable with the concept of "invented" spelling. Give them large sheets of drawing paper and a large soft-leaded pencil. Ask them to write whatever they can — their names, letters, scribbles that "tell" something. Have them share what they have written. You may want to have an "author's chair" or a "sharing chair" so they can read what they have written or tell about their writing.

. After this introduction and discussion about writing, have the children tell you words they would like to write. Put the words they suggest on a piece of paper without showing them to the children. After you have collected several words, pick one for the children to write. Ask them to spell it as well as they can and to use the letters on their desks to help them.

34

Say, "I would like you to try to write this interesting word. Write it as best as you can. Write whatever letters you think are in that word. Pretend you are writing to someone you know."

Encourage all the children to "write" and to tell you what they have written. Some children will only scribble, but many will use letters, and some children will have made appropriate sound-symbol associations. Have the children practice the above types of invented spelling activities for several weeks. Suggest that the children illustrate their words. Display their work on a bulletin board which invites visitors to "Read Our Writing." Add a small disclaimer that says "SPELLING DOESN'T COUNT YET!"

As the children become comfortable with invented spelling, have them use writing as a way of recording and telling. Using active participation and a class BOOK OF LISTS (page 38), incorporate on a daily or frequent basis the listing and metacognitive activites described in the following chapter. On chart paper, set up ABC LISTS (page 41) and, as the children think of items, place each item next to the first letter of the item being listed.

Richard -Kindergarten

Dir sanoelos
Go to miami
Polz go to miam
Peolpe wot toy
To play can you get
Peolpe toy I am
gawig to sta up
all nat book
if you gait
Do you want a toy too?

Sunday is my favorite day of the week.
On Sunday I played with my friends. We played
jump rope all day until we were tired,
then we went home.
                              Nadia

EXAMPLES OF WRITINGS FROM KINDERGARTEN AND FIRST GRADE CHILDREN

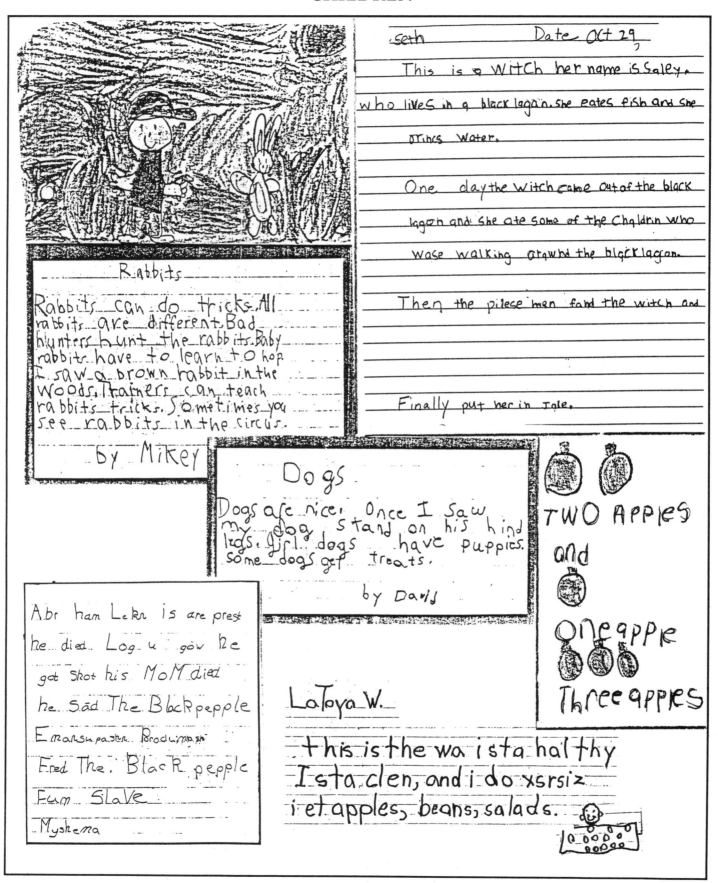

Seth   Date Oct 29

This is a witch her name is Saley. who lives in a black lagan. she eates fish and she drincs water.

One day the witch came out of the black lagan and she ate some of the chaldrin who wase walking arawnd the blacklagan.

Then the pilese men fand the witch and

Finally put her in jole.

Rabbits

Rabbits can do tricks. All rabbits are different. Bad hunters hunt the rabbits. Baby rabbits have to learn to hop. I saw a brown rabbit in the woods. Trainers can teach rabbits tricks. Sometimes you see rabbits in the circus.

by Mikey

Dogs

Dogs are nice. Once I saw my dog stand on his hind legs. Girl dogs have puppies. Some dogs get treats.

by David

TWO APPles and ONE apple Three apples

Abr ham Lckn is are prest he died. Log u gow he got shot his MoM died he sad The Black pepple Emarsupaser. Brodumagh Ered The Black pepple Fum Slave

Myshema

LaToya W.

this is the wa i sta halthy I sta clen, and i do xsrsiz i et apples, beans, salads.

DEVELOPING FLUENCY
BRAINSTORMING, LISTING, AND WRITING FROM KEY WORDS

HOW DO I START?

At some point every writer asks this question. One answer to this question is another question:

"Have you thought of starting with a list?"

What Is a List?

A list is a collection of words and phrases that provides the writer with the raw material for writing on a given topic. It is a collection that confirms to the writer that she/he knows something about the subject. Each item on the list represents a bit of information or a concept related to the topic, and it is through listing or clustering, sometimes called brainstorming, that the student can develop extensive skills for becoming fluent.

Procedures for Listing

We begin teaching listing as the first major strategy for learning to write, and we introduce a procedure called *Active Participation,* described below:

.   Teacher or students choose a topic — for example, DINOSAURS.

.   Then each student WRITES the name of one word or phrase associated with that
       topic.

.   Each person then tells the item he or she has written and everyone adds that item
       to his or her list.

As you will notice, in *Active Participation* every student is responsible for contributing to the group and must write during a writing lesson. That is, the teacher does not serve as the scribe, but rather as the facilitator for the compiling of each individual's list.

Solo and Collaborative Listing

Through *Active Participation* we show the students three ways to expand a list. We have described these three phases of listing as **solo, collaborative,** and **cross-pollinated.**

To begin, we select a topic of mutual interest or one about which the group has prior knowledge. Topics might be pizza, hamburgers, McDonald's, dogs, friendship, television, or anything else related to the students' experiences.

- **Begin solo.** Ask each student to write three to five words or phrases which are associated with the topic. (Example: pizza — great snack, quick service, pepperoni)

- **Collaborate.** Have the students form pairs or small groups of three to five and write individual composite lists. To get a composite list, each student tells those in the group his or her words or phrases. The other students add these words to their lists. Through this process students readily double and triple their word banks.

- **Cross-Pollinate.** After the groups have formed their composite lists, ask one student in each group to select a particularly interesting word or phrase from the group's list and "give it" to the other groups. Each student then adds that item to his/her list.

To make certain that your students understand that sharing of words from a list is a legitimate practice, tell them the slogan

WORDS ARE FREE!

This slogan is important in helping your students distinguish between sharing words and copying sentences, since a sentence is someone else's creative thought or elaborated idea. From these listing activities, students will recognize that they have, as a start, two important resources for beginning a piece of writing — themselves and others.

DEVELOPING A BOOK OF LISTS

After students have learned the three procedures for listing, have them purchase a small notebook (about 6"x 8") which they can name **MY BOOK OF LISTS.** Have them alphabetize the book, leaving several pages between each two letters. Begin by asking each student to write a list of three to five topics that she/he knows something about. Topics are likely to be sports, baseball, football, make-up, rock singers, TV characters, movies, boys' and girls' names, and so forth. Have students share lists and add items which interest them. From this list have students choose one topic (for example, baseball) and write a list of items associated with the topic.

Use the **BOOK OF LISTS** on a daily basis to help students build a personal thesaurus. Suppose your class is reading *Charlotte's Web* or *Great Expectations*. Have the students create categories of lists which can be added to as they proceed through the story. Categories might be Characters, Places, Unusual and Difficult Vocabulary, Quotable Quotes, and so forth. For descriptive writing ask the students to build lists of vivid adjectives and strong verbs. Have them write a list of designer colors (taupe, cimarron, magenta, ecru) and list types of clothing, cars, vegetables, fruits, and other items, all of which can be used for future writing.

The possibilities are limitless. At the end of this chapter (page 46) you will find suggested topics for a total **BOOK OF LISTS**.

The BOOK OF LISTS as a Major Component of Writing

The **BOOK OF LISTS** allows the student to:

- build a personal thesaurus
- keep track of new learning
- have immediate access to vocabulary for writing
- have a huge variety of topics for further development
- write effectively in all areas of the curriculum

Through the **BOOK OF LISTS** your students can begin the process of categorization. It is from such categorization and organization that writing starts to take shape. Below is an example of how you might use a list:

ENDANGERED SPECIES LIST

conservation

ivory

elephants

African Plains

Bald Eagle

carelessness

greed

Sierra Club

birds of plumage

deforestation

From this list your students can set up categories similar to these:

Endangered Species	Products	Places	Organizations
elephants	ivory	African Plains	Sierra Club
Bald Eagle			
birds of plumage			

USING KEY WORDS FROM THE BOOK OF LISTS

After the students have categorized their words, have them practice **sentence composing** by using the words from the lists. Make sure they use at least three words from the list in each sentence. Some examples might be:

- *Conservationists have warned us about the problems we will have if we deforest our land and destroy wildlife, such as the elephant and birds of plumage.*

or

- *The elephant is almost extinct because of the carelessness and greed of ivory hunters.*

After this sentence practice, you can ask your students to work out a tentative plan for writing a paragraph or a longer piece. Have them orally "rehearse" how they might proceed by selecting the **KEY WORDS** they will use for their sentences and then ask them to write those sentences. Then suggest that each student select three more words and add a second sentence that relates to the first sentence. Continue this practice so that your students can easily compose paragraphs and statements from **KEY WORDS**.

WRITING FROM KEY WORDS USING "BOUGHT" LISTS

Throughout school students encounter thousands of words that come from the content areas, spelling lists, dictionaries, and thesauruses. We have named this vocabulary "bought" lists because they come primarily through text material **bought** by the schools. These words can also serve as "starters" for writing.

For example, students might select a list of words from a thesaurus or book of synonyms and use those words to write a descriptive passage, as illustrated below:

- Entry word — **ANGRY**

  Synonyms: wild, enraged, untamed, frenzied, fierce, rabid, mad, ferocious, raging

  Passage: *The frenzied lion approached his prey. He was enraged because he had been unable to capture the elusive, untamed zebra. Mad with hunger and raging with anger, this king of the jungle had never before been so wild and ferocious.*

- Entry word — **HEAT**

  Descriptive words: sultry, parching, smothering, simmering, scorching, blazing, sweltering, oppressive, blistering

  Passage: *For two months now the explorers had known nothing but heat — blazing, scorching, oppressive heat. A persistent, sultry sun sent down unremitting rays, parching the soil and every bit of remaining life in this simmering land. The relentless, sweltering heat would soon smother their own lives.*

ABC LISTING

One of the most exciting procedures we have used in the classroom is **ABC LISTING.**
In **ABC LISTING** we have the students write the letters A to Z vertically on an 8½ x 11 sheet of paper:

A

B

C

D

etc.

We then use a topic which the students either have studied or are studying. As an illustration, we will use *The American Revolution* and will assume that the students have completed studying this topic in class. As a summary of the lesson, we ask each student to recall as many words or phrases about the Revolution as possible and to write each word or phrase next to the letter with which it begins. For example, for the letter G the students should write "George III."

Each student works "solo" for about three to five minutes. After you call time, have the students form groups of three to five to collaborate by sharing and adding to their lists. When the students have completed this task, call on a spokesperson from each group and have that person select an item from the collaborated list and "give it" to the other groups in the class, or "cross-pollinate."

You will find that your students will want to achieve closure by getting at least one item for every letter. At this point you can suggest that they use the textbook or other written material, especially the index, to find related information. Below is a sample ABC list on the American Revolution compiled by a group of fifth graders.

THE AMERICAN REVOLUTION FROM A TO Z

A   Attucks (Crispus), Major Andre, Arnold (Benedict)
B   Boston, Burke (Edmund)
C   Constitution, Cornwallis
D   Declaration of Independence
E   England
F   France, Franklin (Benjamin)
G   George III, "Give me liberty or give me death"
H   Henry (Patrick), Hessians, Hancock (John)
I   Indians
J   John Jay, John Paul Jones
K   Kings
L   Lafayette
M   Marion (Francis)
N   North Carolina, New Hampshire, New York, New Jersey
O   "One if by land, two if by sea"
P   Paine (Thomas)
Q   Quartering of Redcoats
R   Redcoats, General Rochambeau, Ross (Betsy), Revere (Paul)
S   Stamp Tax
T   Tea Party
U   United States
V   Valley Forge
W   Washington (George)
X   eXtraordinary times*
Y   Yorktown
Z   Zenger (Peter)

*Because there are relatively few words that begin with the letter X, you can allow the students this form of word play to increase the pool of "X words."

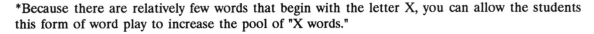

Undoubtedly you can add much more to this list and perhaps you can see the potential of this type of listing. Here are several of our suggestions for using **ABC LISTING**:

.   Use **ABC LISTING** as an "Advance Organizer" when you start a unit. Suppose you plan to study the digestive system. Ask the students to make their ABC lists and individually write as many items as they know (in advance) about the digestive system. Use the solo, collaborative, and cross-pollinated procedures.

.   From this Advance Organizer list you can determine what **prior knowledge** your students **collectively** have about the topic and you can plan and pace your lessons accordingly. If they already know a great deal, move quickly; if their knowledge is scant and vague, provide them with more background.

.   Use **ABC LISTING** to have your students keep track of key concepts and people. As you will notice about the ABC list on the American Revolution, there are items about people, places, and events. As your students read or discuss a topic, have them write important items next to the appropriate entry letters.

USING ABC LISTING TO DEVELOP METACOGNITION

Metacognition is the conscious awareness of one's knowledge. We can think of metacognition as the ability to answer two significant questions:

What do I know that I know?

and

What do I know that I don't know?

By knowing what you know, you are able to elaborate upon or discuss the topic. You can decide you want to know more or you can bypass that topic to spend more time learning something else. By knowing what you know, you have a sense of your "expertise."

By knowing what you **don't** know, you can put yourself on the path of inquiry. "I've never heard of...," "I need to know about...," "I should ask...," "I should look up...." Students who know what they know and know what they don't know become your class achievers. We suggest referring back to the ABC list on the American Revolution as an example, using the following strategies through **ABC LISTING**:

.   Begin by having the students look at their lists. Ask the students to put a check mark next to each item they know "something" about. ("Something" can be as simple as "I know that Thomas Paine wrote something about the Revolution.")

.   Ask the students to pick out one of these items to write about.

.   Ask the students to write the following statement on a separate piece of paper: *I know that I know something about... (put in the item).* Then ask them to write a brief one-sentence statement about that item.

.   Call on different students to tell their classmates something they know by reading their sentences.

.   Then ask the students to put an X next to each item they believe they know nothing or very little about. Ask them to pick one of these items and write, *I know that I know nothing about... (put in the item).*

.   Have students share what they know that they do not know by reading their sentences. Then have the student who contributed the item provide the information. Other students can add whatever information they have on the "unknown" topic.

.   The students who had not known anything about that topic then write, *I now know... (put in information).*

On the American Revolution your classroom participation might proceed like this:

Teacher:	*What do you know that you know?*
Student 1:	*I know that I know something about the Tea Party. That was when some colonists dressed up as Indians and threw tea overboard.*
Teacher:	*What else does somebody know about the Tea Party?*
Student 2:	*The Tea Party took place in Boston.*
Teacher:	*What else does somebody know?*
Student 3:	*The British were very angry and punished the colonists.*
Teacher:	*What do you know that you don't know?*
Student 1:	*I know that I don't know anything about Peter Zenger.*

Teacher:	*Who contributed the name Peter Zenger? What do you know?*
Student 2:	*I know that Peter Zenger was a newspaper writer.*
Teacher:	*What else does somebody know?*
Student 3:	*He got into trouble for saying bad things about the government?*
Teacher:	*What else does somebody know?*

Through this process you will notice that you are discussing and/or reviewing the topic. However, instead of being the dispenser of information, you let your individual students exchange and share their collective knowledge. They are also using writing to keep track of what they previously knew and of the new knowledge they are acquiring.

ABC LISTING is appropriate for just about every subject and topic, such as:

Mathematics — Abacus to Zero

Geography — Austria to Zaire

Historic Persons — Susan B. Anthony to Peter Zenger

Plants — Anemone to Zinnia

Clothing — Apron to Zipper

Foods — Asparagus to Ziti

GETTING TOPICS FOR WRITING THROUGH ABC LISTING

By using Active Participation/Solo Listing, you can have your students develop a list of topics for writing all through the school year. This is the procedure:

. Assign each student in your class a different letter. Have each student then think of a topic that begins with his/her assigned letter and write the topic next to the letter.

. Ask each student to tell the word or phrase he/she wrote.

. Ask each student to write the new words on his/her list.

Below is a partial list of topics which we collected through **ABC LISTING**. Yours will certainly be different and your students will have "ownership" of topics to write about. You can also have the students enter the most interesting topics in the **BOOK OF LISTS** to use for future writing activities.

Suggested Topics from A to Z

This list was developed using active participation. The students were asked to write the alphabet on an 8½ x 11 sheet. Then each student was assigned a letter and asked to think of a topic beginning with that letter. The topics were then "composited" and students were asked to enter the topics that were of interest in their own **BOOK OF LISTS.** In addition, they also entered those topics they needed to know as part of their curriculum.

- Animals, Athletes, American Heroes and Heroines, Astronauts
- Baseball, Boys in Fiction, Black Americans, Bubble Gum
- Cats, California, Canada
- Dogs, Dwellings, Dinosaurs, Dragons
- Ethnic-Americans, Elephants, Explorers, Earrings
- Friends, Foreign Words, Flowers, Freedom
- Girls in Fiction, Gods and Goddesses, Gymnasts,Getting Ahead
- Homonyms, Hawaii, Health, Happiness
- Inventors, India, Impossibilities
- Jobs, Jokes, Jump Rope Rhymes, July Vacations, Jellybeans
- Kings, Kingdoms, Keyboard Instruments, Kites, Kittens
- Lads and Lasses, Languages, Lovers in Literature
- Mythological Characters, Map Terms, Musicians, Marriage
- Native-Americans, Norse Gods, Nursery Rhymes, Numbers
- Oceans, Octogenarians, Opposites, Operas and Operettas
- Presidents, Photographers, Politicians, Power
- Queens, Quadruplets, Quintuplets, Quacks
- Roman Leaders, Rhinoceros, Racing Cars, Railroads
- Slang Words, Superstitions, Songs, Sportswomen
- Tongue Twisters, Texas, Transportation, Taxes, Theater
- Uniform Wearers, Universities, Uganda, Usurpers
- Vacations, Victories, Villains, Venomous Snakes
- Women of Fame, Witches, Weather Symbols, Woodchucks
- X-Words, Xylophones, X-Rays
- Youths in Literature, Yachts, Yesteryear, Yearly Events
- Zoos, Zoographers, Zoologists, Zodiac, Zithers, Zaire

ACTIVITIES FOR LISTING AND BUILDING METACOGNITION

WHAT DO YOU KNOW THAT YOU KNOW?

. What items in the room do you have a name for?

. What parts of the body can you name?

. What colors do you know?

. What streets in your neighborhood can you name?

. What jobs can you name?

. What clothing items can you name?

. What TV and book characters do you know?

WHAT DON'T YOU KNOW THAT YOU CAN FIND OUT ABOUT?

. What items in the room don't you have a name for?

. What parts of the body don't you have name for?

. What colors are around you that you don't have a name for?

. What items are in your kitchen that you can't name?

. What jobs do people in your school do that you don't have a name for?

HOW MANY WORDS CAN YOU THINK OF?

. What words can you think of when you hear the word cold? hot? school? friend?

summer? fall? winter? spring?

To enhance oral language and to make the children aware of the organizational system of the **BOOK OF LISTS** or of **ABC LISTING,** have the children say the following statements during listing activities:

"I know that I know something that I use in the kitchen. It's a spoon and it begins with the letter S."

or

"I know that I don't know what to call that 'thing' on the window. Can somebody tell me its name?" Another child (or the teacher) answers: "I know that I know that it is called a window shade and it begins with the letter W."

At the beginning stages of this activity, you may want to write the names of the items on the class chart. Later the children should have their own ABC lists for writing the words.

- Write a designer color. (solo)

- Collect 9 more color words from your colleagues. (collaborate)

- Write the name of an automobile. (solo)

- Collect 9 more automobile words from your colleagues. (collaborate)

- Write a substitute word for " beautiful". (solo)

- Collect 9 more "beautiful" words from your colleagues. (collaborate)

- Choose one automobile from your list. Use as many designer colors and "beautiful" words as you can to help you write four or five sentences which will SELL your automobile.

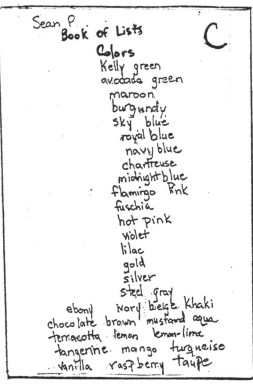

Sean P.
Book of Lists   C

Colors
Kelly green
avocado green
maroon
burgundy
sky blue
royal blue
navy blue
chartreuse
midnight blue
flamingo Pink
fuschia
hot pink
violet
lilac
gold
silver
steel gray
ebony   ivory beige khaki
chocolate brown mustard aqua
terracotta lemon lemon-lime
tangerine mango turquoise
vanilla raspberry taupe

Diane   B

Beautiful
pretty
dainty
lovely
fair
gorgeous
attractive
delicate
bonnie
magnificent
comely
charming
elegant
fascinating
indescribable
luscious
marvelous
ravishing
spectacular
cute

You've got to buy this black and red 1990 Porsche for only $12,500,000. It goes up to 210 mph. So go to Porsche World and test drive it and get $50 back. The 1990 Porsche even has tinted windows, beige interior, a bass stereo, air conditioning, and a Ferrari engine too. It rides nicely and smoothly and has cruise control. So go to Porsche World.

by Marcos

Summary of "Start-Up" Strategies

GETTING STARTED

GOAL: To teach students procedures for gathering words related to topics

PROCEDURAL LABELS

Brainstorming -- Stating words or phrases that broadly relate to a topic

Listing -- The actual writing of words or phrases

Solo Listing -- Writing one's own words

Collaborative Listing -- Incorporating words/phrases contributed by others

Cross-Pollinating -- Small groups contributing to a master list of words

Active Participation -- The procedure in which each student is asked to contribute one word or phrase (idea) to enlarge a group's word bank

Collective Knowledge -- The total corpus of words (ideas) gathered through brainstorming, listing, and active participation which becomes available to all the students

THROUGH THESE PROCEDURES, STUDENTS LEARN THAT

WORDS ARE FREE !

USING ABC LISTING TO BUILD CULTURAL LITERACY THROUGH A KNOWLEDGE-BASED CURRICULUM

E.D. Hirsch, Jr., in his book *Cultural Literacy* (1987), refers to the decline of "shared knowledge" among American youth. He states:

> They [American students] know a great deal. . . . The trouble is that, from the standpoint of literacy and their ability to communicate with others in our culture, what they know is ephemeral and narrowly confined to their own generation. Many young people strikingly lack the information that writers of American books and newspapers have traditionally taken for granted among their readers from all generations. Our children's lack of inter-generational information is a serious problem for the nation. The decline of literacy and the decline of shared knowledge are closely related, inter-dependent facts. (p.7)

While we don't wish to imply that all our nation's ills can be solved by teaching students to write, we do believe that we can effectively add to our children's knowledge through writing and through what we have named "knowledge-based learning" or what Hirsch refers to as "cultural literacy." We offer the following suggestions which you can easily expand upon in your own classroom.

From kindergarten on have your students know the names of the states which they can learn through these suggested listing and metacognitive procedures:

. Have the students set up a category in **THE BOOK OF LISTS** or on a chart titled *FIFTY STATES OF THE UNITED STATES*. They then write the alphabet as a framework for entering the names. Of course, there will not be states for all the letters.

. Using Active Participation/Solo Listing, have each student write the name of one state. Kindergarten and first grade children can tell you the names if they cannot write them.

. Collect the names of states selected by the students through the use of the following questioning strategies:

Teacher:	*Tell me the name of the state you wrote, Lisa.*
Lisa:	*I wrote Florida.*
Teacher:	*Yes, Florida is a state. We'll write it next to the letter F.*
Teacher:	*What state did you write, Ben?*
Ben:	*Miami.*
Teacher:	*No, Ben, Miami is not a state, but we'll list it when we do cities.*

- Respond, "*Yes, ... is a state; no, it is not a state, but we'll list it when we list cities.*"

- Help the students collect the fifty states by playing a "*Yes, it is*"/"*No, it is not*" game. Ask a student to tell the name of a state. Have another student say either "*Yes, it is a state*" or "*No, it is not a state.*" Eventually your students will know which are the names of the states and which are not. As each student names his/her state, place it on a large ABC chart as illustrated below:

FIFTY STATES OF THE UNITED STATES

A	Alabama, Alaska, Arizona, Arkansas
B	
C	California, Colorado, Connecticut
D	Delaware
E	
F	Florida
G	Georgia
H	Hawaii
I	Idaho, Illinois, Indiana, Iowa
J	
K	Kansas, Kentucky
L	Louisiana
M	Maine, Maryland, Massachusetts, Michigan, Minnesota, Mississippi, Missouri, Montana
N	Nebraska, Nevada, New Hampshire, New Jersey, New Mexico, New York, North Carolina, North Dakota
O	Ohio, Oklahoma, Oregon
P	Pennsylvania
Q	
R	Rhode Island
S	South Carolina, South Dakota
T	Tennessee, Texas
U	Utah
V	Vermont, Virginia
W	Washington, West Virginia, Wisconsin, Wyoming
X	
Y	
Z	

Develop related activities about each state (see page 53) that include historical items, state flag and flower, motto, and so forth.

KNOWLEDGE-BASED INSTRUCTION
WRITING ABOUT THE STATES

Suggested Activities (to be used as appropriate for age and grade)

1. Each student in a class becomes responsible for gathering information on one state and learns to fill out the "data" sheet:

   Name of State ....

   Boundaries of State ....

   Area .... Population ....

   Year Entered Union ....

   Capital City ....

   Other Major Cities ....

   Major Industries ....

   Major Places of Interest ....

   Nickname ....

   State Bird ....

   State Flower ....

   State Motto ....

2. Write diamantes, haikus, letter-name poems about states.

Sunshine State

Gulf Coast   *Atlantic Ocean*

Tampa *Miami* *Tallahassee*

Tourists *Oranges*

Florida

3. Use **THREE REASONS WHY** and variations of **THREE REASONS WHY** (page 146).

   There are three reasons why Florida is popular with tourists.

   Three exciting places to visit in Florida are ....

   I enjoy living in Florida for these three reasons .....

   Three people who made Florida famous are ....

A	area, add, acute
B	base, binary
C	cone, cylinder, circle, cube, circumference, curve, centimeter
D	diameter, diamond
E	equal, equilateral, ellipse
F	fractions, factors, foot
G	graph, geometry
H	horizontal, height, hexagon, hemisphere
I	integer, isosceles, inch
J	juxtaposition
K	kilometer, kilogram
L	length, linear
M	multiply, millimeter
N	number, numeral
O	octagon, obtuse, oval
P	polygon, pentagon, pentameter, parallelogram, pyramid
Q	quadrangle, quadrant, quadrilateral
R	rhomboid, rectangle
S	square, sphere, semicircle, scalene
T	triangle, trapezoid, tangents
U	unit
V	vector
W	width
X	x-factor
Y	y-factor, yard
Z	zero

MATHEMATICAL WRITER

You can use your mathematics vocabulary to create interesting sentences and stories. In the geometric figures below are nouns, verbs, and adjectives from your math textbooks. Write **nine** sentences using a word from each geometric shape in each sentence. You may add any endings you need to the words.

EXAMPLE

volume   reduce   measurable

Reducing our **volume** of weapons, without any **measurable** loss of strength, will be a significant gain for our nation.

angle	associate	angular
area	bisect	circular
cube	commute	computerized
diameter	compare	cylindrical
fraction	distribute	diagonal
graph	divide	digital
triangle	equalize	equivalent
cylinder	expand	horizontal
pyramid	intersect	numerical
square	multiply	parallel
zero	subtract	triangular

CHECKLIST FOR EDITING

• Did you use a word from each geometric figure in every sentence?
• Did you check your capitalization, punctuation, and spelling?

KNOWLEDGE-BASED INSTRUCTION
WRITING AND GEOMETRY

Suggested Activities (to be used as appropriate to age and grade)

1. Have the art teacher develop activities using a variety of geometric forms. Then have children write: (a) how they made their figure, and/or (b) a set of directions telling how to make that figure.

2. Use the **DEFINITION MODE** (page 174) to explain the attributes of different forms. Write a compare/contrast essay explaining the differences between a triangle and a rectangle.

3. Have the children write the procedures for measuring different geometric forms using the appropriate mathematical vocabulary.

4. Write poetry — diamantes, haikus, concrete poems.
    Example:

    TRIANGLE
    Simple plane angles,
    Obtuse, Isosceles, Scalene,
    Sitting in the desert,
    PYRAMID

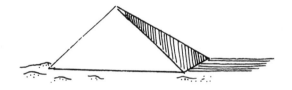

5. Have children observe and record items that use geometric figures (roofs, windows, doors, ice cream cones, drinking glasses) and put their recordings in the **BOOK OF LISTS**.

6. Have children collect items of different geometric figures — musical triangle, saucers, balls, prisms, etc. Label them and have the students write a letter to a "Martian" explaining the use of a particular item.

LITERATURE CHARACTERS FOR KNOWLEDGE-BASED INSTRUCTION

A   Alice, Arthur (King), Androcles
B   Beauty/Beast, Bo-Peep, Boy Blue
C   Cinderella, Charlotte, Cheshire Cat
D
E   Elephant Boy
F   Fairy Godmother, Frog Prince
G   Goldilocks, Goose Girl, Georgie-Porgie
H   Hansel and Gretel, Humpty Dumpty, Henny Penny
I
J   Jack (Beanstalk), Jack (Nimble), Jack Sprat, Jack Horner
K   King Cole, Knave of Hearts
L   Lancelot, Little Red Hen
M   Miss Muffett, Mary (Quite Contrary), Mother Goose, Mother Hubbard, March Hare
N
O
P   Peter (Pumpkin Eater), Puss-in-Boots, Polly and Suki, Pippi Longstocking
Q   Queen of Hearts
R   Rapunzel, Rumpelstiltskin, Red Riding Hood
S   Snow White, Sleeping Beauty
T   Three Pigs, Three Bears, Taffy, Templeton, Thumbelina
U   Ugly Duckling
V
W   Wee Willie Winkie, Wilbur, Wonka (Willie)
X
Y
Z

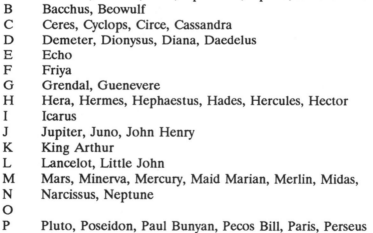

A   Artemis, Athena, Ares, Aphrodite, Apollo, Achilles
B   Bacchus, Beowulf
C   Ceres, Cyclops, Circe, Cassandra
D   Demeter, Dionysus, Diana, Daedelus
E   Echo
F   Friya
G   Grendal, Guenevere
H   Hera, Hermes, Hephaestus, Hades, Hercules, Hector
I   Icarus
J   Jupiter, Juno, John Henry
K   King Arthur
L   Lancelot, Little John
M   Mars, Minerva, Mercury, Maid Marian, Merlin, Midas,
N   Narcissus, Neptune
O
P   Pluto, Poseidon, Paul Bunyan, Pecos Bill, Paris, Perseus
Q
R   Robin Hood, Roland
S   Saturn
T   Titan, Thor, Terpsichore,Theseus
U   Uranus
V   Venus, Vulcan
W   Woden
X
Y
Z   Zeus

EXTENDING BRAINSTORMING AND LISTING INTO THE CURRICULUM

Create MORPHOLOGY CHARTS — Morphology is that branch of grammar or linguistics which deals with how words are **affixed**. (Prefixes and suffixes are particular types of affixes.) Every native speaker learns the affixes of his language according to the way he hears them in his speech community. A speaker of standard English, for example, would say, "She wants to build new friend**ships** so that she will no longer be so **un**happy." This use of affixes permits a speaker to expand his linguistic structures and move him towards a more "mature" use of language, a necessary requirement for learning to write. Word lists can, therefore, provide the basis for morphology charts as described below:

. Have your students set up their notebooks with these categories:

NOUNS	VERBS	ADJECTIVES	-ly ADVERBS

. Show them how to classify major vocabulary words using the **MORPHOLOGY CHARTS,** as in these examples for the words "think" and "friend":

NOUNS	VERBS	ADJECTIVES	-ly ADVERBS
thought	think	thoughtful	thoughtfully
thoughts	thinks	thoughtless	
thoughtfulness	thought		
	thinking		
friend	befriend	friendly	
friends	befriends	friendlier	
	befriended	friendliest	
friendship	befriending		
friendships		unfriendly	
friendliness			

57

. Have students compose sentences which use the same words, but as different parts of speech, as in this example:

> *I've had several **thoughts** about **friendships**. First, a good **friend** is **thoughtful**. Second, I **think friends** should never be **unfriendly**. Finally, I can **befriend** only those people who are known for their **friendliness**.*

. Use **MORPHOLOGY CHARTS** for teaching your students spelling and the parts of speech. (See the chapter *Grammar for Grammar or Grammar for Writing, page 218,* for a further explanation of morphology.)

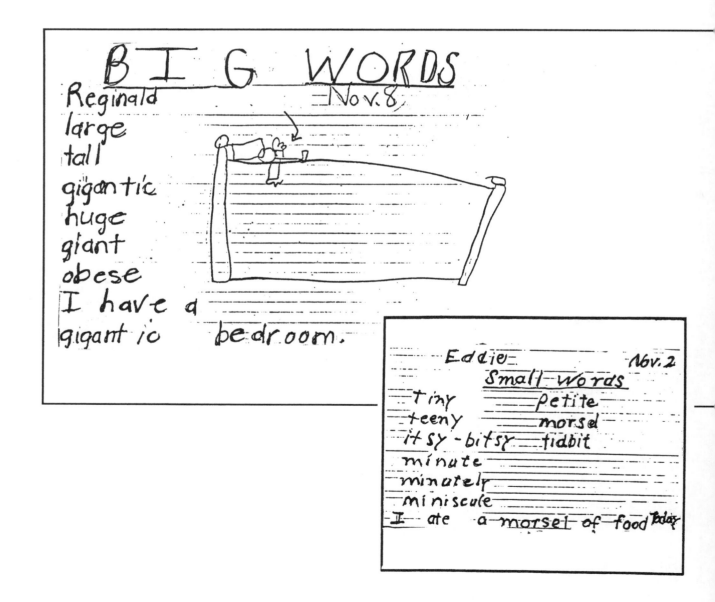

STUDENT ACTIVITY FOR VOCABULARY DEVELOPMENT THROUGH LISTING

ACTIVITIES:

- Look around you. Do you have vocabulary for whatever you can see? One word? Many words? Write a list of words that tell what you have observed.

- Share your words with a classmate and add a classmate's words to your lists.

- Pretend you are a detective who must describe his or her observations. Write a five-sentence description using as many words on your list as possible.

- Edit your writing. Is any particular order "better" than the other?

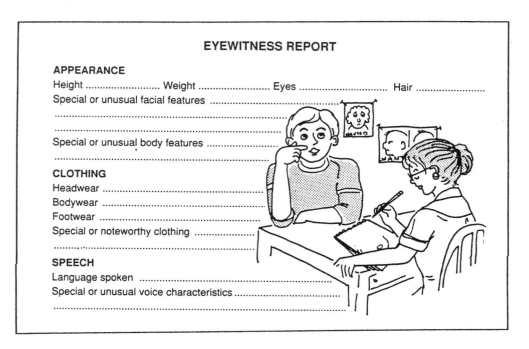

EYEWITNESS REPORT

APPEARANCE
Height .... Weight .... Eyes .... Hair ....
Special or unusual facial features ....
....
....
Special or unusual body features ....
....

CLOTHING
Headwear ....
Bodywear ....
Footwear ....
Special or noteworthy clothing ....
....

SPEECH
Language spoken ....
Special or unusual voice characteristics ....
....

EXAMPLES OF STUDENTS' LISTS AND WRITINGS

Hariyjah

My "One" Words List

1. one
2. single
3. une
4. yote
5. a
6. uni-
7. first
8. only
9. I
10. singular
11. once
12. just
13. unit
14. university
15. unicycle
16. unicorn
17. universal
18. universe
19. uniform
20. unite
21. united
22. United States
23. unique
24. union
25. alone
26. unilobe
27. uniparental
28. unisexual
29. unison
30. unipod
31. unipersonal
32. dollar
33. penny
34. cent
35. monogram
36. monocle
37. unitard
38. solo
39. ounce
40. solitary
41. solitude

Nichole

My "One" Story

Once upon a time there was a lady named Lois, who lived in a one bedroom single apartment with her husband and son. Lois had a son who was the only child. Some days her son would be lonely because he missed his father who worked at the University of Miami. Lois's husband put in a lot of long hours and she and her son were asleep when he arrived home. Lois prayed every day that her family would unite again.

Marie

Book of Lists

C

Creatures

unicorn
horrible
dragon
frightening
monsters
underwater
giant
ogre
troll
cruel
freak
God New
ugly
sharks
serpent
ghoul
Minotaur

18. giant octopus
19. sphinx
20. cyclops
21. mummy
22. fearful
23. beast
24. inhuman

MAMMALS

A-Animals
B-Backbones
C-Cats, Cenozoic Era
D-Dogs
E-Elephants, Eohippus
F-Fox
G-Grows inside mother's body
H-Human beings
I-Impalas
J-Jaguar
K-Kangaroo
L-Live babies, Land
M-Mammary glands
N-No feathers
O-Opossum
P-Platypus
Q-
R-Rabbit
S-Saber Tooth Tiger
T-Tiger
U-
V-
W-
X-
Y-
Z-Zebra

by Aisha

EXAMPLES OF STUDENTS' LISTS AND WRITINGS

METACOGNITION

I know that I know a lot about foxes. I know foxes eat meat. I know they run fast. I know that some are red. They have their babies in a litter.

I know that I don't know much about yaks.

by Tyrone W.

I Know That I Know...

I know that I know a lot about humans. I know that humans eat meat, plants and fish, so they are called omnivores. I know that humans can talk, walk, play, and run. I know that humans are related to the apes.

I know that I don't know a lot about an eohippus. I just know that it is related to the horse and that it is very small.

by Kamilah J.

ABC LIST

A - Animals
B - Backbones
C - Cats
D - Dolphins
E - Eohippus
F - Fox
G - Giraffe
H - Humans
I - Impala
J - Jaguar
K - Kangaroo
L - Live Babies
M - Milk
N - No Feathers
O - Opposum
P - Platypus
Q -
R - Rabbits
S - Saber-tooth Cat
T - Tiger
U -
V - Vertebrates
W - Wolly Mammoth
X -
Y - Yak

MORPHOLOGY CHART

CENTER FOR LEARNING THROUGH WRITING   4th

NOUNS	VERBS	ADJECTIVES	-LY ADVERBS
performance	perform	performative	
performances	performs	performable	
performer	performed		
performers	performing		
act	act	active	actively
acts	acts		
actor	acted		
actors	acting		
actress	activate		
actresses	activates		
activity	activated		
activities	activating		
action			
actions			

CES73
Class 2-413

Kimberly
March 12

I Know That I Know Something about the Soler System I Know that the Planets don't run into each other. I also Know that Pluto takes 248 years to go around the sun. In addition I Know That Mercury is very close to the sun.

EASY WRITER ACTIVITIES FOR BRAINSTORMING

WHAT AM I?

Pretend you are your favorite candy. Write a story about your life.
In your story tell:

- what you look like
- who buys you
- what happens after you are bought

DO NOT TELL WHO YOU ARE. LET YOUR FRIENDS GUESS. Use some of the words from the CANDY FACTORY to help you write your story. Start your story with these words:

Can you guess what I am?

CANDY FACTORY

bubble gum	chewy	birthday	buy
caramel	delicious	friend	chew
chocolate	sweet	money	eat
lollipops	sugary	party	lick
M & M's	tasty	pocket	
peanuts	yummy	prize	
		store	

CHECK YOUR WORK

Can you add more to help your friends guess what you
Are there any words you want to change?
Did you begin each sentence with a capital letter?
Did you end each sentence with a period or question n

EXTRA CREDIT

Make up the name of a new candy.
Write what it is made of.
Draw a picture of it.

THINKING SKILLS
hypothesizing
deciding
imagining

Page 34
BOOK A

WRITING FROM KEY WORDS

THE NUMBER GAME
2, 4, 8, 10

Below are four lists of words which are "spelled" with numbers. Write a two or three paragraph fantasy story or imaginary article using as many of these words as possible. Use the combination of letters and numbers in your writing.

EXAMPLE

2 bad the **4cast 4 2morrow neg8s** any chance of **10nis.**

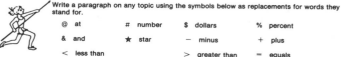

2	4	8	10
2day	4most	appreci8	10der
2morrow	4tune	consider8	10nis
2night	4ead	negoti8	10tacle
2ne	4ce	investig8	10t
2t	4father	depreci8	10sion
2th	4cast	initi8	10ant
2lip	4go	hesit8	10d
2tor	4man	manipul8	10ement
2-2	4sight	bicarbon8	10or
2zday	4give	co-oper8	10th

CHECKLIST FOR EDITING

- Did you use as many words from the lists as possible?
- Are there any more words you can add?

FORGE AHEAD

Write a paragraph on any topic using the symbols below as replacements for words they stand for.

@	at	#	number	$	dollars	%	percent
&	and	★	star	−	minus	+	plus
<	less than			>	greater than	=	equals

ERA/CCR Corp. The Write Track Company

Writing From Key Words
Page 33

THE WRITER'S BOOK OF SYNONYMS

CORPORATION
THE WRITE TRACK COMPANY

Gail Gonzaour   Dr. Helen Erion
Illustrator   Educational Consultant

WORD LOCATOR CHART

PEOPLE

How People **Act**

excited	5	foolish	5	happy	6
mean	6	nice	6	sad	7
shy	7	smart	7	strong	8
talkative	8	tired	8	tireless	8
weak	9	afraid	9		

How People **Communicate**

cry	9	laugh	10	scream	10
sing	10	smile	11	talk	11
write	11				

How People **Do Things**

attack	12	carry	12	dance	12
drive	13	eat	13	exercise	13
fight	14	help	14	jump	14
lift	14	run	15	walk	15

How People **Look**

fat	16	old	16	pretty	16
short	17	skinny	17	strong	17
tall	18	ugly	18	weak	18
young	19				

1

STUDENTS' RESPONSES USING VOCABULARY FROM THE WRITER'S BOOK OF SYNONYMS

Marlene
7GWC!   Reading-english
JHS 22

"How People LOOK"

I have alot of <u>beautiful</u> friends. I like them alot because they look and act <u>fair</u> Alot of guys like my friends because they are <u>proportioned</u> and <u>attractive</u>. But they are also very <u>delicate</u> so the guys have to act <u>comely</u> with them. The clothes they ~~wear~~ wear are pretty so it makes them look <u>dainty</u>. My friend's mother's are very <u>bonnie</u> so I guess they are like their moms. I think it is <u>lovely</u> to have friends like I have.

Magdalena   Reading
7gwc!

Reading
Ice cream is cold, refreshing, rich, creamy, fruity, icy, thick, milky, smooth, and frosty. It's delicious too and don't forget the strawberry on top. Or if you prefer have a cherry instead of a strawberry. And don't forget to have a nice time while it last.

"<u>How things tastes</u>"
Ice cream.

63

BRAINSTORM

USE THE WORDS TO HELP YOU WRITE...ADD ANY ENDINGS YOU NEED

WRITE A MYSTERY STORY
Use as many of these words as you need.

- devil
- dungeon
- ghost
- haunt
- squeak
- storm
- terrify
- thunder
- tremble

WRITE FOR SCIENCE
Use as many of these words as you need.

- adapt
- bear
- den
- food
- forest
- hibernate
- search
- spring
- observe
- survive
- winter
- experiment

WRITE FOR SOCI

Use as many of these w
- adventure
- America
- explorer
- hardship
- settle
- voyage

WRITE YOUR OWN STORY OR REPOR

Brainstorm a list of words from your favorite subject or report.

PLAN THROUGH BRAINSTORMING

A good way to get started writing is to **brainstorm** as many ideas as you can on a topic. Ask a classmate to **brainstorm** with you. When you are ready to write, select those items which you consider helpful for your story or article.

1. How to

be popular
gain weight
get a job
pass a test

2. The many ways to

train a pet
get a room cleaned
earn spending money
get along with a sister or brother

3. Why

watching television is (is not) educational
jogging (or swimming) is good for your health
the school lunch period should be longer (or shorter)
working after school is (or is not) a good idea

CHECKLIST FOR EDITING

- Are there any more ideas you can add?
- Did you add a classmate's ideas to your own?

SENTENCE COMPOSING
WORDS INTO SENTENCES — THE BASIS OF COMPOSING

The basic structure of written English is manifested in the grammatical sentence which, when analyzed or "parsed," appears to be composed of two parts — the *noun phrase,* or the "complete subject," and the *verb phrase,* or the "complete predicate."

The lovely china doll/sat in the family's magnificent living room.

The written sentence is also distinguished by end punctuation marks and the initial capital letter.

These two distinguishing marks of the written sentence — subject/predicate and end punctuation, which are so obvious to the literate adult — are not necessarily apparent to those just learning to write. In fact, speaking and writing have several noticeably different characteristics. For example, all of us learn spoken sentences in early childhood, and these sentences are often different from those which are likely to be written.

Hi.

What's doing?

Not much.

Seen any good movies?

Yeah, one at the Surrey. Pretty good, too. Lots of action.

Good to talk to ya. Say hello to the gang. See ya later!

You can readily notice the absence of complete sentences, except for "What's doing?" which doesn't say much that is complete, or "Not much," an ellipsis for "Not much is doing." The punctuation marks which are added in this conversation only approximate the varied intonation patterns which would be part of such a conversation. Of course, speakers of the language intuitively understand the "deeper" sentence boundaries and could expand these "half-sentences" into grammatically correct complete ones, so that *"Seen any good movies?"* becomes *"Have you seen any good movies?"*

For many students, however, the process of transferring from spoken to written sentences, or from half to complete sentences, is fairly complex. Explanations such as "a sentence is a complete thought" are as baffling as the concept of the sentence itself. Nor do the words "subject and predicate" necessarily help students distinguish grammatical from ungrammatical written forms.

DEVELOPING SENTENCE SENSE

The task for the teacher, therefore, is to help the students develop the intuitive sentence sense which helps them distinguish between full or complete written sentences versus half or incomplete ones. Conversely, the students must distinguish where there are two or more joined sentences that have not been separated by end punctuation. To develop this sentence sense, we begin early in the school year with the following activities:

Words to Build Sentences — Show students how words are analogous to building blocks. Words are, in essence, small items which can be fitted together to state an idea or ideas. For example, we can start with two words:

boy   *truck*

Most of us realize that if other words are added, an idea, expressed as a sentence, can emerge:

The boy has a truck.

From these same two words, different sentences can be made:

Add endings: *The boys have trucks.*
                      The boys' trucks are in the garage.

Rearrange the words: *The truck took the boy home.*
                      The boy took his favorite truck to school.

66

Whole Sentences and Half Sentences — As children hear the word "sentence," they need to have an operational definition. Begin simply by stating that a sentence:

- is usually a group of words
- gives information or tells us something
- usually has two parts — 1) who or what? and 2) has, does, or is what?
- starts with a capital letter and ends with punctuation

Of course, teachers also know that the basic ingredients of a sentence are the subject and predicate, but this concept is often too difficult for the young child or the beginning writer to understand. The teacher must rely on operational information which is observable to the child. We suggest that the teacher use the terms "whole sentences" and "half sentences." For example, write the words:

a new bicycle

Test the definition:

a. Is this a group of words?

b. Does it give some information?

c. Do we think we have a whole sentence or a half sentence? Can we find the two parts?

d. Should there be end punctuation?

It is at point **c** where the students must discover whether "*a new bicycle*" is a whole sentence or part of a sentence. Use a questioning/discovery approach with your students. First, ask a question to which the words "*a new bicycle*" will be the answer. Write the question and write the answer on the board. Do not capitalize the answer when it is a half sentence.

What did you get for your birthday?	*a new bicycle*
What did you see in the hallway?	*a new bicycle*
What would you like to buy?	*a new bicycle*

Have the students discover why you are calling "*a new bicycle*" a half sentence. Guide them into finding a suitable second half to these words. For example, have them join some of the words from the question:

I bought a new bicycle for my brother.
I want to buy a new bicycle .
A new bicycle is in the hallway.

Ask the students why they think you need a capital letter and punctuation for the above sentences, but do not need punctuation for the words "*a new bicycle.*"

Repeat these types of activities frequently. Use the words "whole" and "half," and discuss with the children why some sentences sound "whole" while others appear to be "half."

Have children orally compose dialogues in which they first speak mainly in half sentences and then mainly in whole sentences.

Half Sentence Talk

What's your name?
Jean

Where do you live?
down the street

What do you like to do?
lots of things

How many sisters do you have?
two

Can you come roller skating?
yes

Whole Sentence Talk

My name is Jean.

I live down the street.

I like to do lots of things.

I have two sisters.

I can come roller skating only if my mother says yes.

The Two Parts of a Sentence — Students must have frequent practice in relating the two parts of a sentence until they can "sense" or "feel" when they have a whole sentence. This means they must distinguish not only a whole sentence from a half sentence, but also a whole sentence from a "sentence and a half" or two whole sentences "falsely" joined together. One way to begin is to make a list of every child's name in the class. Put the names under a heading labeled A.

A
Jose
Martha
Frank
Denise

Ask the children if they think each name forms a whole sentence. Ask if they think each name is a sentence or a half sentence. Add a column B and ask each child to provide a word which tells what he or she does. Model the first answer so that you guide the children into providing a verb.

A	B
Jose	*eats*
Martha	*sings*
Frank	*builds*
Denise	*walks*

Continue this type of activity on a frequent basis.

Have the children write a list of animals. Put the word **the, a,** or **an** in front of each word so that the children can observe the noun grouping, technically called the *noun phrase*. Name this column A.

A
the hippo
a giraffe
an elephant
the tiger

Next, brainstorm for a list of verbs. Guide the children in using the **-ing** form of these verbs with "was" or "is."

A	B
the hippo	*was singing*
a giraffe	*is playing*
an elephant	*was sleeping*
the tiger	*is crying*

Every sentence, regardless of its length, can be divided into two basic parts, but the difficulty with this division comes when we move from simple to complex sentences. However, if students continue to work systematically with sentence construction, there is greater opportunity for them to compose and recognize whole sentences in their own writing.

SENTENCE COMPOSING OR SENTENCE SYNTHESIS

Words represent ideas or concepts. The availability of words often gives the student the means of composing. By having several words which are related or associative, the writer can generate an idea which is expressed in a sentence.

Halloween   spooky   mask

We all wore spooky masks on Halloween and scared our friends.

Beginning in kindergarten, and all through the grades, students encounter vocabulary from a variety of sources. There is, of course, their spoken vocabulary which, in the early stages, matches the words from reading and spelling. New vocabulary from social studies, science, mathematics, physical education, and school life is then presented in increasing profusion.

Name Herman
A Halloween Story
I have a spooky costume.
my mask looks like monster.
I scared my friend.

All of this vocabulary can serve for student composing, and indeed should be the basis of composing practice. By using the words from these vocabulary sources, the student can write or compose on a frequent, even daily, basis and can have the opportunity to "try out" the words in varying contexts and sentence arrangements.

Be sure the student composes sentences by using several (two, three, or four) words from his/her spoken or written vocabulary in each sentence, in contrast with composing each sentence using only one word. When the task is to use all three words in the same sentence, the student is less likely to compose "empty" sentences such as:

I see Humpty Dumpty.
I have clothes.
Eggs are good.

When the student is given three words — *Humpty Dumpty, clothes, egg* — and uses the three words in the same sentence, with the option of adding endings, greater possibilities for interesting composings occur:

Humpty Dumpty is an egg who wears clothes.

Eggs spilled on Humpty Dumpty's clothes when he had breakfast.

Humpty Dumpty put on his best clothes and sat down to a breakfast of scrambled eggs.

PROCEDURES FOR DEVELOPING SENTENCE SYNTHESIS

.   **Select an Item of Interest to the Students** — Then have the students brainstorm for related or associative vocabulary and write these words in a cluster pattern as shown below:

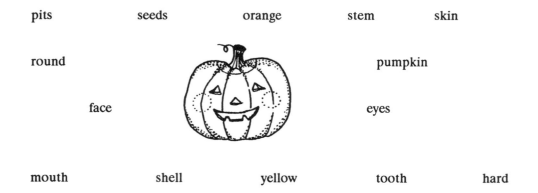

| pits | seeds | orange | stem | skin |

round

pumpkin

face

eyes

| mouth | shell | yellow | tooth | hard |

Have the students orally compose sentences using two or more words from the group in the same sentence. As students become more skilled, they will learn to write varied sentences using the words in different order and in different formats.

The yellow pumpkin had a hard shell and a small stem.

Did you see the round eyes on the funny jack-o'-lantern?

A pumpkin has seeds, a stem, and an orange skin.

. **Use a Picture as a Stimulus** — Select a picture of interest to the students. Have them name all the items they see in the picture and write a list. Then have them compose sentences each of which contains at least two words from the list. Write all the sentences on the board. Then ask the students to organize or sequence the sentences into a story about the picture. (They do not have to use all the sentences.)

. **Compose with Spelling and Reading Vocabulary** — The vocabulary from the spelling and reading program is an excellent source for composing practice. To help your students write fuller and more varied sentences, have them combine three or even four words from their spelling or reading vocabulary into one sentence. You can have the students select the words from their spelling or reading list which combine naturally or easily into sentences. For example, the words might be:

bear wait car yellow land Mars

Possible arrangements are:

The bear waited for the car to stop.

A yellow car landed in the bear's den.

Six men in yellow suits landed on Mars.

. **Use Content Area Words for Composing** — The vocabularies from social studies, science, math, and so forth are excellent sources for composing. In fact, by the time the students are using their content words in writing, they can be asked to form paragraphs or related sentences incorporating KEY WORDS as in the following examples:

raccoon	*nocturnal*	*food*	*environment*	*humans*
woods	*adapt*		*survive*	*winter*

Raccoons *are* **nocturnal** *animals which live in a* **wooded environment.** *Sometimes they get their* **food** *by stealing from animals. They often* **survive** *in the* **winter** *by knocking over garbage cans and eating what* **humans** *have thrown away.*

The math vocabulary can be used for factual or fantasy writing and provides the student with many creative opportunities:

add	*subtract*	*divide*	*multiply*	*equality*

Ladies and Gentlemen: If you elect me to office, I promise that I will **add** *to your joys,* **subtract** *your troubles,* **multiply** *your happiness, and* **divide** *the wealth. Everyone in this town will have true* **equality.**

Beginning in the intermediate grades, students will be required to write extensively for social studies. Essay questions, research reports, biography reports, and opinion statements are all part of social studies writing. To prepare for this writing, students need practice in composing with social studies vocabulary. Here are two examples of students' writing using KEY social studies words:

explorer   *voyage*   *America*   *hardship*   *settle*   *rich*

After Columbus discovered **America,** *many other* **explorers** *went on* **voyages** *to the New World. They* **settled** *all along the coasts and waterways in places they did not know a thing about. They suffered many* **hardships,** *but they believed that they would soon become* **rich** *and have a better life.*

or

Christopher Columbus was an **explorer** *who went on a* **voyage** *to see if he could find the* **riches** *of India. He and his men had many* **hardships** *during their voyage. When Columbus landed, he gave the name Indian to the people because thought he was in India. One day this new place would be called* **America** *and lots of people would come from Europe and other places to* **settle** *there.*

. **Combine Grammar with Writing Through MORPHOLOGY** — As your students gradually become more proficient in combining several words into one sentence, show them how to classify the words into parts of speech using the **MORPHOLOGY CHARTS** illustrated in the previous chapter **BRAINSTORMING** and **LISTING** (page 57).

By categorizing words through **MORPHOLOGY,** the students will understand how sentences result from the combination of at least two different parts of speech — the noun (or pronoun) and the verb. You might first provide your students with a set of words from reading or spelling:

step	*fifty*	*flight*
late	*careful*	*ticket*
tooth	*pay*	*twenty*
thankful	*enjoy*	*time*
ride	*gain*	*sky*
build	*airplane*	*happy*

. Begin by asking the students to list all the words which they identify as people, animals, plants, places, activities, or objects. Place these under a heading called **NOUNS:**

step
airplane
tooth
ticket
sky

. If they are uncertain about which words are nouns, have the students search for words which can be preceded by the word "the" as in "the flight" or "the ride." Tell them that words which combine with "the" are also nouns.

. Have a second column called **VERBS.** To determine which words are verbs, write the following sentence frame:

Today we ....; yesterday we ....

All words which have a form that fits in both slots are verbs.

From the above list, there is:

Today we ride; yesterday we rode.

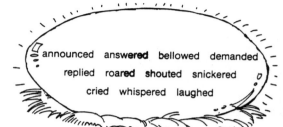

PAST TENSE PRESENTS

announced answered bellowed demanded replied roared shouted snickered cried whispered laughed

Today we build; yesterday we built.

Today we pay; yesterday we paid.

Today we step; yesterday we stepped.

Today we gain; yesterday we gained.

. Have a third column merely called OTHER for words which are more difficult to categorize.

. **Use Sentence Menus** — Have the students compose sentences using a "menu" approach, selecting a word at random from each column. Tell them they can add the word "the" or "a" to start the sentences and that they can add endings to the nouns and verbs. Ask the students if they have composed sentences. If they are uncertain because the sentences "sound" silly or nonsensical, explain that a sentence may tell something "strange" or "true." They are sentences because they have two essential parts — the noun and the verb.

. Ask the students to name the people in their classroom or school. A set of **nouns** will result from this procedure. Then ask the students to state the things they do. The "doing" activities will provide a set of **verbs.** Develop a list of words that describe. **Adjectives** and other descriptive vocabulary will emerge. By asking the students to tell where these people can be, you will get a vocabulary of **prepositions.** Set up these lists according to the most familiar word order of English as shown below:

Adjectives	Nouns	Verbs	Prepositional Phrases
calm	teacher	walk	in/at the desk
young	child	play	in the movies
beautiful	principal	shout	near the playground
gentle	boy	snack	next to the swings
funny	girl	draw	on top of the school
sweet	custodian	laugh	under the table
jolly	cook	sing	inside the cafeteria

After the students have made lists of single words, ask them to think of word groups which contain a noun, technically called a **noun phrase.** Give them an example so the students understand what you are asking for *(green shoe, warm gloves)*. After you have received at least ten noun phrases, divide them in half. Ask the students to compose sentences using two noun phrases in the same sentence:

my gloves   *the cat's paws*

My gloves fit over the cat's paws.

The cat's paws were too small for my gloves.

Vincent
MORPHOLOGY CHART

NOUNS	VERBS	ADJECTIVES	-LY ADVERBS
sweet	sweeten	sweet	sweetly
sweets	sweetens	sweeter	
sweetener	sweetened	sweetest	
sweeteners	sweetening		
	bless	blessed	blessedly
blessedness	blesses		
	blessed		
	blessing		
digest	digest	digestible	
digestion	digests	digestive	
	digested		
	digesting		

77

FOLLOW-UP ACTIVITIES

These follow-up procedures are suggested after the student has composed a variety of sentences:

. Have the student select the "best" or most interesting sentences.

. Make a file or chart of "best" sentences for story starters or story enders.

. Share good sentences orally.

. Publish good sentences. Give the author a "by-line." (Example: Joe Hall, Reporter)

. Use selected sentences for future lessons in improving (expanding, substituting, rearranging).

SUGGESTIONS FOR PUBLISHING SENTENCES

To complete the writing process, students should have their sentences "published." Sentences can be published on oaktag or colored paper. They can be recopied by the student in felt pen or crayon and displayed on bulletin boards. A weekly newsletter can be developed in the classroom where **BEST SENTENCES OF THE WEEK** are published and distributed.

A file of "best" sentences can be kept by students to use when they need story starters or story endings for new composings. Encourage students to get "permission" from classmates to use their sentences. Show them how to "give credit" to the original author of a sentence by placing an "acknowledgement" footnote. (Example: "I would like to thank Jinny for letting me use her sentence as my story starter.")

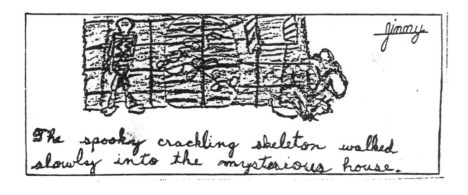

Students can practice writing every day through sentence composing. Gradually, from disconnected sentences they can begin the development of paragraphs. As the students compose sentences, they should follow the editing aspects of the writing process which include:

. composing a checklist with the class or group

. using the checklist to edit for sentence sense and sentence mechanics

The checklist should contain the questions of the task required:

. *Did I use two or more words from the list in each sentence?*
. *Did I use the correct affixes on my words?*
. *Did I begin each sentence with a capital letter?*
. *Did I end each sentence with a period or a question mark?*

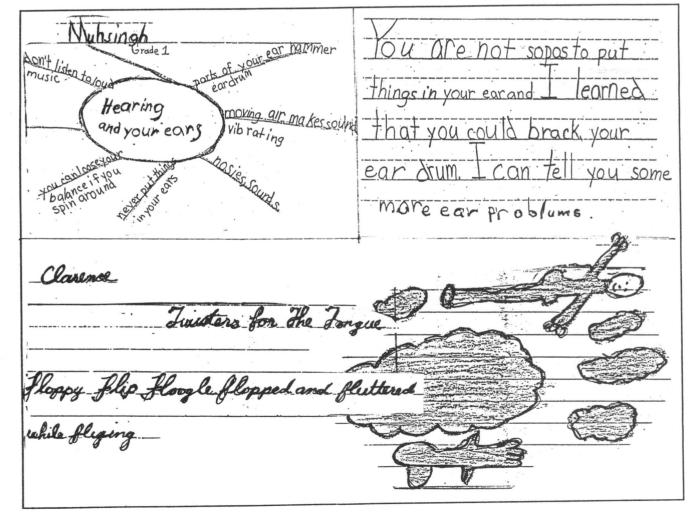

STUDENT ACTIVITY FOR UNDERSTANDING "WHOLE SENTENCES" AND "HALF SENTENCES"

PURPOSE: To develop the understanding of **half sentences** as differentiated from **whole sentences.** The concept of complete vs. incomplete comes when the student recognizes the segments or sectors of a sentence. Have students practice completing charts similar to the one below.

EXAMPLE:

Subject	Verb	Completer
The visitors	*are*	....
....	*walked*	*around the room*
....	*seemed*	*terrified...........*
Many children	....	*in the woods*
Our relatives	....	....
....	*had become*	....
The train	....	*late in the afternoon*

STUDENT ACTIVITY FOR UNDERSTANDING "WHOLE SENTENCES" AND "HALF SENTENCES"

PURPOSE: To develop the students' ability to differentiate between complete sentences and sentence fragments (whole/half sentences).

ACTIVITY

1. Students take turns looking out of the window.

2. The students write what they see.

3. Three or four students work in a group to review the responses and identify whole or half-sentences.

4. The students revise half-sentence talk into complete sentences.

5. Follow up with each student observing something in the room and writing a "whole sentence" about the observation.

6. Have the students share their sentences and identify them as "whole" or "half."

7. Students who have written half-sentences complete the "other half."

SAMPLE EASY WRITER ACTIVITIES FOR SENTENCE COMPOSING

AND THE WINNER IS . . .

The eight animals below deserve awards for being among the largest or smallest animals in the world.

Write an award-winning sentence about each animal.

Use the name of the animal and one verb from the VERB BOX in each sentence.

You can add **-s**, **-ed**, or **-ing** to the verbs.

EXAMPLE: goliath beetle startle

The unsuspecting rabbit was **startled** by the sudden appearance of the **goliath beetle** in the cabbage patch.

blue whale (largest and heaviest mammal)

Siberian tiger (largest member of the cat family)

giant squid (has the largest eyes of any animal

anaconda (longest and heaviest snake)

goliath frog (largest frog)

giant birdwing (largest butterfly)

dwarf pygmy goby (shortest fish)

bee hummingbird (smallest bird)

VERB BOX

approach	lunge
choke	plunge
defend	retreat
destroy	squash
frighten	stagger
gobble	

CHECKLIST FOR PROOFREADING
- Did you begin each sentence with a capital letter and end punctuation?
- Did you check your spelling?

EXTRA CREDIT
Choose an animal that you might want to be. Write a story w
- why you would want to be this animal
- what special or unusual characteristics you would have
- what kinds of things you would do

THINKING SKILLS
deciding
organizing
synthesizing
SENTENCE COMPOSING

BOOK D
Page 1

BODY WORDS

Each sentence has missing words. Put the words from each box into the right spaces. Use the words from the SAME BOX in each set of sentences.

EXAMPLE

toes
wiggle
ten

1. Can you **wiggle** all of your **ten toes** at the same time?
2. "**Wiggle** your big **toes ten** times," said the teacher.

feet
walked
sore

1. I _____ so much that my _____ became _____ .
2. My mother said, "If you _____ on the grass, you would not get _____ _____ ."

mouth
opened
wide

1. The whale _____ his _____ _____ and smiled.
2. "I _____ my _____ _____ and the people got scared," said the whale.

hair
cut
long

1. When your _____ gets too _____ , it must be _____ .
2. "I wish I could _____ my _____ _____ ,"wept the shaggy dog.

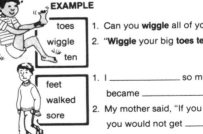

CHECK YOUR WORK
Did you use all three words in each sentence?

EXTRA CREDIT
Write a sentence. Use all of these words in one sentence.

hands   wear   cold

THINKING SKILLS
synthesizing
deciding
SENTENCE COMPOSING

Page 6
BOOK A

SAMPLE EASY WRITER ACTIVITY FOR SENTENCE COMPOSING

ANIMAL FUN

The words on this page will help you write some funny sentences about animals.
Use both words in each box for every sentence you write.
You may add **-s** or **-es** to some of the words.

EXAMPLE

lion
newspaper

Every Sunday morning the **lion** gets up early to read the **newspaper**.
OR
Have you ever seen **lions** read **newspapers**?

sheep
popcorn

whale
flower

pony
basketball

pig
elevator

fox
ladder

deer
sailboat

elephant
baby carriage

owl
bed

CHECKLIST FOR PROOFREADING

- Did you use both words in each box for every sentence?
- Did you begin each sentence with a capital letter?
- Did you end each sentence with the correct punctuation?

EXTRA CREDIT

Choose one of the sentences you like.
Write three or more sentences to tell a story about the animal.
Draw a picture of your story.

THINKING SKILLS
synthesizing
imagining
SENTENCE COMPOSING

Page 7

© Copyright 1987 ERA/CCR Corporation

Book B

EXAMPLES OF STUDENTS' WRITING USING SENTENCE COMPOSING

Mark
nov 30

P.S. 102 2
Class 307

Did you ever see a sheep eating popcorn?

The whale got out of the water to smell a rose.

Mr. and Mrs. Pony played basketball and went to eat breakfast in a restaurant.

Dear Kemwathe

I am writing this letter to inform you that yesterday there was an addition added to our family. My father came home and guess what he brought with him? guess. Nope! He brought a siberean tiger, you know like the one we saw in the zoo. Well that is all for now, See you in school.

TRULY yours,
Angel

P.S. what did you get?

WALL CHARTS TO ILLUSTRATE SENTENCE COMPOSING

COMPOSE A SENTENCE

MAKE IT TRUE OR MAKE IT STRANGE

Compose two sentences. Use
three of the words below the
picture in each of the sentences.
Add as many words as you need
to compose your sentences.
Add any endings you need.

EXAMPLE

• egg • clothes • Humpty Dumpty

1 The **egg** wore **clothes** and
looked like **Humpty Dumpty.**

2 Humpty Dumpty wore
his new **clothes** to go
shopping for **eggs.**

• chase	• police	• car
• hunt	• frighten	• teacher
• sing	• giant	• Jack

CHECKLIST FOR PROOFREADING

✓ Did you use all **three words** in one
✓ Did you add the correct endings?
✓ Did you begin each sentence with a
✓ Did you end each sentence with a pe

© 1985 ERA/CCR Corp.   **THE WRITE TRACK CON**

COMPOSE A SENTENCE

Make it true or make it strange

EXAMPLE:

*The blue whale
somersaulted
in the bathtub.*

Pick a phrase from Column A, a word from
Column B, and a phrase from Column C. Put
them together so that you have a sentence.
Compose sentences that tell both true and
strange events.

A Nouns Phrases	B Verbs	C Prepositional Phrases
hockey star	climbs/climbed	in/on/at the desk
ice skating champion	scribbles/scribbled	inside the closet
long distance runner	croons/crooned	under the sink
stunt pilot	somersaults/	on/under the table
considerate teacher	somersaulted	on top of the house
clumsy dinosaur	paints/painted	on/at the window
giant squid	wrestles/wrestled	on the ceiling
blue whale	whispers/whispered	in the bathtub
	jogs/jogged	

Add your own words and
phrases. Put your favorite
sentences into a book or on cards.

© 1985 ERA/CCR Corp.   **THE WRITE TRACK COMPANY**   *Intermediate 2*

84

IMPROVING THE WRITING PRODUCT

SENTENCE EXPANDING

As we mentioned previously, one way to improve a piece of writing is to add appropriate information or details. Many times a writer reviews her writing, asking herself:

"What must I add to make this writing more interesting, more informative, or more exciting to my audience?"

This concern with improvement for the sake of the reader is the hallmark of the good writer. Thus an essential part of teaching writing is making the student aware of when and how to expand or add to the written product. Being fluent in writing means having the right word or words to add to a previously composed sentence. We begin teaching this strategy of sentence expanding by giving the student the following definition of a sentence:

A sentence is a carrier of information that the writer can "control" to say as much or as little as she wants to say. How much the sentence says is up to the author.

For example, we can show the students this sentence:

Polly put the bread on the table.

While we can be perfectly satisfied with this sentence, the writer may want to provide her audience with more information; so, through "empathy", one of the factors of intelligent behavior, she thinks of what questions her reader might ask:

When did this happen?
Who is Polly?
What kind of bread?
What kind of table?
How did Polly do this?

Now the new sentence might read:

Just before dinner was served, Polly, the young guest at the Mayer's home, put the freshly-baked bread on the family's exquisite dining room table.

Although the expanded sentence may not always be a better sentence, writers learn that certain details provide the reader with a clearer understanding or greater imagery. As students become more proficient with language, they learn to construct sentences that carry meaningful information.

Two main purposes can be accomplished with sentence expanding. First, through expanding, the individual sentence becomes a carrier of related ideas, giving the reader a better grasp of the writer's words or message. Second, the basic sentence can be expanded to become a topic sentence containing supporting ideas which can be developed further. In this way the student is introduced to a procedure for developing a paragraph.

Crestview's, "Write On!"

Name: Dionne

Date:

Sentence Expanison
Easy Writer Pg. 9 1to6
The muddy elf lived in the wild woods
Everyday the dark dwarves went fishing
in the shiny river. The pretty fairy brought
me a wide gift. I saw a mean witch
fly on an ugly broom stick. The friendly
trdl wouldn't let the boy go over the
small bridge. All the terrible monsters
came out of the old cave.

SUGGESTED PROCEDURES FOR SENTENCE EXPANDING

1. Select a short basic sentence similar to types frequently composed by students:

   The woman bought an apple.
   I found a hat.
   The cat climbed a tree.

2. Explain to the students that they can make these sentences tell more or carry more information. For example, if they ask the question **What kind of woman? apple? hat?** or **tree?** they will get adjectives or descriptive modifiers. Point out, too, that when a writer adds a word or group of words, he/she uses a special proofreading mark called a **caret** .

3. Illustrate the use of the caret mark.

   The ⋀ woman bought an ⋀ apple.
   I found a ⋀ hat.
   The ⋀ cat climbed the ⋀ tree.

   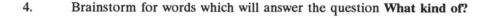

   WORD BOX

beautiful	calm	cruel
dark	friendly	frightened
gentle	huge	hungry	playful
small	soft	tiny	warm

   cuddly
   frisky
   scary
   wild

4. Brainstorm for words which will answer the question **What kind of?**

5. Have the students re-create new sentences, inserting adjectives which the students consider appropriate.

   The *furry white* cat climbed the *twisted old apple* tree.

6. Indicate to the students that other **WH- questions** can produce expansions:

   Where did it happen?

   When did it happen?

   This morning the furry white cat climbed the twisted old apple tree behind the barn.

WORDS AND PHRASES FOR EXPANDING

You can introduce expanding step-by-step by having students add only one part of speech at a time, or you can explore the various types of expanders which can be used to improve sentences. Below is a suggested plan for the order of introducing words and phrases for expansion, followed by sample activities which you can use or adapt for your students.

. Expand with only one adjective:

> *Marie bought a coat.*
>
> *Marie bought a* **warm** *coat.*

. Expand with two adjectives:

> *The boy walked into the house.*
>
> *The* **frightened** *boy walked into the* **empty** *house.*

. Expand with prepositional phrases:

> *The cat is taking a nap.*
>
> *The cat is taking a nap* **on the new electric blanket.**

. Expand with adverbs of time:

> *We played tennis.*
>
> **Early this morning, before anyone else arrived at the courts,** *we played tennis.*

. Expand with adverbs of cause:

> *The firefighter broke down all the doors.*
>
> **Because of the raging fire,** *the firefighter broke down all the doors.*

. Expand with words of quantity (determiners):

> *The children went home.*
>
> **Both** *the children went home.*
>
> **All** *the children went home.*
>
> **Several** *children went home.*

88

USING EXPANDING TO DEVELOP A PARAGRAPH

Often a basic sentence which carries familiar but limited information can become the springboard for "getting started" in writing a paragraph. For example, you can present the students with one of these three sentences, depending on their age and experiential background:

Snoopy is a dog.

Christopher Columbus was an explorer.

Marie Curie was a scientist.

Ask the students to brainstorm for every word or phrase which they associate with (a) **the name mentioned in the sentence** (Snoopy, Christopher Columbus, Marie Curie) and (b) **the noun** (dog, explorer, scientist). Encourage the students to associate freely so that they get a large collection of words. Then have the students write a new, expanded sentence about Snoopy, Columbus, or Curie, using as many brainstormed words as they wish. The result will be an expanded topic sentence which can then be developed into a paragraph.

The following are expanded sentences which have been produced by students at different grade levels:

Snoopy is Charlie Brown's dog and his best friend.

Snoopy is a dog who lives in a doghouse and dreams of bones.

Christopher Columbus was first a sailor and then an explorer who believed in miracles.

In 1492 Christopher Columbus, an explorer, sailed from Spain into an unknown ocean.

Marie Curie, a Polish-born woman, became a Nobel Prize winner for her discovery of radium and was the first woman scientist to receive this honor.

FOLLOW-UP SUGGESTIONS FOR EXPANDING

As part of frequent "warm-ups" or practice, have the students locate or compose **plain** sentences which they can change into **super** sentences through **WH-** expansion.

After the students have written a story or paragraph, ask them to reread their writing and see what they could improve by expanding.

Share sentences orally. Have students tell which sentence they think is more interesting, the plain or the expanded one. Note, however, that long sentences are not always better. Students must evaluate sentences on the basis of **whether or not they carry important or essential information.** Publish **super sentences** which the students have selected as their best examples.

As with sentence composing or synthesis, expanding should be incorporated into the daily language arts program. Here too, spelling and content area words can be used as the basis for developing expanded sentences.

To reinforce your students' editing skills, add the following items to your editing chart:

QUESTIONS FOR EDITING BY EXPANDING

.   *Can I make my sentences more interesting by adding adjectives or other describing words?*
.   *Can I make my sentences more interesting by answering more WH- questions?*
.   *Are my sentences carrying enough information to my audience?*

WHEN?   **WHERE?**   **WHY?**

WHAT KIND OF?

RESOURCE LIST OF EXPANDERS

You may want to put these words on charts and keep them available for the students.

Prepositions
above
alongside of
around
at
away from

behind
beneath
by

down
far

in
inside
into

Adverbs of Place
near
nearby
next to

off
on
on top of
out
outside
outside of
over
to
towards

under
up

never
now and then

occasionally
often
once in a while
once upon a time

rarely
recently

sometimes
soon

today
tomorrow

usually

yesterday

Adverbs of Cause
as a result of

because

even though

in order to

on account of

so that

Words of Quantity (Determiners)
all
any

both

each
every

few

lots of

many

none
numerous

several
some

Adverbs of Time
after
afterwards
always
at the same time as

before
by and by
during

earlier than

for a long time
frequently
from time to time

in a few minutes
in the mornings

last week
lately
later than
long ago

many times
many years ago

The soothing candle was glitting^er peacefully in a shabby shack.

The deep sea diver leaped from the ship because he was very fearless.

The daring acrobat is practicing his dangerous act for tonight's show.

Eary Writer
Getting the Facts
Expanding Sentences

1. My frightenet puppy came home last night because he was scared of his shadow.

2. The artist drew a picture about me because he wanted to be in the hall of frame.

3. The spectacular boy went skating on the sidewalk last afternoon.

4. The intelligent girls built a treehouse in their back yard out of wood.

SAMPLE ACTIVITIES FROM "EASY WRITER"

EXPAND INTO THE FUTURE

Most of us wonder what we'll be like in ten, twenty, or thirty years from now. Look into your own crystal ball and complete the sentences below with as much information as you can. Predict what you think will be happening to you at some time in the future.

EXAMPLE:

(Twenty) years from now I will be <u>thirty-three years old.</u>

(put in number) years from now I will be . . . . years old.

I expect to have achieved the following goals:

1. ....
2. ....
3. ....

I may be living in/at ....
and doing the following:

1. ....
2. ....
3. ....

At that time of my life, I will be making future plans which will include:

1. ....
2. ....
3. ....

CHECKLIST FOR EDITING

- Did you add as many details as possible?
- Are there any other ideas you wish to add?

FORGE AHEAD

Interview a person who is about the same age as you have written about. Ask that person to tell you:

- what their goals were when they were your age
- what goals they have for their own future
- what advice they can give you for achieving your own goals

THINKING SKILLS
deciding
qualifying
imagining
EXPANDING

BOOK F
Page 9

WRITE A SENTENCE—GET A STORY

In the **BOX OF STORY STARTERS** are three sentences.
- Choose the sentence you like the most.
- Copy the sentence on a piece of paper.
- Write as many questions as you can about that sentence.
- Begin your questions with these words:
  What? Where? When? Why? How? Who?
- Write the answers next to the questions.
- Make up answers to the questions.
- Use the answers to write a story. Make your story interesting.

EXAMPLE

The girl had a surprise.

Who is the girl? . . . . my cousin Lisa
What was the surprise? . . . . a new-born puppy
Who surprised her? . . . . her friend Ben
Where was the surprise? . . . . in a big box
When was the surprise? . . . . last Saturday night
Why did she have a surprise? . . . . . . it was her birthday
How did she feel? . . . . excited and happy

Example of first sentence: Last Saturday night, my cousin Lisa got a new-born puppy.

> **BOX OF STORY STARTERS**
> 1. The child found a cat.
> 2. The Princess made a wish.
> 3. A big box landed in my room.

CHECKLIST FOR PROOFREADING

- Did you answer your questions?
- Did you read your story aloud?
- Did you begin each sentence with a capital letter?
- Did you end each sentence with the correct punctuation?

EXTRA CREDIT

Make up your own sentence starter.
Have a friend ask you questions about your sentence.
Write a story using your sentence starter and the answers to help you.

THINKING SKILLS
deciding
sequencing, synthesizing
SENTENCE EXPANDING

Page 14

Book B

SAMPLE WORKSHEET FOR
EXPANSION ACTIVITIES

EXPAND WITH ONE DESCRIBING WORD

Rewrite each sentence using a describing word. Put the describing word where you see the *caret* mark (ʌ). You can pick from the words in the box or you can use your own words.

Example: Billy's kite got caught in the ʌ tree.

Billy's kite got caught in the *oak* tree.

1. The ʌ puppy ran away.

2. We have a ʌ hamster in our room.

3. I watched a ʌ movie last night.

4. My mother baked a ʌ cake.

5. The teacher gave me a ʌ book to read.

6. We planted a ʌ tree in the garden.

7. The ʌ tiger ran from the hunter.

8. Billy and Jane watched the ʌ snake crawl.

9. I took a bite of the ʌ chocolate.

10. In camp we had to jump into the ʌ water.

CHECKLIST

1. Did you put in a describing word where there is a caret mark?

2. Did you begin with a capital letter and end with a period?

3. Put a star next to two sentences that *you* could use to start a story.

4. Use one of the sentences you have chosen as a *story starter* and write the rest of the story.

Words You Can Use to Describe "What kind of?"

size:	big, large, small, tiny, long, short, tall, high, low, gigantic
shape:	round, flat, square
color:	red, orange, yellow, blue green, purple, brown, white, black
taste:	sweet, bitter, delicious, sour, tasty
weight:	light, heavy, fat, thin, skinny
speed:	slow, fast, quick, speedy
feelings:	scared, scary, frightened, brave, kind, gentle, happy, sad, weepy
Other describing words:	clean, dirty, cold, cool, hot, warm, icy, funny, silly, ugly, old, young

SAMPLE WORKSHEET FOR
E X P A N S I O N   A C T I V I T I E S

EXPAND WITH TWO DESCRIBING WORDS

Rewrite each sentence using two different describing words. Put the describing words where you see the *caret* marks (Λ). You can pick from the words in the box or you can use your own words.

Example: The Λ cat chased the Λ mouse.

The *skinny* cat chased the *frightened* mouse.

1. The Λ bird fell out of the Λ tree.

2. The Λ man yelled at the Λ boy.

3. My mother bought me a Λ coat and a Λ hat.

4. We looked up in the Λ sky and saw Λ clouds.

5. The Λ baker gave me some Λ cookies.

6. I dived into the Λ water and found a Λ stone.

7. The Λ girl had to fight the Λ monster.

8. The teacher read us a book about Λ witches and Λ ghosts.

9. We ate Λ hamburgers and Λ french fries.

10. We went down the Λ river in a Λ boat.

CHECKLIST

1. Did you use two describing words where there are caret marks?

2. Did you begin with a capital letter and end with a period?

3. Put a star next to two sentences that *you* could use to start a story.

4. Put a double star (**) next to the sentence that would start a story. Use that sentence as a *story starter* and write the story.

Words You Can Use to Describe "What kind of?"	
size:	big, large, small, tiny, long, short, tall, high, low, gigantic
shape:	round, flat, square
color:	red, orange, yellow
taste:	sweet, bitter, delicious, sour, tasty, juicy, crispy
weight:	light, heavy, fat, thin, skinny, slim
speed:	slow, fast, quick, speedy
touch:	hard, soft, smooth, rough
feelings:	scared, scary, frightened, brave, kind, gentle, happy, sad, weepy
Other describing words:	clean, dirty, cold, cool, icy, warm, hot, funny, silly, pretty beautiful, ugly, old, young

GAMES FOR EXPANSION

ALLITERATIVE ADD-A-WORD
Many new descriptive words can be learned from this activity.

How to Play:
The first player begins a sentence. Each player will add one word starting with the same letter. Thus, if adjectives are being added, the description might be something like this:

"Jane is _____ ."

Player 1: artful.

Player 2: able.

Player 3: alert.

Player 1: attentive.

Player 2: active.

Player 3: amiable.

Each player is given only a limited amount of time to think of another word to add to this list. When no more words can be added, a new list is begun with the next letter of the alphabet.

ALPHABETICAL ADVERBS WITH CHARADES
This game has many educational values. It introduces the child to adverbs, it fosters creativity and inventiveness, and it builds vocabulary.

How to Play:
Begin with a sentence containing an active verb that can be modified by a series of adverbs. These adverbs must be added by each player in turn, in alphabetical order, but in a way that makes sense.

Here is one possible start:

"The pilot flew the plane _____ "

Player 1: **a**rtfully.

Player 2: **b**umpily.

Player 3: **c**arelessly.

Player 4: **d**angerously.

Player 5: **e**nthusiastically.

Player 6: **f**rantically.

Before revealing the word, each player, with gestures or pantomime, acts it out, and the other players try to guess what it is, using as their clue the initial letter and the charade.

WORD PAINTING

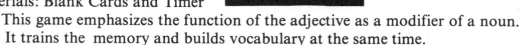

Materials: Blank Cards and Timer

This game emphasizes the function of the adjective as a modifier of a noun. It trains the memory and builds vocabulary at the same time.

Preparation:

Prepare a deck of cards appropriate to the abilities and interests of the players, e.g., *monkey, name, magician, bicycle, mountains, greeting, friend,* and *home.*

How to Play:

The first player, drawing the top card of the deck, holds it up for the other players to see. He must now suggest, within a given time, some adjective that will "paint" the noun. Thus, if he picks the card *home,* he might say, "Happy home."

Now the next player must think of another adjective to paint the same noun—perhaps *unhappy* or *newly built.* The game proceeds in this fashion until a player either repeats some adjective that has already been given, or cannot think of another adjective within the time limit. It then becomes his turn to pick the next card from the top of the deck and to begin another round.

Variations:

1. One way of making the game more difficult, as well as instructive, is to require that each player give two appropriate adjectives to paint each noun, e.g., *polite, peristent inquiry; amusing, fictitious name; loud, hearty greeting;* etc. This is a good way of teaching the use of precise, vivid language.

2. The game can also be made more challenging by beginning with a deck that includes cards with nouns for which there are a relatively limited range of appropriate modifiers—*nourishment, sickle, ownership, audition, breadth, compatriot,* etc. Of course, the time limit would have to be adjusted with the increase of difficulty.

3. Finally, the procedure can be reversed: the words written on the cards may be all adjectives—in effect, different kinds of "paint"—and the players may be invited to use them to draw different pictures. In this case, too, it is possible to pass from relatively easy types of adjectives—*good, clean, smooth*—to those more difficult.

ADD-A-WORD GAME

1. Write a word (noun).
2. Add a color word.
3. Add a sensory word.
4. Draw a picture.

Word	Add-a-Color Word	Add-a-Sensory Word
table	brown table	rough brown table
kitten	black kitten	black soft kitten
sweater	orange sweater	soft orange sweater
puppy	brown puppy	brown soft puppy

EXPAND AND ENRICH A SENTENCE
ASK WH- QUESTIONS

Expand and enrich your sentences by asking **WH-** questions:

WHAT KIND OF? HOW MUCH? HOW MANY? WHY?
WHO? WHOSE? WHERE? WHEN? WHICH?

FIRST, write a short sentence.
  • *The students do their homework*
THEN, ask **WH-** questions.

Which students?
- elementary grade
- Ms. Ryan's
- science class
- English class

What kind of homework?
- math
- English
- difficult
- easy

Where?
- in the computer lab
- at home
- in the classroom
- in the science room

When?
- after school
- before dinner
- during recess
- every afternoon

Why
- to g
- to g
- to u

NOW, write an expanded sentence. Use a~~s~~
as you need.

  • After school Ms. Ryan's students do their
    homework in the computer lab so that th
    the word processor.

THE WRITE TRACK COMPAN

E-X-P-A-N-D with
WHAT KIND OF? and HOW?

You can compose interesting sentences by adding important details.

FIRST, write a short sentence.
  The elf swept the floor.

THEN, ask **WH-** questions.

  • **What kind of** elf?
  • **What kind of** floor?
  • **How** did he sweep the floor?

Put a caret mark ∧ to show
where you are adding words.

The ∧ elf   ∧ swept the   ∧ floor.

• unhappy	• carefully	• dirty
• cheerful	• quietly	• wooden
• tired	• angrily	• bare
• frightened	• eagerly	• beautiful
• kind	• quickly	• rough
• generous	• merrily	• unwashed
• merry	• carelessly	• ugly
• grumpy	• wearily	• tile
• hard-working	• gladly	• marble
• nervous	• impatiently	• splintered

NOW, write an improved sentence.
  • The **tired** elf **carelessly** swept the **dirty** floor.
  • The **hard-working** elf **carefully** swept the **beautiful tile** floor.
  • The **nervous, frightened** elf **angrily** swept the **rough, splintered** floor.

THE WRITE TRACK COMPANY   *Primary 3*

SUBSTITUTING
WRITING IT BETTER, CLEARER, AND MORE PRECISELY

Writers must be collectors. They cannot be satisfied with a paltry supply of commonplace, ordinary, prosaic, or mediocre words. Because they talk to a silent or invisible audience, they must be able, through words alone, to communicate ideas, impart information, correspond meaningfully, and be thoroughly, completely, and fully in touch with their readers. All this writers must do without being wordy, verbose, or pompous. Furthermore, they must say what they want to say clearly, lucidly, cogently, precisely, and, above all, simply.

WORD FIND

SPEAKERS VS. WRITERS

Speakers have the privilege of substituting or clarifying what they say by using the phrase "in other words" and then going on to restate their original ideas. Furthermore, speakers often repeat their statements so their listeners know exactly what they mean. The writer, in contrast, must use a different approach to achieve clarification or preciseness. He or she must plan on using "other" words throughout the total writing process, or, "in other words," the writer must frequently seek to substitute precise words for those less exact, or substitute synonyms to avoid tedious repetition, or substitute technical vocabulary for non-technical, or substitute bland, colorless words with a lexicon which is variegated and image-provoking!

Now that we have flexed our "thesaurus muscles," we can look at how *substituting* — another fluency activity — can improve your students' writing.

DINOSAUR FOOTPRINTS

Dinosaurs came in many shapes and sizes--so did their footprints. Some dinosaurs had footprints three feet wide. Scientists study dinosaurs and put them on display in museums.

When a footprint is found in stone, it is called a fossil. A baby Brontosaurus has a three foot long footprint. A baby footprint that large is noteworthy!

Timothy
Grade 3

Jaclyn   – Grade 5

THE ELEPHANT MAN

The Elephant Man was an ugly man; he was grotesque. Everybody would make fun of him because he was beastly looking.

One day a doctor took an interest in him. They found out he was miserable but he was also very brilliant. The elephant man was homely; it was sad that people treated him so badly.

One day a man made so much fun of him that the elephant man killed him. He continued killing and killing until there was only one person in the town. The doctor fixed him up; but the doctor took on a new role. The Elephant Man had four fingers on the one hand. He took off one of the doctor's fingers and both were put in the crazy house.

SUGGESTED PROCEDURES FOR TEACHING SUBSTITUTING

Introduce substituting by utilizing simple, basic sentences which your students have composed or which come from reading and content area materials. Sentences and stories from workbook texts are also good resources for students to practice substituting.

. Select a short sentence similar to types frequently composed by students.

> *The child was sad.*
> *The dog went home.*
> *The boy saw a car.*
> *My friend said she was tired.*

. Explain to the students that they can often replace words which they have repeated or are not interesting, imaginative, or clear.

Examples:

student for *child*

Labrador Retriever for *dog*

auto, Jeep, Chevy for *car*

announced, cried, whispered for *said*

. Show them how to make changes in their writing by crossing out and substituting.

Examples:

The ~~dog ran after~~ the ~~car~~.

The Great Dane bolted after the jeep.

I SAID . . . SHE SAID . . . WE SAID . . .

The word **said** is used too many times in the story below.
Pretend you are an **editor.** Improve this story using words from the **GOLDEN EGG.** Substitute the word **said** with more interesting words. Cross out the word **said** and and put the new word above it.

EXAMPLE   shouted
            The woman ~~said~~ . . . .

GOLDEN EGG

announced   answered   bellowed   demanded
replied   roared   shouted   snickered
cried   whispered   laughed

After Jack climbed the beanstalk, he entered the giant's castle. From the dark hallway, he heard a deep thundering voice.

"Who is there?" **said** the giant.

"I am," **said** Jack.

"Why have you come here?" **said** the giant.

Jack **said,** "I have come to rescue the children who are prisoners in your castle."

"No one enters my castle without fighting me first," **said** the giant.

Jack looked up at the powerful giant and **said,** "I have these magic beans which give me strength."

The giant looked down at the small brave boy and **said,** "You win, Jack. Take the children and leave my castle immediately!"

. Teach the process of substituting through brainstorming and active participation. Underline each word to be substituted and brainstorm for alternatives.

Example: The *boy saw* the *car.*

Substitute Words:

lad	*noticed*	*auto*
student	*observed*	*Buick*
young man	*eyed*	*jeep*
young scholar	*beheld*	*van*
kid	*visualized*	*four-wheeled monster*
chap	*gazed at*	*Trans Am*
fellow	*perceived*	*dragster*
guy	*peered at*	*dune buggy*

. Recreate new sentences:

The young chap peered at the Trans Am.

The young scholar visualized the four-wheeled monster.

The guy eyed the jeep.

SAY IT A BETTER WAY

On this page you will use different words to say the same thing in a better way. You do this by **substituting words.**

EXAMPLE   The dog went home.

What kind of dog?   **puppy hound poodle**   How did it go home?   **ran limped jogged**

dog / poodle

New sentence: The **puppy jogged** home.   **OR**   The **hound ran** home.

Below are five more sentences.
Replace each **bolded** word with a better word from the WORD BOX.

	WORD BOX	
1. The **boy** saw a **dog**.	lad young man student	hound mutt German Sh
2. The **meat** looks **good**.	beef hamburger stew	delicious tasty tempting
3. "I am **glad** to see you," said the **nice** woman.	delighted happy pleased	kind pleasant sweet
4. The dog **ran** across the street **said** the little child.	bounded jogged leaped	screamed shouted yelled
5. The clown with the **sad** face made the children feel **glad**.	tearful unhappy weepy	cheerful jolly happy

① The Student saw a hound.
② The hamburger looks tasty.
③ "I am pleased to see you," said the sweet woman.
④ "The dog leaped across the street," yelled the little child.
⑤ The clown with the weepy face made the children feel jolly.   by Lisalee

Extra Credit
① Tiphany has been good all day. Tiphany has been Spectacular all day.

101

EXTENDING SUBSTITUTING ACTIVITIES INTO READING AND CONTENT AREAS

With reading and writing as merged processes, students should have frequent opportunities to combine both activities in meaningful and enjoyable ways. Sentences and stories from readers and workbooks can be used for student practice in improving writing, an activity we have named **BASAL REWRITES,** which goes as follows:

. Compose simple sentences such as these two examples:

The bad rabbit Peter Cottontail crept under the gate into Mr. McGregor's nice garden.
Mr. McGregor was mad.

. Elicit adjectives or describers:

PETER	MR. McGREGOR	THE GARDEN
naughty	*furious*	*vegetable*
disobedient	*outraged*	*beautiful*
mischievous	*angry*	*newly-planted*
	steaming	*carefully-tended*

. Write new sentences:

The mischievous Peter Cottontail crept under the gate into Mr. McGregor's carefully-tended garden. Mr. McGregor was furious.

. Compose another simple sentence:

The cabbages looked good.

. Elicit adjectives or describers for the noun *cabbage* and synonyms for the adjective *good.*

CABBAGES	GOOD
green	*juicy*
beautiful	*mouth-watering*
fresh	*tempting*
crisp	*tasty*

. Write a new sentence:

The green, crisp cabbages looked tempting and mouth-watering.

. Take a paragraph from a reader or workbook:

Mrs. Hubbard had to shop for food. She got into the car. The car was old. It would not go. Mrs. Hubbard was worried. What would she eat?

. Select several words for which the students can find synonyms.

FOOD	CAR	GO	EAT	OLD	WORRIED
groceries	auto	start	supper	worn out	upset
meat	truck		dinner	run-down	nervous
cold cuts	station wagon		lunch		jittery
vegetables	Chevy		breakfast		
cheese	jeep				
bread					

. Have them rewrite the paragraph, substituting words of their choice. Students who are skilled in language can be encouraged to combine several replacements.

Mrs. Hubbard had to shop for groceries and vegetables. She climbed into the Chevy. It was run-down and would not start. Mrs. Hubbard was nervous and upset. What would she have for supper?

WRITING A CLASS THESAURUS

Most students love interesting and unusual words, but they are not likely to use them in their daily writing. They are more likely to use "tired" words such as *big, fat, little, happy, good.* To encourage the use of better words, develop a **CLASS THESAURUS.** Hang up a chart for each "tired" word. Discuss the use of a thesaurus and have the students add substitute words to the charts. Have the students put their initials next to the words they add. Give "extra credit" to the best "word finders." Then have the students transfer these words to their own **BOOK OF LISTS,** which should always be available during writing time.

THE "EVERY STUDENT" THESAURUS OR HOW MANY WAYS CAN YOU SAY...?

SAID	LOOKED	RAN	NICE	BAD
exclaimed	gazed	trotted	friendly	worse
stated	peered	skipped	helpful	poor
cried	searched	hurried	gentle	terrible
demanded	stared	moved	warm	horrible
ordered	glanced	sped	inspiring	evil
whispered	sighted	operated	good-natured	wicked
shouted	regarded	progressed	kind	corrupt
mentioned	attended	glided	generous	heinous
blurted	viewed	flowed	cheerful	inferior
screamed	inspected	bounded	loving	inept
giggled	directed	pursued	happy	ill
chuckled	followed	galloped	funny	awful
laughed	scanned	loped	peppy	fierce
gasped	observed	fled	relaxed	false
acknowledged	noticed	charged	thoughtful	immoral
ranted	watched	scampered	cooperative	naughty

BIG	LITTLE	SAD	HAPPY	GOOD
huge	small	unhappy	lively	excellent
giant	tiny	sorrowful	gay	fine
gigantic	microscopic	downcast	jolly	terrific
monstrous	minuscule	gloomy	pleased	kind
tremendous	minute	disconsolate	glad	generous
gargantuan	slender	melancholy	content	worthy
large	Lilliputian	depressed	delighted	humane
wide	petite	discouraged	joyful	pure
important	narrow	downhearted	joyous	benign
influential	thin	dejected	satisfied	benevolent
immense	paltry	dismal	favored	valid
massive	modest	miserable	thrilled	loving
bulky	slight	pitiful	zestful	wonderful
stout	demure	woeful	jocular	caring
heavy	elf-like	unfortunate		
voluminous				

USING SUBSTITUTING TO REVISE FOR AUDIENCE

An important aspect of writing is "voice" — the formality or informality of one's writing. In the world of computers we have the term "user friendly" which means that the computer's voice or way of telling you something is hopefully simple and clear and sounds like "your friend." In teaching writing, we can show students when and how to change voice according to the audience. Here are some suggestions:

- Begin by changing from FORMAL to FRIENDLY. Give the students a letter similar to the one below which was written to someone's grandfather:

Dear Grandfather:

I regret that we have been unable to spend time with you recently. However, I would like to inform you of our latest activities. The week was highlighted by an outing to the local carnival. Cotton candy and jellied apples were enjoyed by all. Unfortunately, my enjoyment was lessened after my third jellied apple, at which time I could no longer separate my lips. I would appreciate your response and some indication of what you have been doing.

Your respectful grandchild,
Randy Kalus

- Have the students rewrite the letter, giving it the expected friendly tone. Follow up with similar examples, including imaginative correspondence between two famous people who had been friends. Here is another example of inappropriately formal writing which the students can revise for voice:

Dear Mr. Ruth:

I have recently signed a contract with the New York Yankees and am delighted to be able to serve with you on the same team. Since 1920, when you left the Boston Red Sox to become a member of the Yankees, your baseball career has been outstanding. For the past five years I have observed your amazing hitting ability and I am hopeful that I can emulate your success. I look forward to being your colleague on the Yankee team.

Yours very truly,
Louis Gehrig

. Now have the students change the inappropriate voice in the letter below from FRIENDLY to FORMAL:

Dear Gov,

How've you been? My teacher says I have to write to you. So what's been happening on the budget? Won't you have enough money for books and other stuff? And taxes? My mom says you already raised taxes. Drop me a line.

Regards,
Kim

. Again, use a famous person from history who has written inappropriately to another famous person and have the students "fix" the voice in a letter like the one below:

Dear Belva: (Belva Ann Lockwood)
You're some spunky gal trying to be President of the USA. I know those guys out there will call you weird. But they don't have enough brains to even let women vote. So while I'm rooting for you to beat the pants off Mr. Cleveland, I don't think you've got much of a chance. Anyway, cheers.

Nellie (Nellie Bly)

FORMAL GLOSSARY

determined resolute brave courageous gallant venturous difficulty distress discomfort anxiety misery disappointment vulgar indecent common insane demented unbalanced intelligence ability common sense perception understanding ridiculed derided laughed scorned lampooned encouraging hoping expecting confident optimistic defeat triumph overturn conquer defy prospect outlook hope expectation success luck victory progress achievement mastery

CHECKLIST FOR EDITING

- Did you substitute as many words as possible to make the letter more formal?
- Did you read the letter aloud to be sure you made the necessary grammatical changes?

FORGE AHEAD

Write a formal letter to a leader in your community, congratulating him or her for a particular accomplishment.

GET RID OF YOUR OLD, YOUR BORING, YOUR TIRED WORDS!

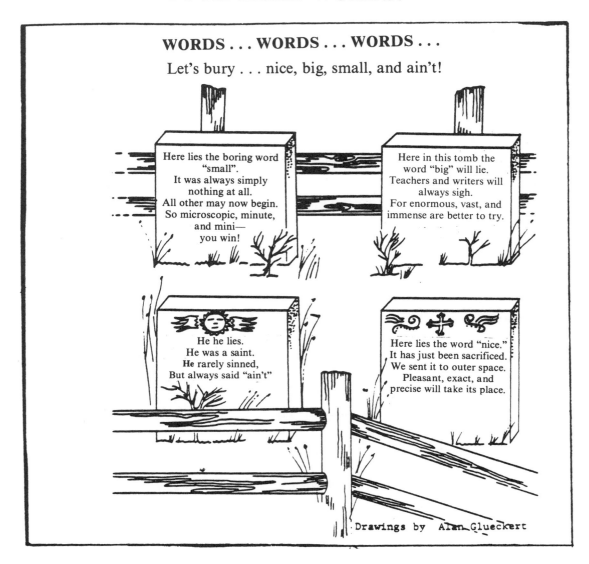

WORDS . . . WORDS . . . WORDS . . .

Let's bury . . . nice, big, small, and ain't!

Here lies the boring word "small".
It was always simply nothing at all.
All other may now begin.
So microscopic, minute, and mini—
you win!

Here in this tomb the word "big" will lie.
Teachers and writers will always sigh.
For enormous, vast, and immense are better to try.

He he lies.
He was a saint.
He rarely sinned,
But always said "ain't"

Here lies the word "nice."
It has just been sacrificed.
We sent it to outer space.
Pleasant, exact, and precise will take its place.

Drawings by Alan Glueckert

Add the following items to your editing chart.

. *Can I improve my sentences by substituting boring, tired words with better words?*

. *Can I improve my writing by changing the way I start my sentences?*

. *Have I used my BOOK OF LISTS or a thesaurus to improve my writing?*

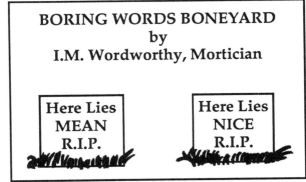

BORING WORDS BONEYARD
by
I.M. Wordworthy, Mortician

Here Lies
MEAN
R.I.P.

Here Lies
NICE
R.I.P.

submitted from a Cherry Creek School

EXAMPLES OF STUDENTS' WRITINGS USING SUBSTITUTING

WHERE THE RAINBOW ENDS

One Spring morning a rainbow was shining across the meadow. Suzy ran out the front door to see if it was real because she had never seen a rainbow before. She went to get her big sister, grabbed her hand and with a dash they both flew down the steps. Suzy showed her sister the rainbow. Her sister said, "It's a rainbow with lots of joy of course! Let's go see what is at the end of it." When they got to the end, there was a pot full of sparkling gold.

Each day they returned to the pot of gold and filled up two large paper bags with the gold until the bags were almost too heavy to carry. On the fifth day the pot of gold was half empty. They carried it into their back yard and thought about all the joy this gold would bring to the meadow in which they lived.

Raynelle

Regina
I am a jack-o-lantern who is friendly, a large pumpkin who talks to children, and cheerful pumpkin that likes to go to the movies. I have a gigantic smile. I have one nose and two eyes. I am huge and fat. I am happy when children are around me. I am peaceful all the times.

Melanie:
Holiday Treasury Book
Once there was a princess. The lass had long curly hair. The damsel was lovely. The miss had a huge family that always ate alot, but she hardly ate a thing. That is why the maiden is so slim. The female is now so skinny people think she is an up side down pencil!

STRUTHIOMIMUS DAY

The sound of Pterodactyls had thundered through the land. That awoke Struthiomimus. He ran to a lake. Nearby was a Protoceratops. The Protoceratops had just laid five eggs. The Protoceratops left the nest. Struthiomus ran to the nest.

Suddenly, Protoceratops was being chased by a Tyrannosaurus. Struthiomimus could now eat Protoceratop's eggs. After that, he went to a big lake. A Megalosaurus started to chase him. He tripped over a rock and fell into the lake. The Megalosaurus dove in after him. What they didn't realize was that they couldn't swim. The Megalosaurus drowned.

Luckily, some waves pushed Struthiomimus to the land. At sunset, after a bad day, he went to sleep near some bushes.

Karl

MARINE BIOLOGY

When you study animals that live in the sea,
It is called marine biology.

There are animals with shells,
There are animals with smells,
There are animals that swim with glee,
And others that are a big mystery.

Some fish are green, some fish are blue,
Some fish will even bite you.
I like to study fish you see,
Because I love marine biology.

Margaux

EXAMPLES OF STUDENTS' WRITINGS USING SUBSTITUTING

A "GOOD" STORY

On this page is a story in which the writer describes everything as good. You can improve this story by changing or substituting the word **good** with more interesting words.

Use the words from the SILO or use your own words.

Cross out the word **good** and put the new word above it.

When you have finished, read your story aloud.

EXAMPLE:

hard working
the ~~good~~ farmer

Once there was a good farmer. He lived in a good house with his good wife. He had three good children and a good dog. Not far away was a good town. Whenever the weather was good, the farmer and his family would take a good trip to town. They always had a good time.

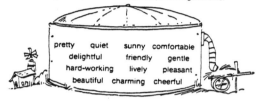

pretty	quiet	sunny	comfortable
delightful		friendly	gentle
hard-working		lively	pleasant
beautiful		charming	cheerful

CHECKLIST FOR PROOFREADING
• Did you substitute interesting words for the word good?
• Did you read your story aloud?

FORGE AHEAD
Write a story in which you describe everything as bad.
Reread your story and substitute the word **bad** with words that are more interesting.
Examples: horrible, nasty, mean

FERRIS WHEEL THESAURUS

Writers use a **thesaurus** when they need a **varied** vocabulary. Improve or revise the invitation on this page by using the words in the **ferris wheel.** You can add, substitute, or rearrange the words. You may also add your own words.

EXAMPLE

Please come to a party.
Revised: We wish to invite you to an evening of gala enter...

diversion
entertainment
recreation
relaxation
pleasure

joviality
laughter
merriment

festive
jovial
pleasant
jolly

festival
social gathering
carnival

entertain
enliven

comic
comedian

humorous
witty
keen-witted

riddles
puns

amuse
delight
please
thrill

rose garden
under a colorful
tent

Please come to a party.
It will be held in a nice place.
We will have fun.
Everyone who will be there
is fun to be with.
A funny Magician will make you
laugh.
A funny person will tell jokes.
You will be glad you came.

CHECKLIST FOR PROOFREADING
• Did you use as many varied words as you could in your revised invita...
• Did you check your spelling and punctuation?

FORGE AHEAD
Use the words from the ferris wheel to write an entertaining story. Your st... can be fact or fiction.

Extra Credit   Dena

November 15,

Once there was a ~~bad~~ (mean) woman. She lived in a ~~bad~~ (horrible) city with her ~~bad~~ (nasty) husband. Her husband was a ~~bad~~ (terrible) shoemaker. They ~~have~~ (had) one ~~bad~~ (alwful) boy and one ~~bad~~ (spoiled) girl. And they had a ~~bad~~ (grumpy) cat and a ~~bad~~ (loud) dog. On ~~bad~~ (ugly) days they always had a party. They are such ~~bad~~ (unhappy) people.

① You are called upon to attend an evening of majestic entertainment.

② It will be held at a magnificent circus and we will stay under a very colorful tent.!

③ You will find it very entertaining and pleasant at the gathering.

④ You will find everyone attending the party very courteous and helpful.

⑤ A hilarious excorcist will entertain us with riddles and jokes that will amuse everyone.

⑥ Also, a very entertaining and funny man will tell very amusing and hilarious jokes.

SAMPLE ACTIVITIES FROM "EASY WRITER"

FRIENDLY TO FORMAL

Below is an imaginary letter written by the British statesman Edmund Burke to Benjamin Franklin. However, the letter is written in too informal a style for the relationship between these two men.

EXAMPLE

Informal: Dear Ben,
       How is everything these days? Going well, I hope.

Formal: Dear Mr. Franklin:
       I hope that your present circumstances are well situated and that you can report on good tidings.

Dear **Ben**,

I hear that **things** in the Colonies are in **bad shape.** We heard that a group of **rascals** dumped some of our **good** British tea into Boston harbor. Those **guys** made quite a **ruckus** painting their faces and **carrying on** like a **bunch of fools.**

I can't believe that you Americans want to **split** from us British. King George isn't that **bad.** He just thinks he's some kind of **big shot** who can **boss little guys** around. But he **won't be around that long.** So just **hang in** with us.

Keep in touch and send my best to the **wife** and **kids.**

       Warmly,
       Ed

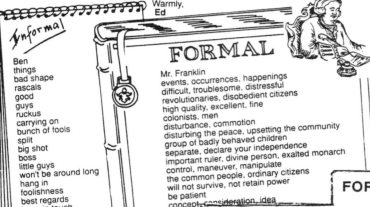

Informal

Ben
things
bad shape
rascals
good
guys
ruckus
carrying on
bunch of fools
split
big shot
boss
little guys
won't be around long
hang in
foolishness
best regards
keep in touch
wife
kids
Ed

FORMAL

Mr. Franklin
events, occurrences, happenings
difficult, troublesome, distressful
revolutionaries, disobedient citizens
high quality, excellent, fine
colonists, men
disturbance. commotion
disturbing the peace, upsetting the community
group of badly behaved children
separate, declare your independence
important ruler, divine person, exalted monarch
control, maneuver, manipulate
the common people, ordinary citizens
will not survive, not retain power
be patient
concept, consideration, idea
respectful
please re
Mrs. Frar
children,
Edmund

CHECKLIST FOR EDITING

- Did you substitute all the bolded words?
- Did you reread your letter to make sure it sound

FORGE AHEAD

Write a formal letter to a classmate info
incident.

FORMAL TO FRIENDLY

Below is an imaginary letter written by the great Yankee first baseman, Lou Gehrig, to the great homerun hitter, Babe Ruth. However, this letter has been written in too formal a style. Rewrite the letter so that it becomes more personal and friendly.

EXAMPLE

Formal: Dear Mr. Ruth:
       It has recently come to my attention....

Informal: Dear Babe:
       I just heard....

Dear Mr. Ruth:

I have recently signed a contract with the New York Yankees and am delighted to be able to serve with you on the same team. Since 1920, when you left the Boston Red Sox to become a member of the Yankees, your baseball career has been outstanding. For the past five years, I have observed your amazing hitting ability and I am hopeful that I can emulate your success.

I believe that the Yankees made a wise decision when they arranged for your leaving the Boston Red Sox. While your pitching record was clearly outstanding, especially during the World Series playoffs, you truly should concentrate on your ability as a hitter. I especially took note of your record of twenty-nine home run hits when you were still a pitcher for the Red Sox.

I look forward to being your colleague on the Yankee team and anticipate great success for both of us in our association as outfielder and first baseman.

       Yours very truly,

       Louis Gehrig

CHECKLIST FOR PROOFREADING

- Did you make your letter as friendly and informal as possible?
- Are there any other changes you can make?

FORGE AHEAD

Write a letter to a sports personality whom you admire.
Tell: • why you admire this person
     • how you hope to become successful in your own life
Decide if you will write your letter "formal" or "friendly".

SUBSTITUTE A BETTER WORD

Choose a better word for **GOOD** and **NICE.** Use the better words from the **WORD BOX.**

EXAMPLE

        comfortable
    I have ~~nice~~ boots.

              creamy
    The ice cream is **good.**

1. The police were very **nice** to the children.

2. "These apples are **good,**" said the farmer.

3. Betty found a **nice** kitten outside her door.

4. The teacher said, "I feel **good** today."

5. All the children laughed at the **nice** clown.

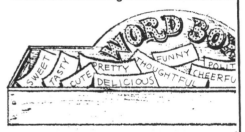

CHECKLIST FOR PROOFREADING
✔ *Did you write better words for* **good**

THE WRITE TRACK COMPANY

SUBSTITUTE
AND SAY IT BETTER

Get rid of, throw away, discard old, tired, dull, boring words. Substitute new, imaginative, exciting, powerful words.

The **nice** woman	**said,**	"I feel **sad** today."
kind	cried	unhappy
pleasant	stammered	gloomy
gentle	screamed	miserable
happy	stated	broken-hearted
understanding	whispered	depressed
friendly	mumbled	tearful
caring	moaned	wretched
sympathetic	remarked	hurt
concerned	announced	blue

OR

The **big** ape	**saw**	the **happy** boy.
large	looked at	jolly
tall	noticed	pleased
enormous	observed	smiling
gross	glanced at	merry
tremendous	sighted	laughing
overweight	eyed	chuckling
great	scanned	delighted
giant	spotted	joyful
huge		jubilant
super		
oversized		

THE WRITE TRACK COMPANY *Intermediate 5*

MOVING, REARRANGING, AND COMBINING
THE MATURATION OF STYLE

"Move the word happy from the second sentence into the first sentence. Then, make your second sentence your third sentence, because the third sentence really belongs with the first sentence. The last sentence of your second paragraph should become the first sentence of your third paragraph. And, to get variety, move the adverbs and prepositional phrases to other places in your sentences."

The writer has two main responsibilities to the reader. He must organize the writing so that the reader can follow his thinking; and he must hold the reader's attention. To fulfill these tasks the writing must be logical and organized and written with varied and well-constructed sentences that maintain the interest of the reader.

Logical ordering and varied sentence structure are often achieved through the process of moving or rearranging words, phrases, sentences, or paragraphs from one position to another. Moving requires the writer to distance herself from what she has already written in order to discover how she can say it better. She must review her sentences as carriers of information and determine if she has given the proper emphasis through placement. Then she must review whether each subsequent sentence clearly relates to what has preceded. Finally, she must look at the sentence groupings or paragraphs and ask whether each one follows the other.

Many of the changes which the writer makes during this revision stage require moving, rearranging, and combining. Fortunately, with the advent of the word processor, rearranging is less tedious than cut-and-paste and, if your students have access to a computer, they should practice this important revision skill as often as possible.

112

PROCEDURES FOR TEACHING STUDENTS TO MOVE, REARRANGE, AND COMBINE

Tell the students that they can often improve the style and organization of their writing by moving certain words or phrases from one position to another or by combining short, choppy sentences that repeat information. Your objectives at this stage will be to have the students:

- shift adverbs of time to change emphasis or to avoid beginning their sentences in the same way

- shift prepositional phrases from final to initial position as appropriate

- use transition words or phrases to avoid the repeated use of "and," "so," or "and then"

- use *-ly adverbs* in initial, medial, or final positions

- shift from active to passive construction or vice-versa as appropriate

- rearrange or regroup sentences or paragraphs for improved sequencing

---

Walter

1. Repeatedly, the Boston Celtics have won game after game this year.

2. Eventually, they will win the championship.

3 Despite all of the injuries they are still the best team.

4 However, they still may loose in the playoffs.

5 But, I don't think that they will loose.

6 At the time they win, I want to be there.

7 Therefore, I will have to go to Boston in June

8 Nevertheless, the trip will be worth it because the Celtics are my favorite team.

SUGGESTED ACTIVITIES

. Build a list of adverbs of time. Brainstorm for a list of words and phrases which answer the question WHEN? Depending on grade level and ability, the list can include the following adverbs of time:

a month ago	next time	finally
a year from now	now	frequently
in the afternoon	once upon a time	never
later in the day	now and then	often
long ago	tomorrow	occasionally
many years ago	yesterday	rarely
at dawn	today	seldom
as the sun rose	recently	suddenly
by evening	lately	usually

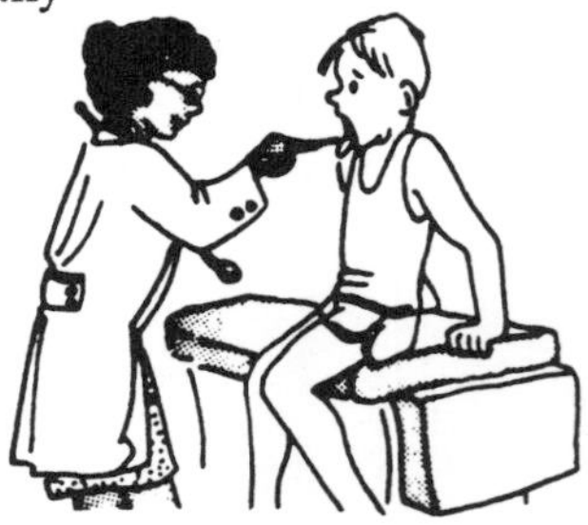

. Select a short sentence to which adverbs of time can be added, as in:

We go to the movies.

I hope to be a doctor.

The queen turned into a witch.

. Tell the students that words which answer WHEN are called adverbs of time and can often be put at the beginning or end of a sentence. There are also several adverbs of time which can be inserted before or after the verb (medially).

. Have the students experiment and discover how these adverbs "sound" in different positions. Encourage them to shift verb tenses to match the "time," as shown below:

(Later) we will go the movies (later).

(A year from now) I hope to be a doctor (a year from now).

(At midnight) the queen turned herself into a witch (at midnight).

. Ask the students to explain why they might use adverbs of time in different positions.

Reasons might be:

    . to change the emphasis or importance of key ideas

    . to vary sentence openings

    . to avoid repeating words such as "and then" or "and so"

. Introduce the proofreading symbol for moving words

and have the students compose new writings or edit previous writings using

Sleeping beauty Chad fell 2nd asleep.
One dark night
On the chair.

A Nurse a nurse is what I want to be.
Nice clean uniform.
Up early in the morning.
Ready at all times.
Saving the sick.
Emergency room at all times.
Stephanie
Gr. 2

115

PREPOSITIONAL PHRASES

Procedures for teaching prepositional phrases can be similar to those for teaching adverbs. Brainstorm for a list of words which answer the question WHERE? Words to include are:

above	beyond	in	on top of
against	beside	inside (of)	over
alongside of		into	out (of)
around	down		outside
at		near	
away (from)	far	next to	under
before		off	upon
between		on	up

Have your students compose sentences using these prepositional phrases in various positions in sentences, as in the examples below:

The cat climbed.....

    above the barn.

    between the buildings.

    down the tree.

    inside the chimney.

    on top of the stove.

.....we spotted a pigeon.

    Above the barn

    Between the buildings

    Alongside the beams

    Next to the apartment house

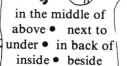

in the middle of
above • next to
under • in back of
inside • beside
on top of
underneath

TRANSITION WORDS

Transition words may not enter a child's written vocabulary until the intermediate grades. They have to be introduced gradually and practiced frequently in sentence composing in order to assure application into full-length writing products. The transition words can be taught in sets as follows:

. Introduce *suddenly, often, finally.* Have the students orally and then in writing compose sentences which use these words in varied positions, as in the following examples:

Suddenly it began to rain.

We were suddenly caught in a downpour.

The storm came up suddenly.

We often visit our grandparents.

Often we have pumpkin pie.

Grandma loves to have us visit her often.

Finally the tow truck arrived.

The tow truck finally arrived.

The tow truck arrived, finally.

. Continue with *seldom, frequently, occasionally, rarely.*
. Add *gradually, usually, eventually.*
. After students have had practice in composing with the above adverbs, introduce the use of more mature forms such as *however, therefore, consequently, nevertheless.* The use of these words has to be clearly explained and students have to practice using them in composings and compositions, as shown below:

HOWEVER indicates contrast or something unexpected.

It began to snow heavily. However, our car with its front wheel drive made it through.

NEVERTHELESS is similarly used.

It began to snow heavily. Nevertheless, our car with its front wheel drive made it through.

THEREFORE means the expected follows.

It began to snow heavily. We, therefore, had to give up our trip to New York.

CONSEQUENTLY is used to indicate the results which follow.

It began to snow. Consequently, all activities were cancelled.

-LY ADVERBS

The **-LY ADVERB** answers the question HOW? and, as with other adverbs, may have an initial, medial, or final position in the sentence. The ability to use **-LY ADVERBS** usually emerges in fourth grade or later and is best introduced in the intermediate grades.

Since most **-LY ADVERBS** originate from adjectives, students can compose sentences which use both forms in order to observe the distinctions. The following adjective/adverb pairs can be practiced in composing:

naughty/naughtily	angry/angrily
nice/nicely	amazing/amazingly
open/openly	bright/brightly
painful/painfully	brief/briefly
pitiful/pitifully	charming/charmingly
quick/quickly	careless/carelessly
quiet/quietly	dangerous/dangerously
rapid/rapidly	daring/daringly
sad/sadly	eager/eagerly
sparing/sparingly	energetic/energetically
sudden/suddenly	gentle/gently
tender/tenderly	generous/generously
terrible/terribly	happy/happily
vicious/viciously	hungry/hungrily
wild/wildly	interesting/interestingly
willing/willingly	loving/lovingly
wonderful/wonderfully	loud/loudly
youthful/youthfully	merry/merrily
zestful/zestfully	mysterious/mysteriously

PASSIVE TO ACTIVE OR ACTIVE TO PASSIVE

While most children in the elementary grades use the active form (The dog bit the man.), the use of the passive can be introduced in fifth or sixth grades (The man was bitten by the dog). Since the active form is usually preferable, students should perceive the use of the passive as an alternative form only when sentence variety is needed or when there is a shift of emphasis.

VOICE: PASSIVE TO ACTIVE OR ACTIVE TO PASSIVE

Most children in the elementary grades use the active voice, as in, "The dog bit the man." The use of the passive voice can be introduced in fifth or sixth grades, as in, "The man was bitten by the dog." Since the active voice is usually preferable, students should perceive the use of the passive as an alternative form only when sentence variety is needed or when there is a shift of emphasis. Some examples are shown below:

The child told a story.

She told about elves and goblins.

(Emphasis is on the child.)

The monkey ate all the peanuts.

(Emphasis is on the monkey.)

A story was told by the child.

It was about elves and goblins.

(Emphasis is on the story.)

All the peanuts were eaten by the monkey.

(Emphasis is on the peanuts.)

REARRANGED SENTENCES FOR IMPROVED SEQUENCING

Whole sentences can be moved around to change emphasis or to add variety, as in the examples below:

ORIGINAL

Karen gave her dad a new wallet.
It was his birthday.

Bill loved to work in his garden. He planted seeds for broccoli, string beans and carrots. Every day he carefully watered his plants.

REARRANGED

It was Dad's birthday.
Karen gave him a new wallet.

Bill planted seeds for broccoli, string beans and carrots. Every day he carefully watered his plants. Bill loved to work in his garden.

There are times, too, when paragraphs or whole sections can be moved around to improve the writing. Students should be made aware of cut-and-paste procedures when they are doing research or other lengthy pieces of writing and they decide to move whole sections of text.

> I wish to be a brilliant, kind
> pediatrician
> Working in my antiseptic
> office
> Skillfully.
>   Kwame
>
> I wish I were a brilliant
> lawyer speaking in my
> comfortable office.
> Helpfully.
>   Natalie

119

INFINITIVE PHRASES

Intermediate and older students can be guided into composing sentences that begin with infinitive phrases, which consist of "to" plus a verb, as in "to run" or "to read."

. First, compose a sentence which includes an infinitive:

*We are learning **to add** two fractions.*

. Separate the sentence after the main verb:

*We are learning/**to add** two fractions.*

. Have the students compose a sentence using the second half of the sentence.

***To add** two fractions, we have to. . . .*

. After the students have generated several of these types of sentences, they should read them aloud in order to hear their sound.

Students can be given additional practice in starting sentences with infinitives by using phrases taken from the content areas:

To measure a room.....

To get change.....

To understand equations.....

To convert to the metric system.....

To find a route to China.....

To stay in good health.....

To prevent the spread of slavery.....

To sail around the world.....

To reach the North Pole.....

To become a great scientist.....

To study bacteria.....

To get rid of germs.....

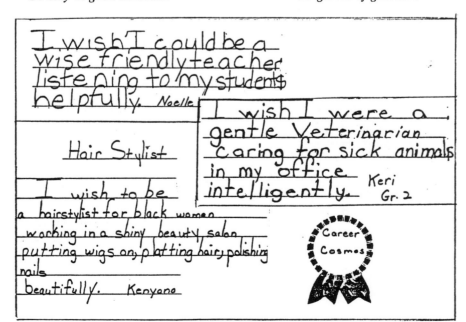

I wish I could be a wise friendly teacher listening to my students helpfully. *Noelle*

Hair Stylist

I wish to be a hairstylist for black women working in a shiny beauty salon putting wigs on, plotting hair, polishing nails beautifully. *Kenyono*

I wish I were a gentle Veterinarian caring for sick animals in my office intelligently. *Keri Gr. 2*

Career Cosmos

PARTICIPLES (PAST AND PRESENT)

Participles are forms of verbs which are used to perform the functions of verbs, adjectives, or nouns. Participles can be used by students after they have had sufficient practice with simpler verb forms. In conjunction with their work on combining, students can attempt sentence construction with participles. You may also want to incorporate the use of participles in sentence composing activities. One way to show rearranging using participles is described below:

. First, have the students make up a sentence using the *-ing* form of a verb with one
      of the auxiliaries — *is, are, was, were.*
  Example: *The child **is swimming** in the lake.*

. Then have them use the same *-ing* form as a participle and construct a new sentence.
  Examples: *My friend is **staying** at my house.*
  ***Staying** at my house is fun.*

  *The elephant is **eating** peanuts.*
  ***Eating** peanuts is an elephant's favorite activity.*

  *I am **playing** football.*
  ***Playing** football is dangerous but fun.*

  *We are **taking** vitamins.*
  ***Taking** vitamins is necessary for good health.*

  *The new sports cars are **racing** at Indianapolis.*
  ***Racing** at Indianapolis is exciting.*

The *-ed* form (past participle) can be similarly developed.

Examples: *The King **prevented** Columbus from making a fifth voyage.*
      ***Prevented** by the king from making a fifth voyage, Columbus died broken-hearted.*

      *The British **defeated** the French in North America.*
      ***Defeated** by the British in North America, the French gave up Canada.*

SUBORDINATORS

Subordinate clauses can often be moved to improve sentences. Students should practice changing the positions of main and subordinate clauses, as in the following examples:

I was tired because I got up early.
Because I got up early, I was tired.

I would travel every year if I could have my way.
If I could have my way, I would travel every year.

I hope to be a geographer when I grow up.
When I grow up, I hope to become a geographer.

I love candy, even though it makes me fat.
Even though it makes me fat, I love candy.

INTRODUCING PARTICIPIALS

You can write interesting sentences by using participial phrases. Below are seven sentence starters with the **-ed** or **-ing** form of the verb. Complete each of these starters with facts from mythology or from your own creative ideas. Be sure to put a comma after the participial phrase.

EXAMPLE: The Cyclops was **angered by Odysseus's trickery.**

Angered by Odysseus's trickery, the Cyclops vowed to make the Greeks' journey home long and difficult.

1. King Midas realized he had made a mistake by asking for the golden touch.
   By asking for the golden touch, King Midas . . . .

2. Prometheus sacrificed his life for the men and women on earth.
   By sacrificing his life for the men and women on earth, Prometheus . . . .

3. Pandora was determined to discover the contents of the beautiful box left by the gods.
   Determined to discover the contents of the beautiful box left by the gods, Pandora . . . .

4. Bellerophon rode across the sky on the winged horse, Pegasus.
   Riding across the sky on the winged horse, Pegasus, ...

5. Persephone ignored her mother's warnings.
   Ignoring her mother's warnings, Persephone . . . .

6. Achilles' mother dipped him in the River Styx.
   By dipping him in the River Styx, Achilles' mother . . . .

7. Icarus and Daedalus wanted to escape from the tower of King Minos.
   Wanting to escape from the tower of King Minos, Icarus and Daedalus . . . .

PRACTICING WITH COMMERCIAL MATERIAL

Students should be given the opportunity to move words, phrases, and sentences in stories from their workbooks and from other simply written material. Emphasize that they are to rearrange words within sentences without changing the basic meaning.

Below is a story similar to those found in workbooks:

Betty liked to take care of the animals.

She milked the cows in the morning.

She fed the pigs after that.

The horses were her favorite animals.

She liked Marybel, the mare, best of all.

Possible moves:

Betty liked to take care of the animals.

In the morning she milked the cows.

After that she fed the pigs.

Her favorite animals were the horses.

Best of all, she liked Marybel, the mare.

Take a paragraph from a reader or workbook. Put each sentence on a separate card. Have the children move the sentences to different parts of the story to see if the story (1) makes sense and (2) sounds better. Encourage the students to use a variety of beginning words to improve the story:

ORIGINAL STORY	**POSSIBLE MOVES**
Buddy gave his sister flowers.	*Buddy always gave his sister a*
Today was her birthday.	*present for her birthday.*
Buddy always gave his sister	*Since today was her birthday, he*
a present for her birthday.	*gave her flowers.*

SENTENCE COMBINING — ADDING, DELETING, MOVING

The written form which we associate with mature literary style often consists of complex clauses united by transitional words, participles, and various coordinators. Research has shown that the well-constructed complex sentence not only sounds better from a literary viewpoint, but actually transmits to the receiver a more comprehensive and cohesive message. For example, the isolated sentences below may be difficult to process:

Evelyn Rothstein reported on her workshop meetings.
She met with sixth grade teachers.
They had been complaining about their students' problems.
The problems were in writing.
Several students wrote the way they spoke.
Many students had immature sentence structure.
Very few students could revise their sentences and paragraphs.

As an alternative, the three combined sentences below carry all the information as the seven abrupt sentences above, and they show more complex relationships among the ideas:

Evelyn Rothstein reported on her workshop meeting with the sixth grade teachers who had been complaining about their students' problems in writing. The teachers complained that several students wrote the way they spoke. Many had immature sentence structure, and very few could revise their sentences and paragraphs.

Research has also shown that, by about age nine or ten, children's spoken language contains most or all of the essential syntactic elements needed to construct complex forms. However, to apply these forms proficiently in writing, children must have specific practice in the construction of complex sentences. Mellon and others (1969) have shown that children of varying abilities can improve their combining ability (syntactic fluency) through such practice.

PROCEDURES FOR SENTENCE COMBINING

The purpose of sentence combining and embedding is to have students construct sentences which:

. are more appropriate for written (in contrast to spoken) form

. reflect the maturation of language

. convey meaning more clearly

. add variety to sentence formats

Introduce sentence combining after your students have had practice in adding, deleting, and rearranging words. Have your class or group generate two simple sentences which could be connected with **and**, such as:

I bought a dog.
I bought a cat.

Ask them how they would combine the two sentences into one and have the children literally cross out the second **I bought** and add the word **and:** I bought a dog *and a cat.* Ask if they have changed the meaning. Also ask their opinion as to which sentence they would prefer if they were writing. Accept all answers, even if some children prefer the longer style. Their opinions will gradually change with maturity.

Now add more information about the dog and cat.

The dog was big.   *The cat was small.*

Have the students combine. Some might select the subordinate clause form:

I bought a dog which was big and a cat which was small.

Others might perceive the embedding option:

I bought a big dog and a small cat.

Always discuss with the group whether the combining has retained the original meaning and whether they feel such combining has improved the writing.

Using the following approaches, continue to give practice in combining:

. Combine related sentences which repeat words. Set them up in **ladder** form so that the students can observe the techniques of **deleting** and **combining.**

Example: *I like swimming.*

             I like tennis.

             I like hiking.

Combined: *I like swimming, tennis, and hiking.*

or

Example: *The Pilgrims left England.*

             They came to America.

             They met the Indians.

             They celebrated Thanksgiving.

Combined: *The Pilgrims left England, came to America, met the*

             Indians, and celebrated Thanksgiving.

. Have the students write several sentences which repeat the same phrase and then have them combine both sentences.

water: *We use water for washing.*

             We use water for drinking.

Combined: *We use water for washing and drinking.*

France: *France helped the United States in the American Revolution.*

             France had her own revolution.

Combined: *After France helped the United States in the*

             American Revolution, she had her own revolution.

television: *I like to watch television.*

             It is fun to watch television.

Combined: *I like to watch television because it is fun.*

Use some of the original sentences composed by students in previous lessons. For each sentence, have them write a second sentence that is related in meaning to the first sentence. Then have them combine the two sentences, using as many various arrangements as possible — coordination, subordination, and embedding. Do this with the whole class first and then have the students work individually.

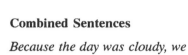

Examples:

Original Sentences	**Combined Sentences**

The day was cloudy.

We couldn't have a picnic.

Because the day was cloudy, we couldn't have a picnic.

Elephants' tusks are made of ivory.

Ivory is a precious item.

Ivory, a precious item, comes from elephants' tusks.

Firefighters help to save people from danger.

Firefighters work hard.

Firefighters work hard when they have to save people from danger.

Combining with Apposition

. Begin with a simple sentence.

> *The lion lives on the African Plains.*

. Brainstorm for words that describe a *lion*.

> *The lion is a(n)...........................animal.*
>
> strong   fierce   wild   intelligent   hungry

. Set into apposition.

> *The lion, a strong animal, lives on the African Plains.*

. Combine

> *The lion, a fierce, strong, intelligent animal, lives on the African Plains.*

Combining with Verb Phrases

. Begin with a simple sentence.

A mail carrier is a community helper.

A mail carrier ....

delivers mail   *works in the post office*

. Then combine the short sentences.

A mail carrier is a community helper who works in the post office and delivers mail.

Using Material from Readers

Use primary grade text material from children's readers for practice in combining **short, choppy** sentences.

Original

I like to walk in the country.
I can see beautiful flowers and a clear sky.

I can't see the trees.
I can't see the lake.
I can't see my house.

Combined

I like to walk in the country where I can see beautiful flowers and a clear sky.

I can't see the trees, the lake, or my house.

128

ABC STORIES

Teachers have frequently complained that many students seem to limit their sentence openers to *the, we, so,* and *and then.* Reminding students to vary sentence openers has usually been unsuccessful. The following activity, which we call **ABC STORIES,** can alert your students to the variety of words they can use to start sentences:

- Have your students brainstorm for topics of interest. The topics can be on sports, music, favorite people, current events, or school subjects. After you have a list of about ten topics, give the following instructions:

  "Start your first sentence with a word that begins with the letter A, the second sentence with the letter B, the third sentence with the letter C, and so forth. Continue your story at least up to the letter M. If you can or wish, you may continue to the letter Z."

From time to time students may need help in thinking of words to start their sentences. We suggest that both you and other students in the class offer a list of words to choose from. For example, a student might ask, "What word can I use for D?" Suggestions might be *during, did, Donna, depending, determined,* and so forth. Then have each student select the word he/she thinks is suitable.

After this practice, encourage your students to use the following variations:

- Rewrite a well-known folk or fairy tale starting your first sentence with a word that begins with A; then proceed through the alphabet.
- Start a story with the letter Z and go backwards through the alphabet.
- Use the letters of your name to begin each sentence of a story or article about yourself.
- Use the letters of places, titles, or objects (acrostics) to begin each sentence in a paragraph about these topics. (See ALPHABET ACROSTIC in the box below.)
- Brainstorm other variations on the same idea.

Add the following items to the editing chart or checklist:

- *Can I improve my writing by moving words or phrases?*
- *Can I improve my writing by moving any sentences within the paragraphs?*
- *Can I improve my writing by moving or changing around any paragraphs?*
- *Can I start my sentences with adverbs, participles, or transitional words?*
- *Should I use some form of ABC starters or acrostics to get sentence variety?*

SAMPLE EASY WRITER ACTIVITY FOR COMBINING

START WITH TEN, END WITH FIVE

Below are directions that tell how to train a pet. Write these directions in a better way. Join each pair of sentences. Write **five** new sentences.

EXAMPLE

Give your dog good food.
Give your dog fresh water.
Give your dog good food and fresh water.

How To Train Your Dog

1. You can train your dog to beg.
   You can train your dog to sit.

2. Show your dog that you love him.
   Show your dog that you trust him.

3. When he begs give him a cookie.
   When he begs pat him on the head.

4. When he sits give him a hug.
   When he sits tell him he is a good dog.

5. You will be happy.
   Your dog will be happy.

CHECKLIST FOR PROOFREADING

- Did you combine your sentences with the word **and**?
- Did you take away the words you didn't need?

EXTRA CREDIT

Read the story below. Combine the sentences so that you will have a better story.

After the school play, Kevin went home.
Erica went home too.
Susan went for ice cream.
Richard went for ice cream.

ALPHABET ACROSTIC

You can vary your sentence beginnings by using a system called acrostics. In acrostics, you start each sentence with a word that begins with a specific letter of the alphabet. Choose one of the topics below or use your own topic. Then write one or two paragraphs in which you begin each sentence with a letter that is in the name of the topic.

EXAMPLE

Topic: **MONEY**
"Money," she mused.
"Owning everything I've ever wanted.
Now that's the way to live.
Everything in the world will belong to me.
Yes, money will change my life."

EXAMPLES OF STUDENTS' WRITING   USING ACROSTICS

AN ABC STORY: SNOW WHITE

Any day was good for Snow White.

But she had a problem, because her
mother wanted her out of her house.

"Could she do anything about this?",
she wondered.

Day by day, life seemed darker and
darker to her.

Everyone in the town felt terrible
about her situation.

Finally her mother made her leave, for
good.

Gundy, the woodchopper was sent to kill
her.

He could not do it and he sent her into
the forest instead.

Ice cold wine and bread was given to
her by this kind man.

Jumper, the rabbit met her and thought
she was the nicest and prettiest lady
he had ever met.

Kindness was written all over her as
she was introduced to all the animals
in the forest.

Late that morning she shared her bread
and wine with them and they took her
to a quiet cottage.

Maybe no one was home......

Nervously she turned the doorknob.

Opening the door, she was very afraid.

Peaking in the door, she saw a big
mess.

Quietly Snow White and the animals
checked the house.

Right away she began to clean, polish,
and fix up the cottage until it was
shining brightly.

Snow White had no idea that at this
very moment her mother was preparing a
poison apple for her.

Taking care of the house was Snow
White, when the Seven Dwarfs returned
from work and it was love at first
sight.

Unaware of the danger, Snow White
received the poison apple the next
day, and when the dwarfs came home
they found her lying on the ground.

Very sad were they, as they made a
special bed for her to sleep on.

When the prince arrived, he gave her a
kiss and she woke up.

Xavier was the prince's name.

Yesterday she became a princess.

Zebras, rabbits, deer, and all kinds of
animals lived in the palace with her,
happily ever after.

by SHANA

EXAMPLES OF STUDENTS' WRITING   USING ACROSTICS

SOFTBALL
by
Kiki

Softball is a fun thing to do. **O**ther people will come to see you play. **F**riends are there cheering for you. **T**eams cheer too. **B**ig kids on the team hit the ball very far. **A**ll the people go wild then. **L**ots of people voted for our team. **L**ots of people throw flowers at us.

BOWLING
by
Tammy

Bowling is the best sport. **O**bserving the ball rolling down the alley is fun. **W**ithout bowling there would be no reason to have any sports. **L**eaving the bowling alley is the worst part. **I** like to bowl a lot. **N**ever refuse to go bowling with a friend. **G**o alone if you need to.

BASEBALL
by
Nicholas

Bases are loaded. **A** lot of players are ready. **"S**afe!" calls the umpire. **E**rrors happen during the game. **B**alls fly as high as they can. **A**ll the fans are cheering for the Mets. **L**efty pitchers strike out many batters. **L**ast inning and the batter hits a homer— the game is over.

SKATING
by
Natalie

Skating is a fun thing to do. **K**ids love going skating. **A** skating rink is a fun place to be. **T**hings hang from the skating rink. **I** am able to skate really well. **N**o one that I know can skate better than me. **G**irls love skating.

FOOTBALL
by
Dean

Football is fun. **O**ffense is a good position. **O**ffense is fun. **T**ackling is tough and bad. **B**usting linebackers is my favorite thing. **A**ction is the best part of football. **L**inebackers are thw worst. **L**ooping around the guy and trying to make a toughdown is hard.

BASEBALL
by
Scott

Baseball is an awesome sport. **A**ll sports are good, but baseball is the best. **S**oftball is the same as baseball only for girls. **E**at gum while you play because it gives me power, and it might for you too. **B**eginners become better. **A**ll people try their best. **L**uck is also in the game. **L**ast, it is fun.

Singing
Diane

Singing is my favorite activiy. I wish I could sing in the next concert. "Never yell a lot or you won't be able to sing," Mrs. Bearman always says. Girls usually have the higher voices, but not always. It would be wonderful if I could be a singer when I grow up. Nothing will stop me from trying . Girls are really better than boys at singing anyway! (Just kidding.)

Sing
Beatrice

Some people like to sing, like Mrs. Berger. In winter, we had a winter concert and everyone sang. Now we are singing in the music room. Going to the club on Main Street is what you can do if you want to sing some more.

A PIANO

A piano is a beautiful sounding instrument,

But being a piano is not easy.

Children bang on my keys.

Don't they think they will damage me?

Even though I am not alive, I have feelings too.

Feeling good about yourself is when you play a nice song.

Goodness, that's a pretty song.

Having humans touch me softly feels very comfortable.

I love having grownups play Christmas carols.

Jazz music hurts my ears.

Kind people play nice and easy.

Living inside a piano is fun most of the time.

Moving around is hard when someone is playing.

Not everyone likes the piano, but I do.

Overweight people hurt my keys.

Piano teachers are the nicest people in the world.

Quiet! Someone is about to play.

Really, I like being played by children.

Sometimes I don't get played on for days.

Today is a busy day for me; a child is having a piano class.

Unexpectedly I get banged on; I am going to need to get tuned.

Vases get placed on me; they are heavy, but I can handle it.

Water spills on me occasionally.

Xylophones are something like me.

Yippee!!! It is 8:00 P.M.

Zzzzz!!! Rest at last!

Kamica
Grade 5

IRA SLEEPS OVER
RETOLD BY CLASS 3B

At Ira's house, while getting ready to sleep at a friend's house, he thought about his teddy bear. Before going to Reggie's house he wondered if he should bring his teddy bear Tah Tah. "Consider this," his sister said," "Won't your friend laugh at you?" "Don't worry, he won't laugh at me," exclaimed Ira. Excitedly, he ran down the stairs to ask his parents what he should do. Fearfully, he thought that his parents might agree with his sister. "Go son," they said, and take your teddy bear. Reggie won't laugh. "Holding his teddy bear tightly he hugged it and decided to leave it home because of what his sister said.

In Reggie's house, they played a lot of games, had a pillow fight and a wrestling match. Just then Reggie's father came in and said, "Good night." Kindly, Reggie said,"We can still tell ghost stories.;" Let me get something first," he said, "My goodness," Ira said, "Is that a teddy bear?"

Now Ira felt lonely so he went home and got his teddy bear. Opening the door, everyone was astonished to see Ira. "Please may I come in and get my teddy bear?," asked Ira. Quickly he got Tah Tah, ran across the lawn to Reggie's house and hugging his teddy bear fell fast asleep in bed.

HOME ALONE
by
Chris

Home Alone is a great movie. Observe it carefully so you don't miss any good parts of it. Miss part of it and you will be sorry. Eat popcorn while you're watching the movie. A great part is when the two robbers try to rob Kevin's house. Lots of parts are funny. Other people enjoyed the movie as much as I did. Now is the time to see it before it goes out of the theater. Enough of the movie is funny so go see it.

BART SIMPSON

Bart Simpson ia a cartoon character. As a cartoon character, I wonder how Bart feels. Remember, Bart is only a cartoon. There was an episode where Bart tried to grow hair like Homer's. Sometimes I miss watching "The Simpsons." I was angry when my brother wouldn't let me watch "The Simpsons." My mother was angry when I wouldn't let **her** watch them! Possibly I will get use to them if I watch them once more. Sometimes I don't watch "The Simpsons" because I don't like them. Once I was watching "The Simpsons" and I fell off the chair. Now when I watch "The Simpsons" I sit on the floor. .

Schakia

THE SIMPSONS

EXAMPLES OF STUDENTS' STORIES

EAST RAMAPO 5TH GRADE GROUP COMPOSITION

The Pilgrims

A long time ago people called Pilgrims lived in England. But they didn't like it there because the king made them go to the same church as he did. Consequently, they sailed from England to Holland for their religious freedom.

During their stay in Holland they had no land for farming, and their children had to work. Eventually, the Pilgrims decided to sail from Holland to the colonies.

From Holland to the Colonies was a long journey and they took two ships, the Speedwell and the Mayflower. Going to the colonies, the Speedwell began to fall apart because it was not made for the ocean. However both ships went back to Holland and the Pilgrims got off the Speedwell and got on to the Mayflower. In that case everybody was very crowded on the Mayflower and didn't have a very good trip to America.

Jokingly, one of the crew members said, "I see land," and there really was land which they named Plymouth Rock after Plymouth, England. Kind Indians greeted the Pilgrims.

Little facts about America were known to the Pilgrims and they needed to know things about how to grow corn, what food in America was edible, and what animals lived there. Massasoit, the chief Indian, and Samoset agreed to tell them everything they needed to know if the Pilgrims, with their weapons, would guard the Indians from another Indian tribe.

Now the Pilgrims were thankful and, to thank God, they had a big feast of turkey, deer, berries, nuts, wild grapes, cranberries, squash and pumpkin which they called Thanksgiving.

Observing the history of the Pilgrims, Abraham Lincoln, as President, made Thanksgiving a national holiday on the fourth Thursday of November.

As he walked on to the court his stomache swirled nervously.

Basketball was his favorite sport.

Calmly he whent throug his pregame warm ups.

During the coach's speach in the locker room he tried to consintrate on the game instead of the huge crowd.

Everything that could happen whent thraugh his head winning, losing, being a hero, being the goat.

Finally the buzzer sounded and the team ran out on the court.

Go, team, Go Go Go the crowd cheered.

Hysterical fans donced and screamed

Ice is what his stomach felt like when the coach shouted he would be starting.

Just as the game had gotten under way he took a shot that barely knocked the rim. →

Krap he thought to himself

Luckily he sank his next three baskets to give his team the lead.

Moving quickly he stole the ball

Nimbly he dribbled down the court

Open for the shot, he jammed it home.

People in the stands whent crazy.

Quickly he ran back to get on defense.

Relentlessly he played.

Steals here, blocked shots here he was great.

Turning, jumping, twisting he scored at will.

Until at last he knew they were going to win.

Very quickly he glanced at the clock, 0:50 seconds left.

When the buzzer sounded he was carried of the floor

Xylaphones in the band played.

Yelling fans stormed on to the floor

Zanily they chanted his name.

SAMPLE EASY WRITER ACTIVITIES FOR MOVING AND REARRANGING

SELDOM, OCCASIONALLY, RARELY

Some adverbs are used to answer the question **how** or **how often.** These words are used in different parts of a sentence.

Copy the sentences below. Add one adverb from the **ADVERB FILE** to the beginning, middle, or end of each sentence (Hint: Put the adverbs in different parts of your sentences.)

EXAMPLE

To get home from school, we walked.

To get home from school, we **usually** walked.

1. People prefer artificial plants to living plants.
2. When there is a problem, there is a solution.
3. An army that advances, retreats.
4. Refusals will bring agreements.
5. During the middle of last winter we were freezing.
6. A guilty person may be judged innocent.
7. The young thoroughbred horse was a winner.
8. In a crowded bus people are polite.

ADVERB FILE

frequently
now and then
from time to time

rarely
occasionally
once in a while

usually
seldom
sometimes
often

CHECKLIST FOR PROOFREADING
• Did you use the adverbs in different parts of the sentences?
• Do your sentences make sense?

EXTRA CREDIT
Write a letter to your teacher telling about yourself. Use the words from the ADVERB FILE to explain as much about yourself as you can.

THINKING SKILLS
deciding
sequencing

MOVING AND REARRANGING

BOOK D
Page 26

©Copyright 1987 ERA/CCR Corporation, PO Box 650, Nyack, NY 10960

MAKE THE TRANSITION

Below are nine sentences which need transitional words. Complete each sentence by choosing a transitional word or phrase from the **LIST OF TRANSITIONALS** below.

EXAMPLE:

. . . . colonists complained about taxation without representation.
Repeatedly, the colonists complained about taxation without representation.

1. the Revolutionary War broke out at Lexington and Concord on April 19, 1775, very few colonists wanted independence.

2. . . . . their differences with England, most colonists merely wanted the right of self-government within the British Empire.

3. . . . . . . Parliament and King George refused to allow the colonists to levy their own taxes.

4. . . . . King George demanded that all British subjects remain loyal to the crown and fight against the colonists.

5. . . . . King George removed the colonies from his protection and blockaded their ports.

6. . . . . the colonists hoped that King George would come to his senses and listen to their arguments.

7. . . . . the British enlisted the help of hired Hessian troops and incited the Indians to fight the colonists.

8. . . . . the colonists had no choice but to rebel.

9. . . . . the embittered colonists declared their independence on July 4, 1776.

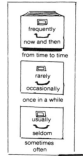

NEVERTHELESS... FURTHERMORE

LIST OF TRANSITIONALS

at last   at the time   but   consequently   despite   eventually   finally   frequently
furthermore   however   in addition   nevertheless   repeatedly   therefore   thus

CHECKLIST FOR EDITING
• Did you have to add or omit any words?
• Do your sentences make sense?

FORGE AHEAD
Compose eight original sentences using eight of the above transitional words or phrases.

Copyright ERA/CCR Corp. The Write Track Company
0809 Book H

Combining and Rearranging
Page 14

WALL CHARTS TO ILLUSTRATE COMBINING

MEET THE APPOSITION

*You can improve your sentences by using **apposition**. In **apposition** you **combine** sentences and **remove** unnecessary words.*

- **FIRST,** write a sentence about a person or animal.
  Harry Houdini was a famous magician.

- **SECOND,** delete the word "was."
  Put a comma after the name and after the last word.
  Harry Houdini, a famous magician, ...

- **THIRD,** finish the sentence with new words.
  Harry Houdini, a famous magician, delighted audiences with his daring tricks.

HERE ARE OTHER SENTENCES WHICH USE APPOSITION.

The raccoon is a nocturnal animal.
*The raccoon, **a nocturnal animal,** is rarely seen*
Eleanor Roosevelt was a great humanitarian.
*Eleanor Roosevelt, **a great humanitarian,** beca to the United Nations.*

IMPROVE THESE SENTENCES BY USING APPOS

Christopher Columbus was a daring explorer.
Marie Curie was a determined scientist.
My best friend is a terrific cook.
The lion is the largest animal of the cat family.

COMBINE SHORT, CHOPPY SENTENCES

One way to improve your writing is to **join** or **combine** sentences.

EXAMPLE

Billy has a puppy and a kitten.
The puppy is brown and the kitten is white.

Billy has a brown puppy and a white kitten.

Below are three pairs of sentences to be combined. Write the new, combined sentences on a sheet of paper.

1. I like grilled hamburgers.
   I like crispy French fries.

2. French fries taste good when they are sizzling hot.
   French fries taste good when they are crispy.

3. I put pickles on hamburgers.
   I put ketchup on French fries.

CHECKLIST FOR PROOFREADING

✔ Did you use the word **"and"** to combine your sentences?
✔ Did you take away the words from the second sentence that are the same as the words in the first sentence?

MOVE AND REARRANGE WITH ADVERBS OF TIME

You can write better sentences by moving **adverbs of time.** **Adverbs of time** can be at the beginning, middle, or end of a sentence.

What are you doing **NEXT WEEK?**

NEXT WEEK I am having a party.

LAST MONTH I had a party.

I was busy **LAST MONTH** and couldn't come to your party.

Do you **USUALLY** go away this time of the year?

USUALLY I go to tl
I **RARELY** miss a g

ONCE IN A WHILE I go to the beach, although **NOW AND THEN** I stay home all summer.

It's been good spea
Let's get together F
TO TIME.

How about **TOMORROW?**

TOMORROW will l

© 1985 ERA/CCR Corp.   **THE WRITE TRACK COMPANY**

MOVE AND REARRANGE WITH -LY ADVERBS

Words which end in **-ly** and answer the question **HOW?** are called adverbs. They can be placed at the beginning, middle, or end of a sentence.

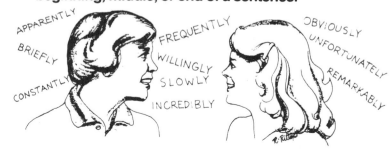

- **APPARENTLY,** you haven't learned your adverbs.

- **OBVIOUSLY,** you're right!

- Tell me, **BRIEFLY,** what you plan to do.

- **UNFORTUNATELY,** I haven't the faintest idea.

- I notice you have been studying **CONSTANTLY.**

- Yes. I study **FREQUENTLY** and **WILLINGLY.**

- Seldom am I so patient, but I will **CAREFULLY** and **SLOWLY** explain -ly adverbs again.

- You are **INCREDIBLY** kind and **REMARKABLY** generous.

© 1985 ERA/CCR Corp.   **THE WRITE TRACK COMPANY**   *Intermediate 8*

138

FRAMES: BRIDGE TO FULL-LENGTH COMPOSING

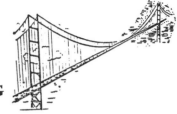

A framed sentence or paragraph is an outline using key or structure words with open spaces for the writer to supply his/her own words.

Example: *When Jack .... his grandmother, he ....*

In a frame such as the example above, the student has the option to complete the frame with as many words as he chooses.

When Jack said good-bye to his grandmother, he felt very sad because he knew he might not see her again for a long time.

Framed sentences and paragraphs are particularly helpful to those students who initially have difficulty writing on their own. These frames often serve as a bridge to original writing. Framing is similar to *cloze* (completing a paragraph where a word has been deleted). In framing, however, the student is encouraged to complete the *slots* with expanded phrases rather than with only one or two words. Frames can easily be constructed from basal readers, social studies and science texts, library books, or other available written materials.

PROCEDURES FOR COMPOSING WITH FRAMES

. Introduce frames by presenting to students two related sentences that have missing parts. Make sure the students skip lines and leave enough space for adding information. Below is a suggested format for an introductory frame:

> *The .... sat down.*
> *He/She/It was very ....*

. Have the students individually decide who or what sat down and ask them to complete the first sentence. Tell them they can use more than one word such as the *young musician.* Then ask them to complete the second sentence with any word they wish. We suggest that you encourage your students not to use the word *tired,* but to find other more interesting words such as *happy, worried, thrilled, nervous, elated,* etc.

. List on the board the students' words.

famous astronaut   *thrilled*

huge monster   *hungry*

patient teacher   *frustrated*

wild tiger   *worried*

. Then have the students add to the frame. Tell them to use the caret (∧) to add details such as:

What kind of person or animal?

When did the person or animal sit down?

Where (on what) did he (she/it) sit?

Why was she (he/it) worried, hungry, thrilled, etc.?

How did he/she/it go about sitting down?

. When the students have completed the additions or elaborations, ask them to invent and write their own original third or concluding sentence. Have the students share their completed frames by reading to each other or to the class. You will notice that most of the "stories" now have a beginning, middle, and end. If there is interest, have the students edit, recopy, and publish their framed stories.

EXAMPLE OF STUDENT WRITING USING FRAME "The . . . . sat down."

The aging President settled down at nine o'clock in the den, because he was very exhausted. He was very exhausted because he had just come from a press conference, and they asked him many questions on foreign policies. So as soon as he got home that night he took his shoes off and relaxed.

FRAMES TO DEVELOP SEQUENCE AND LOGICAL ORGANIZATION

Various types of "open frames" can be used to help students develop sequencing of ideas, supporting details, and paragraph structure. An open frame is an organizing structure or scheme that guides the writer with sentence openers or "place holders," such as:

Once upon a time there was a ....

Every day......................................

One day......................................

or

When I woke up this morning, I noticed......................................

A few hours later......................................

By evening......................................

We suggest the following plan for using open frames:

. Give the students as many sheets of paper as there are sentence starters. They would use three sheets for the above frames.

. Ask the students to complete *only* one sentence for each of the three sentence starters. The three sentences should relate to each other so that there is a brief outline. Have them *indent* each time they begin with a new starter sentence.

Page 1:	*When I woke up this morning, I noticed that my dog had not slept with me last night.*
Page 2:	*A few hours later I noticed that she had not eaten the food that I left out for her.*
Page 3:	*By evening I saw my dog's face in the window.*

. After the students have outlined the story with starter sentences, tell them to return to each sentence on its separate page and add elaboration or details. Suggest that they write three or four additional supporting sentences for each of the three "place holder" sentences.

141

THE "MAGIC WHO"

One of the most useful sentence frames for building elaboration skills is the structure which uses the word "who," as in the following examples:

*The most important character in this story is Charlotte **who** devotes her life to rescuing a runt pig from death.*

or

*Emmy Noether was a mathematician **who** had to publish her research under a man's name.*

or

*I am a fifth grade student **who** enjoys working in the science laboratory.*

Introduce the use of the "**MAGIC WHO**" by beginning with a simple composition titled *"Who Am I?"*

. Have students write the frame:

   I am a(n)................ who................ .

. Tell the students to give themselves an identity *(student, friend, daughter, pitcher,* etc.) and complete the frame by explaining some aspects of their identity.

. Have them repeat the frame two more times, each time writing a new identity of a different type:

   I am a daughter who helps my parents prepare meals.
   I am a friend who loves to go dancing with my friend Jan.
   I am a pitcher who has won three games for my team.

. After the students have completed their frames, tell them to revise this "first draft" by deleting "I am" in sentences two and three, changing periods to commas, and adding the word *"and"*, as below:

   I am a daughter who helps my parents prepare meals,
   ~~I am~~ a friend who loves to go dancing with my friend Jan, ∧and
   ~~I am~~ a pitcher who has won three games for my team.

. Next have them recopy this "second draft" to produce their "finished copy," as below:

I am a daughter who helps my parents prepare meals, a friend who loves to go dancing with my friend Jan, and a pitcher who has won three games for my team.

. After your students have practiced this initial writing activity, have them use similar sentence frames for writing about story characters and famous people using the variation of the **"MAGIC WHO"** in the Famous Person Frame described below.

FAMOUS PERSON FRAME

A variation of the **"MAGIC WHO"** strategy is the following frame for writing about a well-known person of either the past or the present. Using three sheets of paper, have the students set up the following starters, one on each page:

Page 1:   ....*was (is) a(n)....................who*....................
Page 2:   *She /He always wanted (dreamed, hoped, wished)*....................
Page 3:   *Finally, in the year (During the years, After many disappoint-ments,)*....................

When the students have completed this outline, they can research the details and add supporting sentences to each starter sentence. Each of the three starter sentences, along with its supporting sentences, becomes a paragraph in a three-paragraph exposition.

Page 1:   *Amelia Earhart was a pilot who flew across the Atlantic Ocean in the early years of aviation.*
Page 2:   *She always dreamed of being the first woman to navigate her own airplane around the world.*
Page 3:   *Finally in 1937, after many months of preparation, Earhart began her historic, ill-fated flight to circumnavigate the earth.*

143

BOOK REPORT FRAMES

Writing book reports is a long-standing school tradition. Unfortunately many students believe that they must merely retell the story in their own words, forgetting that a more experienced author has already done just that. Frames such as the three outlined below will help your students focus on the "reporting" rather than the "retelling."

Students can use the first frame to tell about the major characters in either a fiction or non-fiction book:

In the book (story, novel, biography) ...., by......................, the most important (interesting, humorous, delightful) character (person) is ....who...................... .
There are several (two, three) other important characters. There is .... who...................... There is also......................who...................... Finally, there is ....who...................... .

The second frame can be used to summarize the book's central problem or theme:

This story deals with the problem (theme) of............ .
The problem is heightened (gets worse) when (as)............ .
The problem is resolved (is solved) when (as)............ .

The third frame enables the students to express their opinions about the book:

As a result of reading ...., I realized (learned, recognized, understood)............... .
I would recommend this book to anyone who............... .

As you will notice, each segment or frame can be used as an independent paragraph to report on a book, or all three frames can be joined for writing a three-paragraph report. Further, each segment can be "expanded" by adding supporting details about the characters, the problem, and the reviewer's opinion. You will find a variety of book report frames in our publication entitled *EASY WRITER.* You may wish to use these activities, or you can develop your own frames.

FRAMES FOR THE CONTENT AREAS

The frames below are helpful for getting students started in writing essays on topics in other content areas such as science, social studies, health, art, music, physical education, or math.

The .... is a .... that (or who)............... . We find .... in such places as .... A .... can be classified as .... It is very similar to .... in that it...............

or

The main characteristics of ....are..............., ..., and...............This organism meets the basic requirements of life by.............. We can compare a .... with a ....in three different ways: (1)...............(2)...............(3)...............

or

...............was a ....who ....He/She patiently waited .... Finally, in the year (or during the years) ....he/she............... .

Again you may wish to refer to the *EASY WRITER* student books for frames which are appropriate for your students' needs and abilities, or you may wish to develop your own.

> Thurgood Marshall
> (The Magic Who)
>
> I am Thurgood Marshall who was a lawyer, who became the first black in the Supreme Court of the United States, and who worked for integrating public schools.
>
> Jimmy

"THREE REASONS WHY": A STRATEGY FOR WRITING PERSONAL, PERSUASIVE, AND EXPLANATORY ESSAYS

You can provide your students with an extraordinarily effective organizing scheme by teaching them the following writing strategy which we have termed "THREE REASONS WHY." The first form of this strategy, **personal expression,** should be set up as follows:

. Have your students take four sheets of paper and number each page 1, 2, 3, and 4, writing the words *Draft Copy* at the top of page 1.

. On page 1, have them write the starter, "*There are three reasons why I ....*"

. Model a response by writing on the board, "*There are three reasons why I* **need a new bicycle.**"

. Ask each student to expand his own starter with one of these verbs: *want, need, like, enjoy,* or *hope.*

. Then ask each student to complete his own starter sentence on page 1, in the way modeled by the teacher.

. Have the students share their responses and check to see that all the students have completed their sentences. You will probably find a variety of topics. Provide time and encouragement for every student to complete her/his sentence.

. Tell the students to skip a line and write the words, "*The first reason,*" or "*One reason,*" or "*First.*" Do **not** have them write the reasons yet, but say you will refer to these starter words as "place holders" and will come back to them shortly.

. Ask them to go to page 2 and write the words, "*A second reason,*" or "*Another reason,*" or "*Second.*" Then go to the third page and ask them to use the place holder "*A third reason,*" or "*Finally,*" or "*Last.*" They should not complete these sentence starters until you discuss them.

. Now tell the students to think of three *significantly* different reasons, one for each place holder. Model different reasons such as:

There are three reasons why I need a new bicycle. One reason is that my old bicycle is broken and totally useless.

Second, with a new bicycle I could get to school by myself.

Finally, I would be able to enter the Springtime Bicycle Race in town and be a winner.

. Tell the students to complete their three starter sentences with their own three significant reasons.

. After the students have successfully written three different reasons, check for understanding by asking several of the students to read their sentences aloud.

. Ask them to write a conclusion on page 4. They should write a conclusion by keeping page 1 in front of them and writing a simple sentence that recapitulates the opening sentence, as in these examples:

These, therefore, are the three reasons why I need a new bicycle.

or

For these reasons, I desperately need a new bicycle.

. When your students have successfully completed several of these **THREE REASONS WHY** outlines, show them how to support each reason with three or four additional detailed sentences. These detailed sentences must refer only to the reason being elaborated upon and not "spill" into the other two reasons.

Inform the students that this genre is called **personal expression** and then proceed to show students how to write a second genre called a **persuasive** essay using a similar model. In this persuasive genre, the student substitutes the words "*we should*" for the word "*I*," as in the following examples:

*There are three reasons why **we should** protect endangered species.*

or

***we should** take multi-vitamins.*

or

***we should** obey traffic laws.*

As they did in the **personal expression** essay, students continue to outline the essay on four sheets of paper and support each reason with several elaborated statements. In the **persuasive essay** the students will most likely have to research information in order to produce a fully developed composition.

Using the same model, the third variation of this genre is the **explanatory mode** in which the student begins with "*There are three reasons why ....*" and completes the statement as a factual description without using the words "*I*" or "*we should,*" as illustrated below:

*There are three reasons why **slavery was introduced in the South.***

or

birds migrate.

or

exercise makes you healthier.

As you will observe, this last form, the **explanatory mode,** provides the student with the structure for writing research essays in the content areas. As students become proficient in using this basic **THREE REASONS WHY** model in all three formats, you can guide them into modifying and adding "style" by deleting repetitive words and adding a full introduction and conclusion as they develop a five-paragraph essay.

There are three reasons why I like my family.
First, I like my family because they support me when I need help in homework, a problem, or when I am feeling gloomy.
Second, when I am sick, they help take care of me so I will get better soon.
Finally, I know they like me.
These are the three reasons why I like my family.
Kamica

ADDITIONAL STRATEGIES USING THE THREE REASONS WHY MODEL

Suppose you want your students to write a composition on any of the following topics or themes:

My Favorite T.V. Show; Helping a Friend; A Good Vacation; My Trip In Space; If I Were Five Inches Tall; and so forth.

They could begin a draft copy as follows:

My favorite T.V. show is ....for these three reasons.

Helping a friend is important for these three reasons.

Going to Lake George with my family is a good vacation for these three reasons.

If I were five inches tall, my life would be different (the same, difficult, wonderful)

for .... (yes, you've got it, "for these three reasons.")

With this basic scheme, your students can write organized pieces that can be developed into three (or more) paragraphs, pages, or even chapters. By stating each reason and supporting each reason with related information, your students will not wander off the topic or write from what we have termed "stream of consciousness." As your students develop sophistication and style, they can vary the scheme, but there must always be some organizational plan that is articulated before writing begins.

Duke Ellington
(Three Reasons Why)

There are three reasons why I like Duke Ellington.
First, Duke Ellington was a composer and a musician.
Second, he was first in modern jazz to give concerts regularly.
Third, he composed nearly 1,000 songs.
Those are the three reasons why I like Duke Ellington.

Caris

149

STUDENT ACTIVITY FOR WRITING

"Who Am I?"

I am a ....

who...

I am also a ....

who...

....

In addition, I am a ....

who...

....

As you can see, I wear many "hats", but I am still me

whose name is..

STUDENT ACTIVITY FOR USING THE "MAGIC WHO " TO WRITE A SUMMARY BIOGRAPHY

EXAMPLE: "WHO WAS PATRICK HENRY ?"

Patrick Henry was a ....who at age..........

could be described as..

For example, ...

....

However, by the time he was .... , he knew that ....

....

So he decided ....

....

In............................... , Patrick Henry had a chance to prove his ability when.............

....

....

As a result of his performance, several important changes occurred in Patrick

Henry's life. First,...

....

In addition, ...

....

Most important, ...

....

....

STUDENT ACTIVITY
FOR WRITING ABOUT ONE OF THE THIRTEEN COLONIES

One of the original thirteen colonies was ....

located ....

This colony was originally settled by...

....

who wanted (hoped, believed)..

....

One of the major leaders in this colony was.................................

....who...

....

From the time it was settled in the year ...., and up to the

start of the American Revolution, the people of (repeat the name of

the colony)..made

their living by.. ,

.... , and ....

....

EXAMPLES OF STUDENTS' WRITINGS USING
THE "MAGIC WHO"

Forrest

The Magic Who
Veterens Day

1. I am a brave soldier who is a hero
2. I am a strong soldier who carries a big flag.
3. I am an American soldier who fought in the war
I am a soldier.

Then we did a Magic Who. I also learned what a Magic Who is. It is a paper numbered down to three and you write one sentence three times but each one has a different ending. Then you put the three sentences together into one good sentence.

The Giving Tree

Monique Davis
"The Magic Who"

1. I am an apple tree who gives apples.
2. I am a loving tree who loves a boy.
3. I am a strong tree who has a swing.

① I am a student at Crestview Elementary who has good behavior,

② I am a beautiful daughter who loves to talk, and

③ I am a sports fan who likes to call games. Lewanda

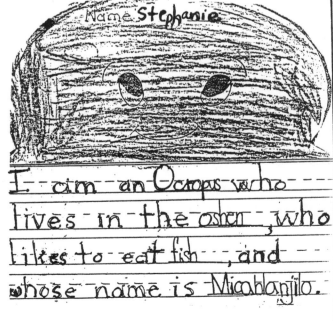

Name Stephanie

I am an Octopus who lives in the osher, who likes to eat fish, and whose name is Micablanjilo.

Mary M. Bethune
(The Magic Who)

I am Mary M. Bethune who worked on a cotton plantation as a youngster, who was the first in her family to learn how to read, who started her own school for blacks, and who won a medal for contributing to education. Geogrey

153

The Ugly Dinosaur   Keith

A long time ago there was a big ugly dinosaur
who always had fights with his wife. He was so
big that when he hollered all the other dinosaur
cried. They fought for at least on hour. He really
got mad.

Every day he would walk out on her.
She got so mad she threw their pots and
pans at him. She decided not to let him
back but she couldn't do that to him.
Finally she didn't let him come back.
So he stayed out in the cold. One day his
wife decided to let him in. When she went
outside she didn't find him but she did a
snowman shaped like him.

A long time ago there was a
gaint Tryasauraus rex who ate 70 men

each day.. A Tryasauraus isa

dinosaur.

Every day the Tryasauraus had

a stumucake. Then he went on
a diet to lose wait.

Finally he lernd to eat 50

less men then 40 men then 30 then

20 then to men and he hollered

It worked.
It worked.
the diet workd

Draft
Oyster Pond
grade 3

154

EXAMPLES OF STUDENTS' WRITING USING
"THREE REASONS WHY" FRAME

Dear Mc Cruz,

There are three reasons why we should have an open campus at McLane High School.

First, it would lessen the problem of running out of food during lunch period. The cafeteria was not built to accomodate the large number of students we have at Mc-Hi. It would enable the cafeteria to provide better service to students who choose to remain on campus for lunch.

My second reason that is allowing students the freedom to leave the campus for lunch teaches them to assume responsibility. They will be responsible to get back on time. Also they will be responsible for choosing where to eat.

My last reason is, it would reduce the number of gangs or student fights on campus by taking students away from getting involved in fights. Felix

---

Marie

Three Reasons Why

There are three reasons why I should do my best in school.

First, I want to get a good education to do the things I want to do in the future. I'd like to get a good job.

Second, I want to help my parents when they need it. I know what my parents expect of me and I will always do my best in school

Finally, I'd like to make my teacher proud of me and of all the things I do.

These are the three reasons why I should do my best in school.

Jodee

Three Reasons Why

There are three reasons why I want to be a zookeeper.

The #first reason why I want to be a zookeeper is because I like to work with animals.

The # second reason is I want to help endangered species.

The # third reason is I want to cure diseases and keep animals from becoming extinct.

Therefore these are the three reasons why I want to become a zoo keeper.

EXAMPLES OF STUDENTS' WRITING USING "THREE REASONS WHY" OUTLINE

There are three reasons

why I want to go back to Taiwan

My First reason is because it's the place

I was born.

Taiwan is a little Island. I was

born in the place that's Near the

Capitol, Taipei, I like it there very

much, especially at Night time because

my mom, my Aunt and I would

go to a department store, and buy

lots of Clothing. The people also

Sell lots of things to eat.

Everything is delicious.

Writing   Lee

There are many alcowhol

abusers across the US and after

you read this piece of writing

think about why you shouldn't

abuse alcowhol. Here are my three

reasons on why you shouldn't abuse

alcohol.

The first reason is alcodhol will

make you sick. It kills of braincells

in about four minutes. It also makes

you sick witch leads to red eyes and d.t.p.

Another reason is to much could

kill you. You could be getting into your

Car and have a bad accident and hurt

you or a cop can ask you questions

and if he finds you drunk he might

take away your licence

The last but not least is you can't

get a good job if you are an alcoholic.

If you don't work you can't eat

because you have no money.

After you read this think about

your own reasons why you shouldn't

drink to much. Those are my reasons

why you shouldn't abuse alcohol.

Why everyone should have more
than 8 pair of socks.   Pary

SOCKS are a very good thing to
have when you need them. I think
everyone should have them.

The first reason is for safety. If
your socks get wet, you can change them
before you get sick and catch amonia. So you
can protect your feet from getting coins
on your feet.

Another reason is for looks. So you
Can have different colors you like and so
you wont look sneezy, and you can through
away the sneezy socks and by some more.

The finall reason you should have more
than 8 pair of socks is for fun. You don't have
to where socks that match all the time.
You can use your amagination, (make
sure they are clean). You can through
them on people and every thing.

Conclusion- The point I'm trying to make
is that if you have a lot of socks, you
wont be stuck with cold, ugly feet.

HELPING OTHERS

Someday I would like to help solve the problem of teenagers commiting
suicide for these reasons.

First, they have everything to live for. They can be doctors, lawyers,
truck drivers, nurses, taxi drivers, athletes or be a teacher like Miss
Shwide. They can be smart and go to college.

Second, suicide is just like running away. You can't solve a problem
with suicide. Teenagers sometimes run away and do dumb things to themselves.
I would like to help them with their problems and tell them that suicide is
not the answer. I would like to help them and show them that people are not
perfect, everybody makes mistakes.

The final reason is when they kill themselves, they leave everything,
their past, their future, their family, friends, and the world too. They
make everybody that loved them suffer.

Now you should know why I would like to help solve the problem of
teenage-suicide.

by Melissa

Susan   Writing

Mrs. Luby

There are 3 reasons why I

never take things from a stranger.

First, it could be poison.

Second, I could get sick.

Last, he might take me.

EXAMPLES OF STUDENTS' WRITING   USING A BOOK REPORT FRAME

My Favorite Character
Charmane

In the story of The Last Puppy, my favorite character is the last puppy who was always last to do everything. I especially like the last puppy because he was very patient. If I were to meet this character in real life, I would say you can be first in my lines.

My Favorite Character
Cheri - Anne

In the story of Harry's New Born Sister, my favorite character is Harry who was jealous of his new born baby sister. I especially like Harry because he tried to act like a baby when he broke all of the baby's toys. If I were to meet this character in real life, I would tell Harry, new born babies need attention.

Story Frame   10/40

In the fable The Poor Old Dog by Arnold Lobel the problem is about a poor old dog who is so poor because he has no house, no food, and clothes with holes all over. This problem gets worse when he finds a ring and thinks its magic and wishes but his wish doesn't come true. This problem is resolved when he sees a sign posted on a log that a rich lady lost her ring and there is a reward for the lost ring and he brings the ring to her. The dog gets alot of money and buys a house, clothes and shoes and is never poor again. Seth

Book Report: BEN HUR

In the book Ben Hur, by Lew Wallace, the most important character is Ben Hur, who was a Jew and a merchant in Jerusalem. There is also Messala, who was a Roman and he hated the Jews. Finally, there is Quintus Arrius, who was a commander of a fleet of galley ships. He also was a Roman who adopted Ben Hur as his son because Ben Hur saved his life.

This story deals with the problems of Messala when he takes Ben Hur's family. The problem gets worse when Messala sends Ben Hur to the galley ship and takes him as a slave. The problem is resolved when Ben Hur gets out of slavery and goes out looking for his family.

As a result of reading Ben Hur, we realized the difficulty of being a Jew and the advanges of being a Roman in the time of Christ. We would recommend this book to anyone who is interested in knowing how the Jews and Romans lived. We also would recommend the movie so people could get a better understanding of life in the time of Christ.

We thought the novel was well written because it was easy to follow. We understood everything that went on; however, there was some difficulty with understanding why the Romans could be so cruel to another human being, but other wise the book and movie was very well written.

STUDENTS' RESPONSES TO USING BOOK REPORT FRAMES

Tyrone
Brentwood

Book report

Swell Job!

The Wizard of Oz
by L. Frank BAUM

The most important person in this book is Dorothy who was lost in the land of oz. This person had a dog named Todo. There were also many other interesting characters. There was the scarecrow who needed a brain. There was a tin man who needed a heart. There was a lion who needed courage. And the witch who wanted Dorothy and the magic slippers.

Travis
Cherry Creek
CO

In the story Farenheit 451, the author, Ray Bradbury, makes the reader aware of the horrifying future where books are outlawed. By introducing the main character, Guy Montag, who is a futuristic fireman who doesn't put out fires, since house are fire-proof, but burns the outlawed books, the reader learns the danger of outlawing books.

The author also presents several other characters who affect Mr. Montag. First, there is Mrs. Montag, Guy's wife, who reports him for reading outlawed books. A second significant character is an old man, who helps Montag plant books in firemen's homes and then later helps him escape from the police. Finally, there is a band of outlaws who accept Montag and let him live with them in the wilderness.

In reading this story, I concluded that the author believes if books become outlawed people will stop thinkin

---

Missy
Cherry Creek CO

Book Report

In the story Anna Karenina, the author, Leo Tolstoy, makes the reader aware of Russian high-society life. By introducing the main character, Anna Karenina, who is very rich and among the best circles of women, the reader learns that even people who can buy anything they want can't buy love and respect once they've done something bad in the eyes of society.

The author also presents several other important characters who affect Anna. First, there is Karenin, who is Anna's husband. He is among the top officials in Russia and takes all cots to protect his name. A second significant character is Alexis Vronsky, who is friends with everyone, very rich, and is in love for Anna, and Anna is in love with him.

In reading this story, I concluded that the author believes that there are many things in life you can't buy or pay to have done for you, for the most important things in life you must work for yourself.

158

SAMPLE EASY WRITER ACTIVITIES FOR WRITING BOOK REPORTS

THE HEART OF THE BOOK

The frame below is designed to help you write a book report in which you discuss two or three significant chapters or ideas. Complete the frame, putting in as much information as you can where there are dots. Expand each paragraph with sentences that answer **wh-** questions. You may change the words of the frame if necessary.

The heart of the book .... by ....begins with the

chapter (introduction, opening) .... The author presents

(explains, describes, discusses) .... He/She makes the reader

aware (understand, recognize) .... Most important, ...

Another significant chapter (segment, section) is devoted to ....

The author's approach is .... In this chapter

the reader also (learns, meets, realizes) ....

This book would be of particular interest to ....

because of ....

CHECKLIST FOR EDITING

- Is there any more information you need to add?
- Did you read your report aloud to be sure it makes sense?
- Did you proofread for spelling, punctuation, and grammar?

FORGE AHEAD

Imagine that the book you have reported on will be produced f
of four or five scenes or situations from different chapters that
tise the televised production.

Copyright   ERA/CCR Corp   The Write Track Company
0708   Book G

USE A FRAME
WRITE A BOOK REPORT

A **FRAME** can help you write a good book report. Use the **FRAME** on this page to write about a story you have read. Copy the words in the **FRAME.** Leave lots of room where there are dots. Fill in each space with words that tell about the story. Add as many words as you need to write a good book report.

EXAMPLE

This book is about a person named **Cinderella** who **wants to go to the prince's ball.** There is also **the wicked stepmother** who **makes Cinderella do all the housework.**

Title of Story ....

Author of Story ....

This story is about a person named ....

who .... There is also ....

who ....·...... Another person in this story is ....

who .... The person I liked reading about

the most was........................... because...........................

CHECKLIST FOR PROOFREADING

- Did you write as much as you could in each space?
- Did you read your story aloud to be sure it makes sense?

EXTRA CREDIT

Write a **FRAME** that can be used to tell about another book you read. You can use some of the ideas below to help you.

- favorite person
- many other interesting people
- most exciting part of the story
- saddest part of the story
- funniest part of the story

THINKING SKILLS
deciding
qualifying

FRAMING

159

SAMPLE EASY WRITER ACTIVITY FOR FRAMING

STUDENTS' RESPONSES TO EASY WRITER FRAMING ACTIVITY

My life began in Kiev, Russia on May 30, 1982. At this time of my life I had a Mother, Father, and grand parents. I lived in a small, brown, apartment with my parents, grandparents, and uncle.

When I was very little we had moved to Italy. I made friends. I was very active, and put rocks in my mouth.

At this time of my life, I have a new addition to my family, a beautiful baby boy named Ryan David. I am almost ten and a student in P.S. 199 Queens, New York. I have a very good writing ability, love to dance, and play the Violin.

Ten years from now I will be nineteen years old. I will be in my last year of college and looking for a job as a writer or fashion designer.

My Autobiography
My life began when I was born in Korea. I soon found out I was a twin. It was being the same age and size as my sister.

From the time I was very little I loved to draw. I enjoyed playing with my twin sister.

At this time of my life I know many different things. I love growing up and learning more and more about life. I hope I never die because I hate leaving life especially my family!

Ten years from now I am going to work and help support my family. I will work as a third grade teacher. Someday I might get married and have children of my own.

160

SAMPLE EASY WRITER ACTIVITY FOR FRAMING

When I WOKE Up This Morning . . .

The **frame** on this page helps tell you the events of a day from beginning to end. Copy the frame on a sheet of paper. **Skip lines and leave lots of room** for writing your own words.

Write either a true or make-believe story of a day in your life.

Use as many words as you wish where there are dots.

EXAMPLE

Last night I spotted a strange object on the roof of my house.

When I woke up this morning	....
An hour later	....
When lunchtime came	....
Later in the day	....
Just before bedtime	....
Finally	....

CHECKLIST FOR PROOFREADING
- Did you write interesting ideas or events?
- Did you reread your story to be sure it makes sense?

EXTRA CREDIT

Write a frame from the story below by taking out some of the words. Ask a friend to fill in the frame.

Once upon a time there lived a poor man and woman who wanted to have a new car. Every day they would say, "We would be so happy if we could have a new car." One morning a frog visited the poor man and woman. It announced, "Your wish will come true. By next week, you will have a new car."

THINKING SKILLS
Deciding
Imagining
Sequencing

BOOK C
Page 18
0304

STUDENTS' RESPONSES TO USING FRAMES

Doreen

When I woke up this morning I noticed that my dog had not slept with me last night. Her hair wasn't in my blanket, my bed wasn't warm, and she wasn't barking at my alarm clock when it went off. I got up and looked all around for her, I looked under the bed, I looked, I looked in the closet, I looked everywhere but I couldn't find her.

A few hours later I noticed that she had not eaten the food that I left out for her I was very surprised. She always eats her food when she wakes up in the middle of the night. But her food wasn't touched. I'm scared, she be hurt.

By evening I saw my dog's nose in the window. I found out that she spent the night with the dog next door. She was alright! Thank God!

Janet

When I woke up this morning I noticed that my hamster grew unusually big and his color was purple, green, and blue. I ran to my mother and father and their faces were green and red and their hair was orange.

A few hours later I came home from school and my hamster was eating my house and the block was invaded by hamsters. I ran to Jenny Walz's house and her dog looked like a hamster. I got really scared.

By evening my mother and father turned back to normal and my hamster turned back to normal but he got much to fat and we had dinner except my hamster.

SAMPLE EASY WRITER ACTIVITIES FOR FRAMING

TELL THREE REASONS WHY

Below is a **FRAME** which helps you write three reasons why you like to do something.
First, decide what you like to do. You can use one of the ideas in the **FUN BOX** or you can make up your own.
Second, copy the frame. Leave lots of room where there are dots.
Third, finish each sentence starter in your own words.

FUN BOX

Some things I like to do:
ride my bike
play with my best friend
go out to eat
take a long trip

FRAME FOR THREE REASONS WHY

There are three reasons why I like to . . . .

. . . .

The first reason is . . . .

. . . .

A second reason is . . . .

. . . .

A third reason is . . . .

. . . .

. . . .

CHECKLIST FOR PROOFREADING

- Did you write what you like to do?
- Did you have three **good** reasons?
- Did you read your writing aloud to be sure it ma

EXTRA CREDIT

Write three reasons why you would like to hav
Use a frame like the one above to help you wri

THINKING SKILLS
deciding
sequencing
PLANNING AND OUTLINING

ESSAY CONTENTS

A **FRAME** is a useful guide for writing essays. Read the **ESSAY STATEMENT** below and the **EXAMPLE** of the opening sentence. Copy the **ESSAY FRAME** as your guide and use it to respond to one of the essays in the **CONTENTS OF ESSAYS**.

EXAMPLE

ESSAY STATEMENT

State three significant differences that caused conflicts between the Indians and the white settlers. Support the differences with specific details.

Opening Sentence:

Three significant reasons for conflicts between the Indians and the white settlers were differences in life styles, customs, and use of natural resources.

ESSAY FRAME

Note: Expand each reason by asking yourself **wh-** questions. Your essay should contain between 200 and 250 words.

Three reasons for (differences) . . . . were (are) . . . . , ... , and . . . .

The first reason (state what it is) . . . . (then add three or four support sentences).

The second reason (state what it is) . . . . (then add three or four support sentences.)

The final reason (state what it is) . . . . (then add three or four support sentences.)

As a result (Consequently, Because of) . . . . (restate and conclude).

CONTENTS OF ESSAYS

Causes of the American Revolution (or another American war)
Problems of Pollution
Endangered Animals
Conflicts Between Two Group With Different Cultures
Problems of Drugs, Smoking, or Alcohol

CHECKLIST FOR EDITING

- Did you write an opening sentences giving three significant reasons?
- Did you write three or four support sentences for each reason?
- Did you use **wh-** questions to expand your paragraphs?

FORGE AHEAD

Compile a list of topics which fit this type of frame. Put these topics in a notebook for future use.

Framing
Page 21

WALL CHARTS TO ILLUSTRATE FRAMING

USE A FRAME FOR SOCIAL STUDIES and SCIENCE

Copy the frame and put in as much information as you can where there are dots.

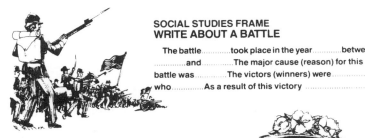

SOCIAL STUDIES FRAME
WRITE ABOUT A BATTLE

The battle............took place in the year............between
.............and............The major cause (reason) for this
battle was............The victors (winners) were................
who............As a result of this victory ....

SOCIAL STUDIES FRAME
WRITE ABOUT A FAMOUS PERSON

.............was (is) a............who............He/She always
wanted to (dreamed of, patiently waited)...............
Finally, in the year (during the years)...............
he/she...............

SCIENCE FRAME
WRITE ABOUT A LIV

The............is a............1
such places as............ar
classified as............It is
in that it............

USE A FRAME WRITE A BOOK REPORT

Copy the **frame** and put in as much information as you can where there are dots.

FRAME 1
WRITE ABOUT THE CHARACTERS

The most exciting/realistic/imaginative/
memorable character in the book............by
............is............who............There are also
several other interesting characters. There is
............who............There is also............who
............Finally, there is............who ....

FRAME 2
WRITE ABOUT THE PROBLEM

This story (book) deals with the problem of...............
The problem becomes worse when...............
The problem is eventually (finally) solved (overcome) when ....

FRAME 3
WRITE YOUR OPINION

From the moment I started to read this story, I knew...............
The book held (or didn't hold) my interest because...............
As as result of reading ....,I...............

OUTLINING INVOLVES THE THINKING PROCESSES OF OBSERVING, DECIDING, SEQUENCING, ORGANIZING, AND SYNTHESIZING.

RESEARCH REPORTS, ESSAYS, DESCRIPTIONS, NARRATIVES, AND OTHER FULL-LENGTH WRITING

The extensive practice which your students have had in sentence composing and sentence improving is preparation for the main goal of writing **full-length** products which are organized and logical. The sense of meaningfulness in a written product results from an organizational scheme which is recognizable to the reader. This scheme or format consists of a *sequence* which the reader can follow and contains *main* or major themes or ideas that are supported (or elaborated upon) by *details* or specific information. An example of this organizational scheme can be seen in the childhood story of *Goldilocks and the Three Bears,* which we have divided into Sequence, Main Ideas, and Support or Elaboration.

Sequence Questions	Main Ideas	Support or Elaboration
What happened *first?*	food not ready to eat	porridge is too hot; bears take a walk
What happened *second?*	Goldilocks enters house; Goldilocks samples food and other items	tastes porridge — too hot, too cold, just right; in bears' house tries chairs — too small, too big, just right; tries beds — too hard, too soft, just right
What happened *third?*	bears return home; are upset at discovery of intruder	Mama's and Papa's porridge, chairs, and beds have been tampered with; Baby's porridge has been eaten; chair has been broken; bed has been slept in
What happened *last?*	bears frighten off Goldilocks	Goldilocks wakes up; is frightened; runs out of house

Many students from primary grades through college struggle and often fail to construct an organizational scheme for writing because they are unaware of basic structures. Instruction in the three-part arrangement of **(1) Asking Questions, (2) Responding with Main Ideas,** and **(3) Adding Supporting Details** can be particularly valuable to students who have difficulty in ordering their written work logically. This three-part arrangement is especially useful for expository writing, which includes narratives, journalism, descriptions, explanations, thesis-proof, and compare/contrast.

PLANNING FORMATS

In order to use this strategy effectively, your students will need to develop **planning formats** to guide their thinking.

. During the pre-writing discussion you might want to reinforce two key points:

1. We write to express ideas, thoughts, or information which are really answers to question such as *who? what? how? what kinds of? why? when?*

2. We always write to an audience — a person or persons who will read or hear what we have written.

. Begin by developing an outline or various outlines with the class or group. Explain that many types of writing contain information that can be answered in the form of **WH-questions,** such as in *what happened? how many? why did it happen?* and *what kinds of?* Name the genre (narrative, journalism, descriptive, etc.) so that the students know which *plan* to use and which *questions* to ask.

. With the students, construct a three-part outline which includes:

. **Questions** which the writer plans to answer

. **Answers** which are brief or general responses to the questions

. **Details** which support each question and its answer

QUESTION	ANSWER	DETAILS
Who went away?	Terry	best friend, kept me company, helped me with homework, told silly jokes
When did it happen? Why did it happen? What did I do? What happened after?		

165

SETTING UP THE QUESTION/ANSWER/DETAIL — Q.A.D.

The **QUESTION/ANSWER/DETAIL** format is an easy-to-use plan which should be practiced by the students in preparation for writing a full-length paper. A sample plan is given below:

First Step: The student receives or selects a topic to write about.

Example: *Keeping Tropical Fish as Pets*

Second Step: The student formulates a set of **WH- questions** on the topic. Not all of the questions will necessarily be used, but as many questions as possible should be asked. Possible questions include:

What are tropical fish?

How do tropical fish make good pets?

What kinds of conditions do they need?

Where can tropical fish be obtained?

What are the best types to get?

Why do people enjoy having fish?

etc.

Third Step: The student selects *main* or *major* questions or those questions which he or she wants to write about and sets up a **Q.A.D.** format as illustrated in the pages following.

Henry Wadsworth Longfellow finds his song in the heart of a friend and that song becomes a symbol of sharing.

RELATE List the things you have done that you believe have influenced or affected the lives of your friends or family. Next to each item, write the name of the person and that person's relationship to you.

SELECT Write the names of people you care about. List them in these categories:

| **Relatives** | **Friends** | **Others** |

CREATE Complete this Q.A.D. outline. Then use it as a guide to write two paragraphs about yourself.

QUESTIONS	ANSWERS	DETAILS
What is my best quality?	**Example:** making people laugh	I tell funny jokes, mimic people, etc.
What affect does this quality have on others?	makes them happy	they forget problems; remember their own funny stories

EDITOR'S CHECKLIST
- ☐ Did you add details to develop your paragraphs?
- ☐ Did you read your writing aloud to be sure you wrote what you wanted to say?
- ☐ Did you edit your work for spelling, punctuation, and grammar?

Suggested Sequence for Developing Q.A.D. Outlines

Chronological Outline: *A Visit to the Firehouse*

. Begin with an opening sentence:

> *Yesterday we went to the firehouse.*

. Set up the Q.A.D. outline:

QUESTIONS	ANSWERS	DETAILS
What did we do (see) first?	*looked at the engines*	*red, shiny, different kinds, hook and ladder the biggest, two people drive it*
What did we do (see) second?	*went on the hook and ladder*	*climbed in, sat in front, sat in back, rang the bell*
What did we do (see) third?	*went upstairs and looked around*	*saw where firefighters rested and played, saw cots, stove, refrigerator, deck of cards*
What did we do (see) last?	*slid down pole*	*was fun, was scary, landed on mat*

. After the outline has been completed, have individual students orally compose the narrative by telling or reading the information from the **Q.A.D.** outline. The teacher should model the composing process by showing how to link or synthesize the opening sentence with the phrases from the three different columns as shown below:

> *Yesterday we went to the firehouse. The first thing we did was look at the engines. They were red and shiny. There were many different kinds. The hook and ladder was the biggest engine. Two firefighters have to drive it. Then we went up on the hook and ladder, etc.*

The News Report Outline

The well-known journalism format of asking *who? what? when? where? how? why?* can be extended into the three-part **Q.A.D.** outline as in the following example:

. Construct or use a headline — *FIRE IN CHEMICAL LABORATORY.*

. Have students write **WH- questions** and provide answers and details.

QUESTIONS	ANSWERS	DETAILS
What happened?	*fire broke out in one of the offices*	*workers were painting; set a bird's nest on fire; fire spread quickly*
Where?	*Standard Laboratories in Nyack*	*a large pharmaceutical company near the river*
When?	*yesterday*	*afternoon, 3 p.m.*
Who?	*100 employees*	*no injuries; everyone evacuated; firefighters helped*
How did it happen?	*fire started accidentally*	*no one knew of bird's nest; paint spilled; fire spread quickly*
What was the result?	*fire put out*	*no serious damage; some water on first three floors; no estimate of damage*

Summary sentences taken from the ANSWER column could be:

> *Yesterday afternoon at 3 p.m. a fire accidently broke out in one of the offices in Standard Laboratories in Nyack. One hundred employees were evacuated and the fire was quickly put out by the firefighters.*

QUESTIONS	ANSWERS	DETAILS
Who are the people making the news?		
What has happened?		
Where did it happen?		
How did it happen?		
When did it happen?		
Why did it happen?		

The students can then write the full article using their notes. Some students may see variations in organization or sequence which differ from the outline. Encourage them to try their own variations and then have the students evaluate which arrangements they prefer.

Example: *Yesterday afternoon at 3 p.m. a fire broke out in Standard Laboratories, a large pharmaceutical company in Nyack. Workers were painting the building when a bird's nest caught on fire and spread quickly. It seemed the workers did not know the bird's nest was there and the fire was considered accidental. One hundred employees were helped to safety by the firefighters. Fortunately, no one was injured. In spite of water on the first three floors, there was no serious damage. The company does not yet have an estimate of its losses.*

Thesis-Proof Q.A.D. Outline

QUESTIONS	ANSWERS	DETAILS
What do I want to prove?(thesis)	*the American Revolution was actually a civil war*	*Americans were divided — Patriots vs. Loyalists*
What is my evidence?	*there were Loyalists in every colony*	*one third of all Americans were Loyalists; conflict was in all states; fought against other Americans*
What conclusions can I draw?(proof)	*we have not fully understood the American Revolution*	*Loyalists not completely understood; we should study history from the "other side" or point of view*

NEVERTHELESS...   FURTHERMORE

169

Using the Q.A.D. Outline with Sentence Starters

. Have your students complete a **Q.A.D.** outline like the one about a hero or heroine below:

QUESTIONS	ANSWERS	DETAILS

Who is the hero or heroine?

When and where did he/she live?

What were the most important accomplishments in this person's life?

What event or events made this person become a hero or heroine?

. Ask the students to use a sentence starter (such as those listed below) as the opener of each paragraph. Possible starters for paragraph one:

One of the greatest heroes/heroines of all times..............

In my opinion .... is among the outstanding.............

A man/woman who achieved greatness as a hero/heroine is.............

In (year or time period), a person of courage, intelligence, and determination...............

If I had to choose one hero/heroine, I would choose..............

Possible starters for paragraph two:

(name of person) was the first man/woman to ....

The most important accomplishments in this person's life were ...., ..., and ....

The outstanding achievements in this person's life were ...., ..., and ....

In (year or time period), (name) accomplished what no one had ever been able to do before. He/she ....

Possible starters for paragraph three:

In spite of many difficulties, (name) was determined to ....

From the time she/he was young, (name) knew that.......... .

In (year or time period), (name) decided to ....

If there had not been........, (name) would not have ....

170

The Q.A.D. Outline for Writing a Description

To "describe" means to tell about the appearance, attributes, and characteristics of an object, setting, or person. A description differs from a narrative in that the description tells what exists independent of time, while a narrative has sequence or chronology. Below is an example of a **Q.A.D.** outline for descriptive writing:

QUESTIONS	ANSWERS	DETAILS
What is a forest?	*a wooded area*	*many trees and other plants live there naturally*
What kinds of plants live in a forest?	*different kinds or a great variety*	*deciduous trees, evergreen trees, tropical trees, flowering plants, bushes, mosses, etc.*
What kinds of animals live in forest?	*different kinds, untamed, wild*	*tree animals, underground animals, cave or den animals, etc.*

After the students have had practice in composing orally from the **Q.A.D.** outline, provide them with a frame for writing their information in sentences. The purpose of the frame is to provide a transition for eventually writing freely and independently.

If you explored a forest, you would find many different kinds of plants. The main plants of a forest are ...., ..., and .... A forest might have ...., ..., and .... trees. There are also...............

171

Additional Suggestions for Using the Q.A.D. Outline in Composing

Some students may continue to have difficulty in organizing the information from the Q.A.D outline. One problem is the formulation of the topic sentence or the "umbrella" sentence. Below are suggested sentence starters with **WH- questions** which can be adapted for students of different ages:

Topic Sentence: *Our senior citizens receive many benefits from living in the city.*

Questions to ask:

Whom are we writing about?

What are the benefits?

How are the benefits received?

What does a city offer?

Where can senior citizens go?

Topic Sentence: *George Washington was a skillful soldier, a dedicated statesman, a civic-minded Southerner, and a planter.*

Questions to ask:

When did he fulfill each role?

How did he come to have such diverse roles?

What did he accomplish in each of these roles?

Topic Sentence: *The ocean has always been of great interest to scientists.*

Questions to ask:

Why are scientists interested in the ocean?

What discoveries have scientists made about the ocean?

What do scientists still want to know?

How will scientific information about the ocean help us?

What background, history, or knowledge can you add about the ocean?

Topic Sentence: *Although most scholars already knew otherwise, the average sailor in Columbus' day believed that the earth was flat.*

For the topic sentence above, what questions would you have your students ask?

Q.A.D. FOR SOCIAL STUDIES

Sample Q.A.D.
New Hampshire

QUESTION	ANSWER	DETAIL
Where is New Hampshire?	Northeast	New England, borders Vermont, Maine, Massachusetts, Canada, access to Atlantic Ocean
What is its population?	one of the smallest states	45th largest state, 4 electoral votes, 2 members of House of Representatives, 600,000 people, 68 people per square mile, settled by Scotch, Irish, Scandinavians, Canadians; after 1890 settled by Greeks, Poles, Russian Jews.
Where do most of the people live?	in small cities	the ten largest cities are: (from largest to smallest) Manchester, Nashua, Concord (capital), Portsmouth, Dover, Berlin, Keene, Rochester, Lanconia, Claremont
What is the nature of its land?	varied, mountains, hills, and some seashore	called Granite State, White Mountains (covers 60%), Lake Winnipesaukee, Connecticut River Valley, Isle of Shoals
What kind of climate does it have?	cold winters, warm summers	average summer temperature 70°, average winter temperature 21°, warmer in valleys, cooler in mountains, average rainfall 39", average snow 61"
What are its natural resources?	forests, water power, vacation area	forests cover 80% of land, White Mountain National Forest, fisheries, tourist areas
How do the people earn their living?	manufacturing, tourism, some farming, lumbering, and quarrying	textile mill products, leather and leather goods (mostly shoes), electrical machinery, electronics, paper, lumber mills, quarrying, farming, tourist industry
What was its history like?	first to declare independence, grew slowly	very slow to grow in population; 1622: given land by G.B.; 1679: became first Royal Province; 1776: first colony to declare independence. 1800: introduction of power machinery, welcomed foreigners for growing industry, became industrial state; 1900's: greatest growth in population and industry
What are its major places of interest?	State Parks, historical landmarks	many national parks for hiking, swimming, skiing, fishing, Mt. Washington, Franconia National Park

WRITING A DEFINITION USING "DEFINITION MODE"

As students move through the grades, they generally shift emphasis from story or fiction writing to expository or factual writing. In exposition the writer often has to explain or define topics or subjects. Below is an effective, organized approach that allows students to construct a clear, unambiguous definition. It shows the students how to separate the *general category* of an item from its *details* or *attributes* and prevents them from defining an item through a singular, vague statement, *"A pencil is something you write with."*

Introduce students to the **DEFINITION MODE** with the following steps:

. Give each student a sheet of unlined paper (8½ x 11) which should be held horizontally and folded into thirds. Title the columns as below and select a commonly used word as an example. Enter the information in each column:

QUESTION	GENERAL CATEGORY	ATTRIBUTES
What is a shoe? A shoe is a(n)	article of footware that	a) is generally made of leather, plastic, cloth b) can be of different types: pumps, sandals, flats, moccasins, etc. c) can be used for sports, walking, running, etc. d) protects the feet e) consists of a sole, a heel, and a top covering

. Have them write the definition by connecting the three parts as in the example below:

What is a shoe?

A shoe is an article of footwear that is generally made of leather, plastic, or cloth. It consists of a sole, a heel, and a top covering that may or may not have laces, snaps, or buttons. There are many different types of shoes such as pumps, sandals, flats, moccasins, and others. Shoes are used to protect the feet. They are also used for different puposes such as sports, walking, running, and dressing up.

. Ask the students to list other common objects and write a definition for each one using the three-part system above. As a practice activity, have students define common objects such as a cup or a pencil and later introduce curriculum items.

QUESTION	GENERAL CATEGORY	ATTRIBUTES

What is a cup?

A cup is a	drinking utensil	that	a) is used for drinking hot and cold beverages
			b) looks like a short cylinder with a handle
			c) can be made of china, porcelain, plastic, or paper

What is a pencil?

A pencil is a	writing implement	that	a) is made of.....
			b) is used for.......
			c) looks like.....

. Have your students practice using **DEFINITION MODE** for writing definition paragraphs on social studies and science topics in your curriculum. Topics to define and write about might be:

> *country, state, city, village, hamlet, settler, colonist, patriot, explorer, astronaut, pilot, sea diver, balloonist, star, planet, moon, asteroid, comet, meteor, tree, grass, weed, bush, seed, root, stem, leaf, flower, etc.*

Defining through categorizing can be used in all subjects, as shown below for social studies and science:

QUESTION	GENERAL CATEGORY	ATTRIBUTES
A continent is a	large land mass that	a) contains political divisions called countries
A country is a	political division that	b) is self-governing
Eleanor Roosevelt was an	American woman who	a) achieved fame as the wife of a president
		b) was a delegate to the United Nations
		c) was a humanitarian who fought for equality
Oxygen is a	gaseous element that	a) humans need for breathing and to survive
		b) is one of the elements in water
		c) is invisible and odorless, etc.

DEFINITION MODE

QUESTION	GENERAL CATEGORY	ATTRIBUTES
What is Florida? Florida is	a peninsula or a place that	a. has a wetland
		b. has a ridge
		c. has a coast
		d. has a beach
		e. has a swamp

Balfour

EXAMPLES OF STUDENTS' WRITING USING THE DEFINITION MODE

DEFINITION MODE

QUESTION	GENERAL CATEGORY	ATTRIBUTES
Who was Osceola? Osceola was...	a young Indian who——	a) was a great warrior b) became the leader for the Seminole Indians c) did not give up easily even when put in prison d) died at age 34.

Sharifa

QUESTION	CATEGORY ATTRIBUTES	
Who was Christopher Columbus? Christopher Columbus was a......	sailor who a) discovered America in 1492. b) believed that the world was round. c) was born in Genoa, Italy. d) always dreamed of sailing even when he was a child.	

Zsanai

Brandon Garvin

DEFINITION MODE

QUESTION	GENERAL CATEGORY	ATTRIBUTES
What is a living thing? A living thing is	a creature or plant that	(a) lives (b) breathes (c) grows (d) eats (e) is healthy

---

DEFINITION MODE
CENTER FOR LEARNING THROUGH WRITING

QUESTION	CATEGORY	ATTRIBUTES
Emotion	a strong feeling such as	love hate happiness proud sadness happiness excitement
Denia		lazy angry silly scared fright hurt

An emotion is a strong feeling such as love, hate, happiness, proudness and sharness!

Definition Mode

Name: Brandon

Question	General Category	Attributes
What is a teacher?	A teacher is a person who	a. teaches children b. gives tests c. gives math work d. teaches people how to write e. makes children learn f. takes children outside g. gives journals to write h. i.

EXAMPLES OF STUDENTS' RESPONSES TO WRITING A DEFINITION

4/1/85

An Apple   Ann

An Apple is a type of fruit that can be eaten, fed to animals, baked into apple sauce, apple pie, baked apples, candy apples, and other stuff. It looks like a big, round, red ball with a stem and leaves. It's made out of a seed and grows on trees. It's juicy and good for a snack. It also has vitamins in it.

What is a Spoon?

A spoon is a type of eating utensil. It's used for eating, moving, slurping and flinging. It is made of plastic or metal. It looks like something that fits in your mouth.

The End

spoon

By
Sandra

The Sneaker

A sneaker is a type of footwear. It is used for running, walking, playing, jumping, keeping your feet warm, and protecting your feet. A sneaker is made of rubber, leather, cotton, string straps velcro, and zippers. A sneaker looks like the shape of a foot. They come in many colors.

The End

Dear Mrs. Rothstein, I made this paragraph from what you wrote on our board, we loved it!

From Kellie Ann

What is a Bed?

A bed is a type of furniture used for lying down, relaxing, resting, sleeping and for comfort.

It is made of wood, cotton, metal, coils, springs, feathers, cloth, and a frame.

It looks like a table with a mattress on it. It has pillows, sheets, comforters, etc.

MARIA
East Islip

SAMPLE EASY WRITER ACTIVITIES FOR WRITING A DEFINITION

Tell What It MEANS
Write A DEFINITION

A definition is a way of telling what a word means. Below are frames to help you write your own definitions. Copy each frame and complete it with as many details as you can.

EXAMPLE

> A **table** is a **piece of furniture** which is used for
> .... (eating, writing, or working on).

1. A **pencil** is a **tool for writing** which looks like ....

2. A **telephone** is a **communication machine** which is used for ....

   ....

3. A **coat** is a **kind of clothing** which is worn when ....

4. A **bed** is a **piece of furniture** that is used for ....

   A bed can have a ...., a ...., and a ....

5. An **apple** is a **kind of fruit** which grows on ....

   An apple has .... on the outside and .... on the inside.

   Apples can be used to make ...., ..., and ....

CHECKLIST FOR PROOFREADING
- Did you put in as many details as you could?
- Do your definitions give a good meaning of the words?

EXTRA CREDIT
   Here are three objects which you have used or seen many

dog   chair   shoe

Write a definition for one of these objects. Pretend you are writing who has never seen these objects.

THINKING SKILLS
Classifying
Observing
Synthesizing

BOOK C
Page 31
0304

FROM GENERAL TO SPECIFIC

A definition is a way of telling what a word means. Below is a three-part system for writing definitions of both general and specific topics.

> First, write the word or topic you are defining.
> Next, write the general category to which the word belongs.
> Last, add the details that are related to the word you are defining.
> (Note: If you are unfamiliar with any of the words or topics, use a reference book.)

EXAMPLE

WORD	GENERAL CATEGORY	DETAILS
a god	is a spiritual being	that has supernatural powers; is immortal; is prayed to
Apollo	was a Greek god	who represented truth and light; made the sun travel across the sky; was a twin of Artemis

1A.	A nurse	is a person	who	....
B.	Clara Barton	was a nurse	who	....
2A.	A president	is someone	who	....
B.	Abraham Lincoln	was	who	....
3A.	A civil war	is	that	....
B.	The Civil War	was	that	....
4A.	An explorer	is	who	....
B.	Marco Polo	was	who	....
5A.	A planet	is	which	....
B.	Mars	is	which	....
6A.	An invention	is	that	....
B.	The cotton gin	is	that	....
7A.	An author	is	that	....
B.	Charlotte Bronte	was	who	....
8A.	An immigrant	is	who	....
B.	Andrew Carnegie	was	who	....
9A.	A musician	is	who	....
B.	Ludwig von Beethoven	was	who	....
10A.	An artist	is	who	....
	Georgia O'Keefe	was	who	....

CHECKLIST FOR EDITING
- Did you write a general category for each definition?
- Did you add as many important details as possible?

FORGE AHEAD

Select one of the specific definitions from above. Use it as the **topic sentence** of a paragraph. Write four or five more detailed sentences about your topic. Use who, what, where, why, and how questions to develop detail sentences.

Copyright ERA/CCR Corp. The Write Track Company
0809 Book H

Planning and Outlining
Page 28

TEST-TAKING WORDS IN THE CONTENT AREAS

Writing in the content areas often means responding to a specific set of key words, the kinds of words frequently used on essay tests. In order for students to respond properly to these words, they must understand the meaning of each word and they must be instructed in how to plan their writing. Frequently used essay words are **analyze, compare/contrast, define, describe, illustrate, prove, summarize.** Below are definitions of these words, examples of questions, and procedures for responding. The **Q.A.D.** (Question/Answer/Details) and the Sentence Frame are used as the basic formats.

Analyze

Definition: To break down a subject into parts and examine critically.

Sample essay: Analyze the effects of the Stamp Tax and Tea Tax on the colonists' attitudes of loyalty towards the British government.

First Step: The writer asks a set of questions before responding.

1.   What were these taxes?
2.   What purpose did they have?
3.   What did Great Britain believe were its taxing rights?
4.   What were the attitudes of loyalty before the taxes?
5.   What were they afterward?
6.   What effect did each tax have on the colonists' attitudes?

Q	A	D
Write out questions	*Give brief answers (general statements)*	*Give details for each general answer*

Second Step: Write a paragraph using information from the **Q.A.D.**

ıpare and Contrast

Definition: To show how things are similar and different.

Sample essay: Contrast the arguments of the Loyalists with those of the Patriots on the issue of declaring independence from Great Britain.

Brainstorm: Arguments of Loyalists, Arguments of Patriots.

Categorize arguments: Issue of monarchy, issue of economic benefits, Issue of freedom.

Write a topic sentence: *There were sharp (clear, cogent, compelling) differences between the Loyalists and the Patriots............*

Support the statement with details of the arguments with each issue serving as a subtopic sentence.

)efine

Definition: Give the meaning by stating a general category and then adding details or description.

Sample: Define *Loyalists, Minutemen, Continental Congress, Letters of Correspondence.*

Set up a three-part frame:

WORD TO BE DEFINED	GENERAL CATEGORY	DETAILS
Loyalists were	*American colonists who*	a) *believed that the colonies had no reason to rebel*
		b) *were loyal to the king*
		c) *etc.*
Minutemen were	*American colonists who*	*etc.*
The Continental Congress was a	*legislative body that*	*etc.*
Letters of Correspondence were a	*series of communications that*	

Describe

Definition: Tell in detail the major features of a person, animal, place, or item.

Sample: Describe the muskets used by George Washington's soldiers.

Set up **WH-Questions.**

      1. What did they look like?

      2. What were they made of?

      3. How did they work?

Add the **Answers** (early rifle, made of metal, rod and bolt-process).

Add the **Details** (describe appearance of rifle; add information on metal, hammering, forging; describe procedure for firing).

In **descriptive writing,** the use of contrast can be helpful (e.g. The musket is an early rifle but, unlike the modern rifle it.............).

Interpret

Definition: Explain inferential ("between-the-lines") meaning.

Sample: Explain the statement, "All *men* are created *equal*," in the context of the times in which it was written.

    First: The writer asks **WH-questions.**

      1. When was it written?

      2. Who wrote it?

      3. Where do these words appear?

Second: The writer defines the literal meaning of each of the key words (*all, men, equal*) and then contrasts the literal meaning with the applied meaning or connotation.

    Example: *all = every,* but may also = *some*

                  men = males, but may also = *white males*

                  equal = same, but may also = *more or less*

Illustrate

Definition: Give **evidence** to show that a statement is true or convincing.

Sample: Prove or persuade the audience that the American Revolution was caused by economic problems in Great Britain.

Questions: What do I want to prove? What is my evidence? What is my conclusion?

Summarize

Definition: Give the key or main points for a detailed topic.

Sample: Summarize the key issues of the American Revolution.

First: Return to all documentation on the topic and "skim" off topic phrases or ideas.

- taxes
- changing attitudes of Loyalists vs. Patriots
- John Locke and democratic philosophies
- emerging pride and power of colonists
- economic problems

Second: Combine these ideas into paragraphs.

The American Revolution was a battle between the Loyalists and Patriots over issues of........., ..., and ....

ASKING QUESTIONS FOR CONTENT AREA WRITING

Students can organize and restate the information from a social studies article by asking a set of general questions which will fit many contexts. In most social studies articles, for example, the following questions emerge:

1. What dates or time periods are mentioned?
2. What names or people are discussed?
3. What places are involved?
4. What special vocabulary is used?
5. What other facts are stated?

Using these questions, the student sets up a **Q.A.D.** outline which then permits him or her to retell or rewrite the information. The form below is a sample of how such a **Q.A.D.** outline would look for writing about the American Revolution.

Q	A	D
What dates or time periods are mentioned?	April 19, 1775	Clash between British regulars and minutemen in the afternoon
What names are discussed?	Gen. Gage, Samuel Adams, John Hancock, Paul Revere, William Dawes, Major Pitcairn	Gage a British general; Adams a Massachusetts patriot; etc.
What places are involved?	Boston, Concord, Lexington, North Bridge, Village Green	etc.
What special vocabulary is used?	minutemen, colonials, redcoats, patriots, volleys, militia, reinforcements	etc.
What other facts are stated?	number of men in battle, number of men killed	etc.

When all these words or phrases are entered, the student can *synthesise* the article. New sub-topics can be formed such as *The Men Who Fired the First Shots, Places Where History Was Made, The Vocabulary of the American Revolution,* or *War is a Battle of Numbers.*

After the students have been instructed in the procedures for writing Q.A.D.'s, they can work independently in creating and developing their own outlines for paragraphs or articles.

STUDENT ACTIVITIES

Purpose: To compose a paragraph about an imaginary animal having the characteristics of several real animals.

Activity: Read this paragraph.

The Elebeaver

The elebeaver looks like several animals you already know. It is about as big as a beaver and has the beaver's flat tail. It has a trunk like an elephant, but it doesn't have any tusks. At the sound of approaching footsteps an elebeaver runs quickly into the nearby forest. Its big elephant-like ears helps it detect even the faintest sounds. It is happy in its own shy way, just eating roots and berries.

. Write a description of your own imaginary animal to a zookeeper. Use the Q.A.D. outline:

- What does the animal look like?
- What can it do?
- How does it protect itself?
- What does it eat?

Purpose: Write a science report on animals.

Activity:
- Select an animal (example: bluejay).
- Write a set of questions relating to the topic.
- Answer the questions using the **Q.A.D.** format.

QUESTION	ANSWER	DETAIL
What animal group does the bluejay belong to?	*bird group*	*covered with feathers; flies, lays eggs, etc.*
What does the bluejay look like?	*like a bluebird with a head crest*	*blue-winged with white markings on wings and tail, blue crest, etc.*
What does it eat?	*a variety of foods*	*acorns, beech nuts, corn and other grains*
Where does it live?	*in a nest*	*found 30-50 feet up on an evergreen; made of twigs and rootlets and lined with grass*

TIPS FOR A RESEARCH REPORT

1. Choose a specific topic.
2. Check resources for information about the topic to determine if the topic is too broad or too narrow.

Examples of *broad* topics:

a. books	f. magazines
b. television shows	g. encyclopedias
c. newspapers	h. museums
d. filmstrips	i. interviews
e. posters	

3. Think about the topic again:
   a. If there is too much information, the topic is too broad. Choose a more specific aspect of your topic and go back to Step 1.
   b. If there is not enough information, go back to Step 1 and change the topic.
   c. If there is enough information, go on to Step 4.
4. Write **WH- questions** for your topic.
5. Organize related questions into categories.
6. Write and answer each question on a note card.
7. When you have answered most of the questions, you will have completed your research.
8. Organize the index cards into the categories established in Step 5. Each category becomes a paragraph.
9. Write the draft.
10. Edit the draft.
11. Write the copy to be "published."
12. Include in the report:

a. cover	d. diagrams
b. table of contents	e. charts
c. pictures	f. bibliography

NOTETAKING

You have selected a topic for your report. Now you will need to gather information from many different sources. How will you do this? Will you copy on paper everything you hear, read, and see? That would be impossible. What you should do is take **notes.** The notes will be made up of *key words* and *main ideas.* A good way to start is to write **WH- questions.** Suppose you are writing about bats. You might write questions similar to those shown below. After you have written your questions and found your material, you will then *skim* (read through rapidly) the article or chapter to see if it has information you can use.

What is a bat?
What does a bat look like?
How are they classified?
How do they contribute to the ecology?
What beliefs do people have about bats?
Where are they found?

Checklist for Outlining

Do I have a complete outline (plan) for my composition?

Do I know exactly what my topic (subject) will be about?

Will I tell a story? Write a description? State an opinion? Prove an idea? Recommend
    a course of action?

Have I asked all the questions I want to answer?

Have I used the answers as main ideas?

Do I have enough details to support the main ideas?

Did I fill my **Q.A.D.** outline with as much information as necessary?

Did I answer each question with as many details as possible?

Did I write a topic sentence to begin each paragraph?

Did I indent each time I began a new paragraph?

After writing the first draft, can I *improve* my writing by:

    . combining some of the sentences?

    . moving words or sentences to make the story clearer?

    . using connecting (transitional words) that clue the reader?

    . using different words (synonyms) that will make the writing clearer?

Michael
Senquence Paragraph

Language
Three Village

How to Make a Capital B

Would you like to learn how to make a Capital B. There are several steps you have to follow. First, you take a pen or pencil. Second take a piece of paper and hold it rightside up. Then, draw a vertical line. Next make a semi-circle the covers half the line on the rightside. Last, create more semi-circle connected underneath to the first semi-circle. Practice this a few times and you'll learn how to make a Capital B.

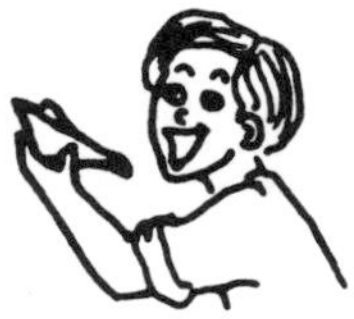

Sharon
January 26,

How to eat Pizza

Would you like to know how to eat pizza? First you cut a slice of pizza from the pizza pie. After you cut it, you use your hands to put it on your plate. Then you blow on it to cool it off. Next you fold it up or leave it flat down. Eat it up! Fifth you take the napkin & wipe up the sauce on your chin. Hope your pizza is good.

EXAMPLES OF STUDENTS' WRITING USING SEQUENCING

If you ever went to Brooklyn, the first question you'd ask would probably be, what are 3 places of interest to visit in the city of Brooklyn. I'll tell you. The first place would be the Brooklyn Bridge, of course. It is over the East River, and connects the boroughs of Brooklyn and Manhattan in New York City. The span is 1,595 feet, and hangs from steel cables which are about 16 inches thick. It was completed in 1883. Total cost of the bridge was about $15 million. John Roebling designed it. When he died, his son Washington directed construction work on it. The second place of interest would be the Brooklyn College. It is a coeducational liberal arts school. It is supported by the city. Besides liberal arts, it offers courses in science and teacher education. Was founded in 1930. Now it is part of the system of colleges known as the city University of New York. And last but not least, the Brooklyn Polytecnic Institute. This institute is a private college of science and engineering. Programs are offered in the day and evening, undergraduate sessions and in graduate school. The extensive research program is conducted in connection with graduate school. It was founded in 1854, reorganized in 1890. If I'd like to see them, I know you would, too!

Sandra
5-3

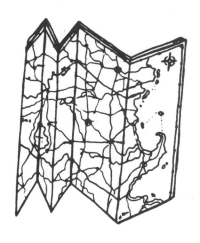

Melissa
5-3

December 4, 1984

When you visit Sayville you can see so much. First, if you want to see a beautiful resteraunt, go to Baron's 4. Baron's 4 has very good food. It has mostly seafood. If you go to the sundeck you will have a great and beautiful view of the bay. On the sundeck you will get alittle bit of a breeze. You can visit Sayville's beautiful church. This church is called Saint Lawrence. Inside it is very pretty. It is also fancy enough if your planning to dress up. Then you can go see some of the many fishing docks for peace and quiet. If you go in the evening you can see the sunset.

Sayville is a quiet and peaceful little town.

Q, A. D. narrative

grade 7
J H S 117

What happened?

I'll never forget April 7 because my father came home and said crossly that he got laid off from his job. I felt scared. I felt scared because I was afraid of what might happen. Then

How did I feel?

I felt sad for my father because he is probably worried sick over the money that he is loosing. I felt so bad for my father. He liked his job a lot. I was also mad at my fathers boss because my father was good at his job and he didn't deserve to be laid off, why should my father suffer and get laid off when some other person should be laid off.

What would I do?

I thought maybe I could get a job and help out, but I already know that I couldn't get enough money for anything. I knew I wouldn't have enough money if I did little things but I could get some money for myself if got a good-paying job so I could go to the movies and not bother my father for the money, I got the job. It wasn't the best job but I got enough money for movies. I took care of horses. I worked for 5 weeks and on Tuesday my father said I could stop working because he got his job back.

EXAMPLES OF STUDENTS' WRITING USING COMPARE AND CONTRAST

Language Arts   Clare
Compare/Contrast Paragraph   Plymouth

School buses and city buses have similarities and differences. Both have seats, although the arrangement of the seats is different. They both have drivers, but the driver of the city bus cannot yell at you or tell you to sit down. Both have doors, but a city bus has two sets of doors, while a school bus only has one. A city bus has more storage space, handles for standing, and carries people to different stops. A school bus has seats in rows, a strict busdriver, and always goes to school. Both have metal, wheels, and engines. We can compare and contrast school buses and city buses in many similar yet different ways.

Strange Comparisons

A book and a teacher are alike because both have and give information. They both should be in a school. They both teach you reading. Also, you can't judge them by their cover.

SAMPLE EASY WRITER ACTIVITIES FOR PLANNING AND OUTLINING

PLAN A LETTER
USE A Q.A.D.

Write a letter to a pen pal, or someone far away who doesn't know you. Below is a plan for writing a letter. Make up your own plan with **Questions, Answers, Details.** Leave lots of room for your answers. Use the ideas from the plan to help you write your letter.

EXAMPLE

QUESTIONS	ANSWERS	DETAILS
Who am I?	a girl or boy	tell: your age; what you look like; who is in your family
Where do I live?	on a farm (or in a city, or in an apartment)	tell about your farm or city or house; tell what it looks like
What do I like to do?	lots of things	tell; your favorite games, places, food

Your letter can look like this:

Dear . . . .

I am a . . . . who . . . .
I live . . . .
I like to . . . .
Please write and tell me . . . .

Your pen pal,

. . . .

CHECKLIST FOR PROOFREADING

- Did you write lots of details for each questic
- Did you write lots of details in your letter?
- Did you read your letter aloud to be sure it

EXTRA CREDIT

Write a letter to someone you know. In th
something funny that happened in school or a
details about what happened.

SOLVE A PROBLEM: USE A Q.A.D.

Below are four questions for writing about a problem. Next to the questions are brief answers. Fill in the **DETAILS** for each question by brainstorming as many ideas as you can. There are **wh-** questions to guide you.

EXAMPLE

QUESTION	ANSWER	DETAILS
What is the problem?	Students are misbehaving in the cafeteria.	noisy, food is thrown, arguing and fighting

QUESTIONS	ANSWERS	DETAILS
What is the problem?	students can't get summer jobs.	which students?
What is the cause?	employers want year-round help only	why?
What are the effects?	students have 2 months with nothing to do	what happens?
What is the solution?	organize a student job corps	how? who will run it? what will it do?

Use the information from the **Q.A.D.** to write a three- or four-paragraph essay about the problem. Each question should be responded to in a separate paragraph.

CHECKLIST

- Can you add more details to each question?
- Does each question represent a different paragraph?
- Did you read your essay aloud to be sure it makes sense?
- Did you check punctuation, spelling, and grammar?

FORGE AHEAD

Prepare your own **Q.A.D.** outline about a problem in your school or community. Use the outline to write a report.

PLAN A REPORT
COMPARE AND CONTRAST

How is a bird like an airplane? How is it different?
How is a dog like a wolf? How is it different?

Questions like these are called **Compare and Contrast.** To answer these questions you need a plan which tells where to start, how to continue, and where to end.

- FIRST **BRAINSTORM**

COMPARE AND CONTRAST CORN WITH APPLES

CORN	APPLES
yellow	red
kernels	fruit
cook	tree
vegetable	juicy
maize	McIntosh
butter	Delicious
pone	orchards
pigs	New York State
field	peel
Iowa	Johnny Appleseed
Indians	juice

- SECOND Organize the details by categories.
  colors, uses, places, history, ways to cook, dif
- THIRD Write a simple topic sentence. You can also s
  support sentence.
  Many things about apples and corn are similar.
  used for ... They both have ...
- FOURTH Write support sentences for each category. C
  compare and contrast.
  Both corn and apples have an interesting hist
  raised by the American Indians and ... Apples
  when Johnny Appleseed ... Both foods were u
  American settlers ...
- FIFTH When you have finished comparing, write a c
  sentence.
  We rarely think of comparing corn with apple:
  about it, there are many similarities as well as

© 1985 ERA/CCR Corp.   **THE WRITE TRACK COMPANY**

WRITE A DEFINITION

What is a pencil? What is a telephone?
What is a continent?

Use the plan below to write definitions.

FIRST *write what you are defining*	SECOND *write the words "is a" or "are"*	THIRD *write the category of the item*	FOURTH *write "that" or "which"*	LAST *add the details*
a **PENCIL**	*is a*	*writing tool*	*that*	*is made of graphite and wood; looks like a stick with a point; may have an eraser; is used for many kinds of writing*

a **TELEPHONE**	*is a*	*communication machine*	*which*	*carries the voice over a long distance; has a receiver and a speaker; is used for messages and conversation*

a **CONTINENT**	*is a*	*large land mass*	*that*	*usually contains one or more countries; has a name such as Europe or Asia; is separated from other continents by water and mountains*

Use the same plan to write definitions for each of these words:
- cup • shoe • chalk • typewriter • river • house
- highway • airplane • soldier • computer

© 1985 ERA/CCR Corp.   **THE WRITE TRACK COMPANY**   *Intermediate 11*

USE A Q.A.D. WRITE A REPORT

Use a plan for writing. Begin by asking **QUESTIONS. ANSWER** the questions. Research the *DETAILS.*

FIRST STEP—
Choose a topic

- *I think I'll write about robots.*

SECOND STEP—
Ask yourself questions about your topic. Get friends and classmates to ask you questions too.

- *What are robots?*
- *What do robots do?*
- *What do robots look like?*

THIRD STEP—
Choose the best or most important questions. Prepare a Q.A.D. outline or plan. Use this plan to write your **first draft.**

QUESTIONS	ANSWERS	DETA
What is a robot?	a mechanical person or animal	its brai follows by con
What does a robot look like?	a monster	can ha arms, l look lil car, ro
What can a robot do?	many tasks that humans do	builds house fights, carrie:

Write your own story or report about a robot
from the Q.A.D. Add your own ideas or informatic

THE WRITE TRACK COMPANY

USE A Q.A.D. TELL A STORY

Ask **QUESTIONS.** *Write the* **ANSWERS.** *Add the* **DETAILS.**

QUESTIONS	ANSWERS	DETAILS
Why are these children crying?	They lost their dog.	little poodle; six months old; name is Tippy; white curly hair; short tail…
What happened first?	They were taking the dog for a walk.	down Main Street; lots of traffic; many people; children just moved; didn't know their way…
Then what happened?	The leash broke and the dog ran away.	**PUT IN YOUR OWN DETAILS.**
Then what happened?	They looked for the dog.	**PUT IN YOUR OWN DETAILS.**
What will happen now?	They will go to the police.	**PUT IN YOUR OWN DETAILS.**

THE WRITE TRACK COMPANY   *Primary 8*

WHOLE LANGUAGE

FROM NURSERY RHYMES TO *JULIUS CAESAR*

To be literate means to be comfortable with both reading and writing. The literate adult reads widely for both information and enjoyment and is able to write clear, organized prose for both occupational and literary purposes. To achieve this level of literacy in adulthood, the child must be actively immersed in the world of books — books that contain poetry, stories, and factual information. The child must hear and share good writing, participate in reading through oral and choral responses, and construct his or her own writing to express ideas, feelings, and opinions. This total involvement in literacy is currently described as *WHOLE LANGUAGE INSTRUCTION*. Some authorities also use the terms "integrated language" and "holistic language."

NURSERY RHYMES

The nursery rhyme is the young child's first introduction to literary language. Children who are familiar with *Jack and Jill, Hickory Dickory Dock, Old Mother Hubbard,* and the dozens of other traditional rhymes have entered the world of poetry and metaphor. If they have heard these rhymes since infancy, they know them by heart, and in knowing them by heart they have a lifelong reference of characters, poetic forms, and literary vocabulary. Because this book focuses primarily on writing, we would like to offer some activities in which you can use nursery rhymes and combine all aspects of language.

We begin with four aspects of language:

LISTEN, RECITE, READ, WRITE

. Select a traditional rhyme that is strongly repetitive and predictable and have the children recite it chorally:

EXAMPLE: Smoking hot!

Piping hot!

What have I got that you have not?

Hot gray peas, hot, hot, hot,

Hot gray peas, hot, hot, hot.

.   Write the poem on a chart and/or make a copy of it for each child.

.   Have the students illustrate the rhyme in as detailed a way as possible. By noting the key words — *piping, smoking, hot, I, you, gray peas* — the students come to "comprehend" the poem.

.   Write a **FRAME** so that the students can rewrite the poem in their own words:

.... hot!
.... hot!
What have I got that you have not?
Hot ....,
    Hot, hot, hot,
Hot ....,
    Hot, hot, hot.

.   Brainstorm possible "substitutions" for the original words: *burning hot, steaming hot, fiery hot, glowing hot, hot crusty pizza, hot baked potato, hot sweet chocolate.*

.   Innovate on the structure of the poem. In the example below, HOT has been changed to COLD and the students can write their own poems:

.... cold!
.... cold!
What have I got that you have ....?
Cold ....,
    Cold, cold, cold,
Cold ....,
    Cold, cold, cold.

. Use the concepts in the rhyme to have the students generate new ideas:

What is hot?

.......................is hot.

What is cold?

.......................is cold.

What else is hot that you've been told?

.......................is hot,

So I've been told.

What else is cold that you've been told?

...................................is cold,

So I've been told.

. Use the poem for expanding vocabulary and rhyming words:

HOT List

cot

dot

lot

pot

tot

What rhymes with HOT?

A bed called a .... rhymes with hot.

What else rhymes with HOT?

A speck called a .... rhymes with hot.

What also rhymes with HOT?

A bunch called a .... rhymes with hot.

THE BOOK OR STORY AS THE SPRINGBOARD FOR INTEGRATING WRITING AND READING (THE READING/WRITING CONNECTION)

Brainstorming and Listing

This activity may be carried out in the following way:

. After your students have heard or read a story, ask each student to write or contribute one word or phrase (active participation) which she/he associates with the story.

> Example from *Charlotte's Web: runt, spider, farm, worried, many animals, friendship, pig, brave.*

. Gather these words on a list and give each student a copy of the collected words. **(ABC LISTING** may be used as a frame for collecting words.) Ask the students to:
   . Use the words to help them retell the story
   . Use the words to write their own story

. Divide the class into groups of three or four students. Each group is given or selects a character from the story. Then ask each student in the group to write three words which he/she associates with the character. The group makes a composite list which is distributed to each member of the group. Each student then writes about that character using the words from the list.

. Ask the students keep a running list of descriptive phrases about the different characters. Examples from Shakespeare's *Julius Caesar* might be *"a lean and hungry look," "an honorable man," "the noblest Roman of them all,"* and so forth. Each student uses as many of these phrases as appropriate to write a description of an historic or fictional character in another piece of literature.

"INTERACTIVE WRITING" — LINKING READING WITH WRITING

One of the most exciting ways to integrate reading with writing is through an activity we call **INTERACTIVE WRITING**. In interactive writing the writer assumes the role of a character in a literary piece and writes to another character in the same piece. By setting up an interactive writing assignment, the student views a story as relationships among characters. An example of such a relationship is illustrated in the childhood story *Little Red Riding Hood.* In this tale, Little Red is the pivotal or central character and, as such, interacts with all the other characters — her mother, her grandmother, the wolf, and the woodcutter. In addition, we can assume other interactions, both explicit and inferred, among the other characters in the story. The diagram below shows these interactions:

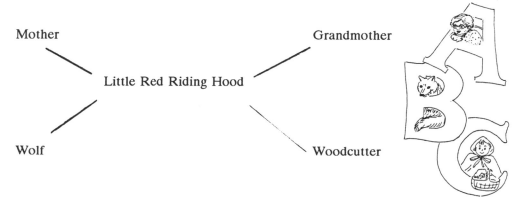

Mother

Grandmother

Little Red Riding Hood

Wolf

Woodcutter

Little Red's mother is obviously related to, and therefore interacts with, Little Red's grandmother. The wolf's treacherous actions toward Little Red must surely affect Little Red's mother. And the woodcutter clearly affects not only Little Red and her mother and grandmother, but brings a major catastrophe upon the wolf, perhaps sending a warning to other wolves who may be contemplating the deception of little girls.

By understanding the interactions of the characters, the student is better able to comprehend both the surface (literal) and the in-depth (inferential) meaning of the story. In the example of *Little Red Riding Hood,* we recognize that there are three types of interactions: 1) familial, 2) antagonistic, and 3) heroic. We can also see how each character impinges upon the other — the wolf is not only an antagonist to Little Red, but also to Little Red's mother, while the woodcutter is friend and hero to everyone but the wolf.

INTERACTIVE WRITING helps the student fully grasp these relationships among the characters. As students assume the roles of the characters, they must decide on the genre they will use in writing to other characters — letters, warning signs, notes, invitations, or even diaries or journal entries. Each piece of writing allows the student to express a specific aspect of the story. For example, students can write the following pieces based on events in the story:

. Since Little Red Riding Hood's mother is planning to send her daughter to her sick mother (Grandmother), she writes a note telling Grandmother of Little Red Riding Hood's forthcoming visit.

. Grandmother could then write a brief response noting the items in the mother's letter.

. Because Little Red Riding Hood is quite young, her mother might draw a map and write clear, sequenced directions for the child to follow.

. The mother could also write several of her recipes which she puts in Little Red Riding Hood's basket.

. The students could list the signposts and milage markers that would help Little Red Riding Hood through the woods.

. The mother writes a list of instructions for Little Red Riding Hood to follow so that she will arrive safely.

. The wolf, in preparation for tricking Little Red Riding Hood, writes out several persuasive approaches to get Little Red Riding Hood to stop and talk to him, since he plans to get into Grandmother's house.

. Grandmother writes a list of games and other activities to keep her grandchild entertained.

. The wolf begs the woodcutter to spare his life and writes a persuasive letter (**THREE REASONS WHY**).

. The wolf writes letters of apology:
    . to Grandmother
    . to Little Red Riding Hood
    . to Little Red Riding Hood's mother

. Little Red Riding Hood, the mother, and Grandmother write thank you notes to the woodcutter.

The above list is merely an example of the possibilities for **INTERACTIVE WRITING;** but even more important is that through such writing the student becomes deeply involved in the characters and the story. Furthermore, every fictional story (as well as biography) lends itself to **INTERACTIVE WRITING.** From this simple beginning in a fairy tale, there is the potential for involving students in writing about almost all literature through the process of interactions among characters. Thus, from *Little Red Riding Hood* in the elementary school, we can move to Shakespeare's *Julius Caesar* in the high school. We suggest the following plan which can also serve as a model for other literature.

USING INTERACTIVE WRITING FOR SHAKESPEARE'S *JULIUS CAESAR*

Begin by giving the students a synopsis or summary of the story. The synopsis serves as an "advance organizer" which permits the students to attend to the details of character development and interactions.

Read the cast of characters with the students and speculate on their roles and relationships with each other. You will note that in this play there are six major groups of characters who relate to Caesar:

- the Triumvirs (Mark Antony, Octavius Caesar, and Aemilius Lepidus)
- the Senators (Cicero, Publius, and Popilius Lena)
- the Conspirators (mainly Marcus Brutus, Cassius, and Casca)
- five friends of Brutus and Cassius (Lucilius, Titinius, etc.)
- wives (Calpurnia and Portia)
- servants and soothsayers

Your students may already have some prior knowledge about the major characters — Julius Caesar, Marcus Brutus, and Mark Antony — and they may be familiar with some of the events of the conspiracy. Have the students discuss and write out an **ABC LIST** for whatever they already know of this story and its characters, thereby uncovering prior knowledge.

Tell the students that during the reading of the play each student will assume the roles of several characters (three or four) which they can choose or you might wish to assign. As these characters, they will write a variety of pieces that will include:

- letters to other characters
- diaries or journal entries
- letters, statements, or articles to newspapers or magazines

Since this play is divided into five acts, every student should plan on writing at least five pieces, one piece for an event in each act.

As the students read each act, they should be thinking of which characters they would like to assume and what interactive writing might have occurred in the historic situation. Have them brainstorm the different types of writing and select those which they find of interest.

For Act I, students could select any of the following **INTERACTIVE WRITINGS** :

- Soothsayer writes to Caesar explaining his forebodings; Caesar responds with his own point of view.
- Cassius writes to Brutus explaining his enmity for Caesar; Brutus responds giving his fears and concerns.
- Casca writes to the Roman Times (newspaper) telling of Caesar's plan to make Rome a monarchy; other Romans dispute Casca's concerns.
- Cassius writes to Casca convincing him of the need for a conspiracy; Casca responds to Cassius' letter.

For Act II, students might write the following:

- Brutus writes in his journal agonizing over his feelings about Caesar.
- Portia writes in her journal agonizing over her husband's strange behavior and her meeting with the soothsayer.
- Calpurnia writes in her journal about her fears and forebodings related to events surrounding her husband.
- Caesar writes in his journal responding to Calpurnia's fears and his own need to present a brave front.

Act III is the heart of the play. Caesar is assassinated by Cassius, Brutus, Casca, and the other conspirators. Caesar says his famous last words, "*Et tu Brute? Then fall Caesar.*" Brutus then makes a feeble attempt to explain to the crowd the reason for his actions and fails to see a threat in Mark Antony, Caesar's friend and defender. Mark Antony, of course, seizes the moment, and in a biting, sarcastic speech, turns the crowd against the men who thought the Roman populace would understand their noble reasons for killing Caesar. There are many writing opportunities that emerge from this act:

- The major conspirators Cassius, Brutus, and Casca each write a persuasive letter to the newspaper explaining their reasons for the assassination.
- Newspaper reports of the assassination are written from the points of view of pro- and anti-Caesar forces.
- An obituary recounts Caesar's political and military accomplishments.
- The coroner prepares an autopsy report detailing Caesar's wounds.
- Various characters in the play (including historic characters related to Caesar, such as Cleopatra) write letters of condolence to Calpurnia.

In Act IV further tragedy follows and the writing might include:

- Letters of anger between Cassius and Brutus showing the growing enmity between the two men.
- Portia's suicide note to Brutus referring to her sorrow and disappointment regarding her husband's actions.

Act V brings the deaths of Brutus and Cassius, both of whom have realized the folly of their acts. Students could now write:

. Entries in Brutus' diary telling of his remorse and sadness as he realizes he has betrayed his friend and has allowed himself to be betrayed.

. Entries in Mark Antony's diary telling of his hatred for Cassius and/or his respect for Brutus.

. Caesar Augustus' plans for carrying forth his uncle's policies for Rome.

From the above assignments, students will not only read the play more intensely, but they will have a much greater understanding of the relationships among the men and women in this story and, in fact, in any other story. Furthermore, by writing in a variety of genres — diaries, letters, persuasive statements, newspaper formats, etc. — they will produce writing that is original, insightful, and, above all, **interesting** to read.

Lashunda

The Leopard and the Lion

One winter day, there was a leopard that was going out to hunt some food down. He hunted down a rabbit. While he was hunting down the rabbit, there was a lion watching him. The lion was hiding behind a bush. When the leopard was on his way home, the lion followed him. Then lion decided to show himself. He walked to the leopard, eye to eye, and snatched the rabbit right out of his mouth. They started to fight. The lion got a bad scratch on the leg, but the leopard had a little scratch on the arm. They stopped fighting and shared the rabbit.

Moral: Share your food.

Lakisha

The Lion and the mouse

Once upon a time, a lion came out and went into his den and laid down. Soon he was fast asleep. A mouse came and ran up his back and on his nose. The lion grabbed the mouse. The mouse shouted please don't take my life away. The lion replied why should I let you go. The mouse whinned, maybe one day I can help you. The lion smiled and let him go. One day, the lion was walking in the woods and hunters had sat a trap to catch the lion. The lion stepped in the trap. The mouse bit the rope. The lion stated I am glad I let you go.

Moral: Do not make fun of the weak.

A MODEL FOR MERGING WRITING WITH READING

WRITING
RESEARCH • EXPOSITORY • LITERARY

READING
INFORMATIONAL • FUNCTIONAL • LITERARY

Skills for Writing

Understands the Task
- writes on topic
- keeps consistent point of view
- indicates sense of audience

Creates an Organization
- organizes logically
- paragraphs correctly
- uses topic and support sentences
- writes conclusions

Distinguishes Between Spoken and
Written Language

- writes complete sentences
- uses varied sentence structure
- uses pronouns appropriately
- uses transitional words
  (however, therefore, etc.)
- uses varied vocabulary

Skills for Reading

Understands the Purpose
- reads to gain information
- reads to locate information
- reads to get "story line"

Recognizes Organization
- follows sequence
- makes use of headings
  and paragraph structures
- identifies topic and support sentences

Understands the Language of the
Writer/Author

- recognizes or "looks up"
  difficult vocabulary
- recognizes idiomatic
  or special vocabulary

READING AND WRITING MERGE FOR
Studying
Reporting
Re-creating
Creating

INTEGRATING WRITING INTO THE CURRICULUM

"How can I add writing to a curriculum already bursting with reading, grammar, spelling, social studies, science, and who knows what else?"

The answer is, don't *add* writing to such a curriculum! Instead, you can integrate, incorporate, include, and use writing in all subjects across the curriculum. Writing, like thinking, is not a separate subject; it is a *universe* of literacy, *supported* by reading, spelling, and grammar. It expresses in tangible form our ideas, beliefs, knowledge, and feelings about every other subject. Writing *is* an essential part of every subject. The suggestions which follow can help make writing an integrated part of your curriculum. Each time your students write, they will be thinking, gathering, organizing, spelling, practicing penmanship, reading, and possibly illustrating. An hour of writing presents an economical way to include four or five subjects. And it offers a brilliant and creative opportunity to lead your students to higher thinking processes by tying several subjects together at once. We call this *interdisciplinary learning*, with writing as the unifier.

MERGING WRITING WITH READING — A HOLISTIC APPROACH TO LANGUAGE

Unfortunately for many students (and teachers), writing and reading have been viewed as two *unrelated* subjects. The basal reader, as well as the reading workbook, often remain separate from writing activities. They are too often taught at separate times without linking them in the students' minds. Reading groups work together for reading, but rarely write about their discussions. Reading workbooks frequently limit writing to underlining, circling, or placing an X — tasks that elicit practically no active participation by students. These rote activities elicit only passive *responding* to someone else's thoughts, rather than active *construction* of the student's ideas.

A meaningful *whole language* program is one in which writing and reading are viewed as two sides of the same coin. To extend the metaphor, a "coin" with only one side would be without value. While the development of reading skills is frequently seen as the single major goal in literacy, the truly educated person must be skilled in both reading and writing. Writing and reading spring from the same origins of oral language in which writing represents the expressive side of language in print, while reading becomes our receptive language. The model below illustrates this idea.

RESPONDING IN WRITING TO READING

After the students have read a story, the teacher can encourage written responses. You may find the following plan helpful:

- Have the students read the story, such as the one below:

The Circus Comes to Town

It was night, but Buddy was still up.

He was sick and couldn't sleep.

He looked out the window of his apartment building.

The street was empty.

Suddenly Buddy saw some red and white vans.

On the vans were signs that said, "Circus."

The trucks went slowly down the street.

Buddy knew before anyone else that a circus was coming to town.

He was happy that he had not been asleep when the circus vans came to town.

- Have students ask and answer **WH- questions** that would result in a summary of the story.

    - **Who** is the most important person or animal in this story? *Buddy*
    - **Where** does this story take place? *in a city apartment building and the street below*
    - **When** does this story take place? *at night*
    - **What** important things happened? *Buddy looked out the window. He saw some vans. He knew the circus was coming.*

- From the answers to these questions, have each student write one sentence combining all the information.

    One night Buddy looked out the window of his apartment house in the city and noticed some circus vans.

· Ask the students to **expand** their sentences, adding and combining still more information.

> *One night when Buddy was sick he looked out the window of his city apartment and saw some circus vans coming down the street.*

· For writing the sequence of events, have the students write answers to the questions below and put the story into sequence:

  · What happened first? *Buddy looked out the window.*
  · What happened then? *Buddy saw some circus vans.*
  · Then what happened next? *The vans went down the street and turned the corner.*
  · What happened finally? *Buddy felt happy he had seen the vans.*

· Show the students how to combine, in their own words, those sentences which *belong* together. They will then have a **summary** of the story.

> *Buddy looked out the window and saw some circus vans. The vans went down the street and turned the corner. Buddy was happy to have seen the vans before anyone else.*

· For expressing **inference,** have the students write answers to these questions:

  · How would this story have been different if it had taken place during the day?
  · How would this story have been different if Buddy had not been sick?
  · What do you think was happening in Buddy's house at the time?
  · What time of year do you think it was, and what are your reasons?

· To express critical and creative thinking, have the students write responses to these questions:

  · What words could you add to each paragraph to make the story more interesting?
  · What descriptive words about Buddy would make him more interesting?
  · What descriptive words about the circus could you use?

Other Suggestions

. From a story in the reader, the student takes a topic sentence and writes more details in his/her own words.

> Example: *On Marla's street there were three houses.*
>
> *The first one was ...(white, shutters, tree in front, etc.)*
>
> *The second one was ...*
>
> *The third one was ...*
>
> *All three houses...*

. From stories, have the students take a topic sentence and ask **WH- questions.**

> Example: *When our country was young, the city of Washington, D.C. was built.*
>
> Questions:
>
> > *Where was it built?*
> >
> > *Who helped design it?*
> >
> > *How was it built?*
> >
> > *What did it look like?*
> >
> > *Who lived in it?*

. From literature, ask the students to take a starter sentence from a story they have read. Have each student ask as many **WH- questions** as he/she can about the starter sentence and then write his/her own paragraph answering those questions.

> Example: *Long ago the people of Japan believed that in the beginning there were only gods who lived in the sky.*

> Brainstorm questions:
>
> > *Where is Japan?*
> >
> > *Who were the gods?*
> >
> > *What did the sky look like?*
> >
> > *When was the "beginning?"*
> >
> > *What did the gods look like?*
> >
> > *What did the gods do?*
> >
> > *What were the names of the gods?*

EASY WRITER ACTIVITIES FOR WHOLE LANGUAGE

NEW RHYMES FROM OLD

Sometimes you can have fun by rewriting old rhymes. On this page are nursery rhymes with some of the words left out. Copy the rhymes and **put in your own words.**

EXAMPLE

Humpty Dumpty went to the fair.
Humpty Dumpty flew up in the air.
All the young women and all the young men,
Were happy when Humpty came down again.

Here is the rhyme as it was written.

Here is the rhyme with words left out.

To market, to market,	To market, to market,
To buy a fat pig.	To buy a ....
Home again, home again,	Home again, home again,
Jiggety jig.	....

Little Miss Muffet,	Little Miss Dillow,
Sat on a tuffet,	Sat on a ....
Eating some curds and whey.	Eating some .... and ....
Along came a spider,	Along came a ....
Who sat down beside her,	Who ....
And frightened Miss Muffet away.	And frightened Miss Dillow away.

Jack and Jill went up the hill,	.... and .... went up the ....,
To fetch a pail of water.	To .... a ....
Jack fell down and broke his crown,	.... fell down and broke his crown,
And Jill came tumbling after.	And .... came .... after.

CHECKLIST FOR PROOFREADING
- Did you substitute interesting words?
- Did you read your rhymes aloud?

FORGE AHEAD
Publish your new rhymes.
- Write them in your best handwriting.
- Draw a picture for each new rhyme.
- Put the rhymes in a book with its own title.

WHEN AND WHERE DID IT HAPPEN?

On this page are sentences about storybook people. Copy each sentence. Add **WHEN** and **WHERE** to tell more in your sentences. You may put **WHEN** words at the beginning or end of your sentence.

EXAMPLE

Little Jack Horner went for a walk.

(WHEN) Yesterday Little Jack Horner went for a walk (WHERE) in the park.

1. Old Mother Hubbard baked some bread.
2. Sleeping Beauty fell asleep.
3. Jack met the giant.
4. Tom Thumb built a house.
5. Little Bo-Peep went for a walk.
6. Peter Rabbit stole some carrots.
7. Simple Simon met a baker.
8. Red Riding Hood saw the wolf.

WHEN	WHERE
early one morning	around the corner
last year	up in the sky
many years ago	in the street
once upon a time	behind a tree
the other day	in the kitchen
two weeks ago	on the chair
one rainy day	in the field
one dark night	next to the school
after lunch	down the hole

CHECKLIST FOR PROOFREADING
- Did you use both **WHEN** and **WHERE** words in each sentence?
- Did you begin each sentence with a capital letter?
- Did you end each sentence with the correct punctuation?

EXTRA CREDIT

Choose a sentence that starts a good story.
Write what happens next.
Write what happens after that.

MIXED-UP MOTHER GOOSE

Many people like Mother Goose rhymes because they are funny or strange. Make up your own Mother Goose sentences using the names of the Mother Goose people in the **PUMPKIN**. Use a verb from the **PAIL** and a verb from the **HORN** in each sentence.

EXAMPLE

Little Boy Blue   jump/jumped   fly/flew

Little Boy Blue jumped through the window and **flew** away into the clouds.

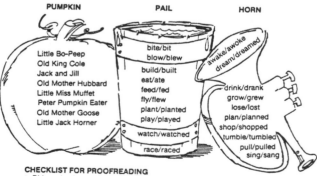

PUMPKIN

Little Bo-Peep
Old King Cole
Jack and Jill
Old Mother Hubbard
Little Miss Muffet
Peter Pumpkin Eater
Old Mother Goose
Little Jack Horner

PAIL

bite/bit
blow/blew
build/built
eat/ate
feed/fed
fly/flew
plant/planted
play/played
watch/watched
race/raced

HORN

awake/awoke
dream/dreamed
drink/drank
grow/grew
lose/lost
plan/planned
shop/shopped
tumble/tumbled
pull/pulled
sing/sang

CHECKLIST FOR PROOFREADING
- Did you begin each sentence with a capital letter?
- Did you end each sentence with the correct punctuation?
- Did you check your spelling?

FORGE AHEAD
Make up questions for your classmates about Mother Goose people or other story characters. Write two or three sentences giving clues.

Examples:

I am an egg.
I fell off a big wall.
Who am I?

I am an old lady.
I have lots of children.
Who am I?

NURSERY NONSENSE

Rewrite the two nursery rhymes below using the words from the cradle as substitutes for the bolded words. You may also substitute your own words. You do not have to make the sentences rhyme.

EXAMPLE

Old Mother Hubbard went to the cupboard
To get her poor dog a bone.
But when she got there,
The cupboard was bare,
And so her poor dog had none.

Rewritten:

The ancient matriarch, Mrs. Hubbard, walked to the cupboard to procure nourishment for her canine. When she arrived, she perceived a non-existent supply of canine victuals. Thus her dispirited domesticated pup remained famished and disgruntled.

1.
Jack and Jill **went** up the **hill**,
To fetch a **pail** of water.
Jack **fell** down.
And broke his **crown**.
And Jill **came** tumbling after.

2.
Little Jack Horner **sat** in a corner
Eating a Christmas pie.
He put in his thumb
And pulled out a plum,
And **said**, "What a **good boy** am I!"

CRADLE OF SYNONYMS

scaled climbed marched scampered ascended
mountain promontory dune highlands knoll peak
obtain procure
bucket canteen barrel cask decanter pitcher
slipped stumbled slid slumped
fractured cracked slit
cranium noggin dome skull
rested relaxed reclined
adding consuming dining munching nibbling devouring gulping chewing
thrust rammed drove pushed jabbed
extricated
exclaimed shouted chuckled cried out
magnificent youth incredible lad amazing chap

CHECKLIST FOR EDITING
- Did you substitute all the bolded words?
- Did you read your writing aloud to be sure you wrote what you wanted to say?

FORGE AHEAD
Find a short newspaper or magazine article. Rewrite the article substituting as many words as you can. Use a thesaurus or book of synonyms.

SAMPLE ACTIVITIES FROM "EASY WRITER"

AND THE MORAL IS

A fable is a **story which** generally uses animals and occasionally uses people to teach a moral lesson. In the **BOOK OF FABLES** below are five morals which come from well-known fables. Select one of the morals and write a fable, using your own characters and plot.

First, develop an outline by answering the questions from the **QUESTION BOX**. Then use the answers to help write your story.

EXAMPLE

Moral: Slow and steady wins the race.

Possible character:

The class bully who thinks he or she is a champion jogger.

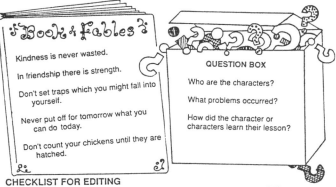

Book of Fables

Kindness is never wasted.

In friendship there is strength.

Don't set traps which you might fall into yourself.

Never put off for tomorrow what you can do today.

Don't count your chickens until they are hatched.

QUESTION BOX

Who are the characters?

What problems occurred?

How did the character or characters learn their lesson?

CHECKLIST FOR EDITING
- Does your fable contain answers to the question in the **QUESTION BOX**?
- Are there any more details you need to add to the story?
- Did you check your capitalization, punctuation, and spelling?

FORGE AHEAD

Turn your fable into a short play. Add dialogue, a time period, and a setting.

Doreen 5th grade Clovis, N.M.

The Spoiled Soup

Once there was a rabbit who decided to cook some soup.

"I think I can cook this soup all by myself," said the rabbit. She began to gather carrots, corn, peas, and potatoes. "This will be a magnificent, delicious soup," she thought.

As she was preparing the soup along came a wolf. "What are you putting in that soup?" asked the wolf.

"I am putting in carrots, corn, peas, and potatoes."

"Oh no," said the wolf. "You must also put in some weeds."

"Well all right if you think so," said the rabbit.

By and by along came a bear. "What are you putting in that soup?" asked the bear.

"I am putting in carrots, corn, peas, potatoes, and weeds."

"Oh no!" said the bear. "You must also put in some berries."

"Well, all right if you think so," said the rabbit.

Later along came a hungry duck. "What are you putting in that soup?" asked the duck.

"I am putting in carrots, corn, peas, potatoes, weeds, and berries."

"Oh no!" said the duck. "You must also put in some fish."

"Well all right if you think so," said the rabbit.

She had no sooner added the fish when along came a giraffe. "What are you putting in that soup?" asked the giraffe.

"I am putting in carrots, corn, peas, potatoes, weeds, berries, and fish."

"Oh no!" said the giraffe. "You must also put in some leaves."

"Well all right if you think so," said the rabbit. The rabbit decided to taste her soup. "This is the worst soup I ever tasted!"

Moral lesson: Too many cooks spoil the soup.

211

THE MALEFICENT MARAUDERS

Malevolio and Maledicta were **maleficent marauders** who, through their evil **maledictions**, **maligned** the **maimed**, the **mendicants,** and the migrants. Nothing could **mitigate** the **macabre** manipulations of these **mendacious malefactors**.

Finally, a **magnaminous magnate** managed to muscle in on these **miscreants**. He gathered the maligned **maelstrom** of humanity and announced:

"Never again will **maniacal** marauders mar your lives. I have hired a multitude of **mercenaries** who will massacre these **misanthropes**, and I will make sure that all humankind will live free of the **machinations** of **meddlesome** manipulators."

VOCABULARY	DEFINITIONS
maleficent	evil
marauders	raiders, plunderers
maledictions	curses
maligned	
maimed	
mendicants	
mitigate	
macabre	
mendacious	
malefactors	
magnaminous	
magnate	
miscreants	
maelstrom	
maniacal	
mercenaries	
misanthropes	
machinations	
meddlesome	

(19 words)

Memory Guide
1. Read the story aloud to anyone willing to liste
2. Write three or four sentences using several of t
3. Write your own story using the vocabulary wo
4. Create a crossword puzzle or word find.

A PITHY PARODY

Here is **a pithy parody** about three **portly** pigs:

The oldest and most **pragmatic** pig had a **portentous presentiment** concerning the **proximity** of a **pernicious** wolf. He promptly proceeded to proclaim his **precarious** predicament to his two **porcine** siblings.

The siblings, who were less **perspicacious** than their older brother, prattled privately that the wolf was too **puny** to **precipitate** a problem and that their pessimistic brother was suffering from **paranoia**.

Unfortunately, the wolf was a **pyromaniac** whose **proclivity** for excitement could not be **placated**. Provoked into **pugnaciousness** by these **presumptuous** pigs, the wolf plundered their personal possessions, precipitating a pathetic life of **peripatetic penury**.

VOCABULARY	DEFINITIONS
pithy	brief
parody	humorous imitation (of a piece of writing)
portly	heavy, stout
pragmatic	practical
portentous	frightening, ominous
presentiment	premonition, warning
proximity	nearness
pernicious	destructive
precarious	risky, dangerous
porcine	piggish
perspicacious	insightful
puny	weak, small
precipitate	hasten
paranoia	delusion
pyromaniac	arsonist
proclivity	inclination
placated	satisfied
pugnaciousness	combativeness, desire to fight
presumptuous	arrogant
peripatetic	wandering, walking around
penury	poverty

(21 words)

Memory Guide
1. Read the story aloud to anyone willing to listen.
2. Write three or four sentences using several of the vocabulary words in each sentence.
3. Write your own story using the vocabulary words.
4. Create a crossword puzzle or word find.

SOURCE: "STAYING AT THE TOP" (ERA/CCR Corp.)

EXAMPLES OF STUDENTS' INTERACTIVE WRITING

<u>WEDDING BELLS</u>
by Charlotte

Mother Goosetown: On July 3, 1990, Bobby Shafto and Mary, Mary Quite Contrary will get married at the Mother Goose Marriage Celebration Studio.

The Priest, Simple Simon, will attend bringing his whole family including his grandma and his aunts.

The food will be served after the marriage and will consist of cake, fruit punch plus other beverages, fruit salad, doughnuts and much more.

When everyone has eaten, there will be a huge parade of about 3,000 people marching down Humpty Dumptyville at around 5:00 in honor of the ecstatic couple.

Both Mary and Bobby are looking forward to the marriage and especially, their first honeymoon, which will be spent on a coastal beach in sunny Florida.

Are you interested in coming to the marriage? If you are coming, please call: M-O-T-H-E-R-G-O-O-S-E before June 23, 1990.

by-Charlotte

MARRIAGE ON THE ROCKS
by Lakeisha

In Mobile, Alabama on June 3, 1990, Mrs. Ruben found herself a little husband no bigger than a thumb. She then bought him a very small horse. In addition, she also bought a tiny bridle and saddle.
Mrs. Ruben celebrated her anniversary by buying her husband some garters and a silk handkerchief. Now that she got him the horse, he goes riding every day for several hours.
Her mom and dad are not very happy about her marriage. Now she wants a divorce.

LaKeisha

EXAMPLES OF STUDENTS' INTERACTIVE WRITING

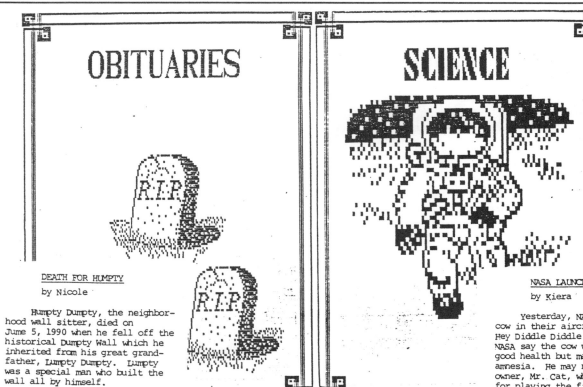

OBITUARIES

DEATH FOR HUMPTY
by Nicole

Humpty Dumpty, the neighborhood wall sitter, died on June 5, 1990 when he fell off the historical Dumpty Wall which he inherited from his great grandfather, Lumpty Dumpty. Lumpty was a special man who built the wall all by himself.

It appears that Humpty broke into 300 pieces after falling. Little Red Riding Hood was an eye witness and told us that she was walking down the street one day and Humpty waved hello. Just then, he fell.

All the king's horses and all the king's men tried to put him together. However, all attempts were unsuccessful.

If you are a close friend and would like to attend his funeral, it will be held at the Dumpty Wall at 12:00 noon. Send flowers to: 101 Dumpty Street
Storyland, Mother Goose
12345

SCIENCE

NASA LAUNCHES COW
by Kiera

Yesterday, NASA launched a cow in their aircraft called the Hey Diddle Diddle. The crew at NASA say the cow will return in good health but may suffer from amnesia. He may not know his owner, Mr. Cat, who is famous for playing the fiddle. The spaceship is expected to enter this atmosphere and land in Florida early next week.

As the Hey Diddle Diddle was traveling, its scanning went off course. They think the spaceship went over the moon and is heading back to earth.

Our cameramen took pictures and found that the scientists' observations were true. The cow mistook a dog for Mr. Cat. Also in view was a dog running away with a spoon.

SPORTS

SPIDER MAKES GIANT WEB
By Ruben

On June 11, 1990, a big contest was held to see which spider was worthy of building the best web for King Tarantula. Sammy Spider, also known as the Itsy Bitsy Spider, astonished the king with his amazing architectural skills.

The dazzling eight-legged insect used his super powers to make the colossal web with his shiny string created from gems. The web shined so brightly that it almost blinded the king. The Itsy Bitsy Spider won a lovely trophy made out of gold because of the massive web that he had spun. Everyone was very impressed.

EXAMPLES OF STUDENTS' INTERACTIVE WRITING

Dear Red,

There are three reasons for you not to go to Grandma's house. You might lose your red cape. You might miss Dad's visit. Last you might get lost.

The first reason is you might lose your red cape, and that would be a catastrophe. For example you might walk by a tree branch and get too close to it and it rips off your cape. If it did that your mom will be crying out her heart.

Secondly you might miss Dad's visit, and you wouldn't want to miss him would you? It wouldn't make him feel good.

Last and most important, you might get lost. For instance you might take a wrong path and then you would really be lost.

These are three reasons for you not to go to Grandma's house.

                    Your friend,
                    John

Jack and the bean stalk.

There are three reasons where Jack should not go up the bean stalk. One is his mother will get mad because she won't know where he is. Another reason is he could fall and get hurt. The last reason is he doesn't know what's up the bean stalk.

One reason is his mother will get mad because she won't know where he is. He will get a whipping because his mother will worry about him and will go looking for him. He will probably get grounded from watching tv and still make him read a book.

Another reason is he could fall and get hurt. He would have to go to the doctor and wear a cast for a week. He may have to give up his skate board for a week. He could not move his arm and could not go swimming in the after noon with his friends. He could not play with his friends and he probably can't go to school for his party.

The last reason is he doesn't know what's up the bean stalk. There could be an alligator that is ready for a person to climb up the bean stalk and charge at him and make him fall and break his leg. I hope he is convinced so go ahead Jack, and make your decision.
                    Jennifer

March 6, 199_

My Dear Princess,

        I am lost in the jungle. Every time I look at someone, I think it is you. But it is not you. It is just my imagination playing tricks on me. I want to see your beautiful face one more time. But, If you find this letter, it is from me. I love you Rapunzel.

                    Sincerely,

                    Your Prince
                    EDDie

Rapunzel
by Colleen T.

ACTIVITY FOR INTEGRATING POETRY AND WRITING

SITUATION WANTED

Read this poem by William Jay Smith.

THE TOASTER

A silver-scaled dragon with jaws
flaming red
Sits at my elbow and toasts my
bread.
I hand him fat slices, and then, one
by one
He hands them back when he sees
they are done.

William Jay Smith has a unique arrangement for getting toast.

RELATE Write a list of the unique characteristics of an animal which could help you get a job done. **For example:** a lion's tail might help you sweep the floor.

SELECT Select one of the animals from the **RELATE** section. Write a list of any other ways this animal could be of assistance. **For example:** The lion's roar could serve as a burglar alarm; or since the lion is king of the jungle, it could be a political leader.

CREATE Imagine that you are an animal with many talents. Write a job description about yourself and tell the services you can offer. The following format is suggested:

NAME . . . . (animal)
HOME . . . .
PHYSICAL CHARACTERISTICS AND CAPABILITIES . . . . . .
TRAINING AND/OR EDUCATION . . . .
. . . .
WHEN AVAILABLE . . . .
REFERENCES . . . .

EDITOR'S CHECKLIST

☐ Did you complete the job description from an animal's perspective?
☐ Did you check your spelling?

ERA/CCR 1984   8   Book A

STUDENT RESPONSES TO

gh58   Mitchel
9-2   4-28-
creative writing

Job. meat cutter
name charles shark
Home -1221 ocean drive. St
physical characteristics. long,
big, white firm body. sharp
carnivorous fangs.
capabilities - able to cut meat
at a speed of 45 (rpm) revolutions per minute
Training. trained by a great
whale and a dolphin.
education - was taught the
basic rules of swimming
and cutting.
when available. when-
ever needed.
references.
1. worked at bottled nose shark
fish deli
2. cut and grinded meat a the
meat market   (grichinis).

Gh88   Lorna
g.2   4-30-

Creative Writing.

Job = taping phone messages (answering machine)
Name = Parrot (Sydney)
Home = 873 #4 Oak Lane Drive.
Valley Stream, Nassau 11382.
Physical characteristics & capabilities
Has feathers a beak, has a long memory
Training and/or education
Attended Harvard University Specialized Speech Education.
When available
Available 24 hours
references
has fantastic memory and needs.
little food; little or no cleaning
up after.

AVAILABLE FROM ERA/CCR CORP.

ACTIVITY FOR INTEGRATING POETRY AND WRITING

ANOTHER LIFE

Read this excerpt from a poem by Henry Wadsworth Longfellow.

THE SLAVE'S DREAM

Beside the ungather'd rice he lay,
His sickle in his hand;
His breast was bare, his matted hair
Was buried in the sand.
Again, in the mist and shadow of sleep,
He saw his Native Land.

Wide through the landscape of his dreams
The lordly Niger flowed;
Beneath the palm-trees on the plain
Once more a king he strode;
And heard the tinkling caravans
Descend the mountain-road.

He saw once more his dark-eyed queen
Among her children stand;
They clasp'd his neck, they kiss'd his cheeks,
They held him by the hand!—
A tear burst from the sleeper's lids
And fell into the sand.

Henry Wadsworth Longfellow writes of a slave's memories of Africa and the time when he and his family were free and noble.

RELATE   Write a list of the words and phrases that you associate with the word **slave**.

SELECT   Select and write the words and phrases from the poem that tell of the nobility and glory of the slave's former life.

CREATE   Imagine that you are the slave of this poem. Write a letter to a relative in Africa telling about your present life and your memories of [...]
Include:
- where you are living
- what you must do for your master
- what is happening to your old (or new) family
- what you would like to know about your relatives who are [...] Africa
- what you are feeling and hoping for

EDITOR'S CHECKLIST
- ☐ Did you include the essential information in your letter?
- ☐ Did you edit your work for spelling, punctuation, and gra[...]
- ☐ Did you read your writing aloud to be sure you wrote wha[...] wanted to say?

ERA/CCR 1984   10
Book B

STUDENT RESPONSE TO ACTIVITY

Chris F.

1)
Servant
Worker
Person
Field
Cotton
Corn
Mean
Master
Whip
Pain
Death
Mistreating
Rest
Dream + hope

2)
Lordly Niger flowed
Palm Trees
Once more a king he strode
Dark eyed queen
Kiss'd his cheeks

Dear Mom + Dad,

I miss you a lot. I am living in the barn of my master's house. At night he locks all the doors and windows, so we can't get out. This man I'm working for, is very mean. I don't like him too much. My master makes me do so much work. When I get up, I have to take care of all the crops. Then I have to feed all the farm animals, That, believe it or not, takes the whole day.

How is little Jenny and Roger doing. I havent talked with them for six years. I miss them just as much. Has father gotten a job yet? I have been wondering. Are you, mom, still working in our fields? I always loved our fields. I hope Roger and Jenny are doing well in school.

I never told you this before, but I want to own my own store. I'm going to sell the freshest and most delicious fruits ever imaginable. It's going to be the greatest.

Well, I have to cut this letter short, because I have to go to bed. Have to start working early. Give my love to everybody.

AVAILABLE FROM ERA/CCR CORPORATION

GRAMMAR FOR GRAMMAR OR
GRAMMAR FOR WRITING

THE BATTLE OVER GRAMMAR

The battle over grammar is still raging. To teach it or not to teach it, or to teach it occasionally, seems to be the question. There are those teachers who remember fondly the odd practice of diagramming sentences and who continue to teach subject and predicate, compound and complex sentences, direct and indirect objects, and the recognition of transitive and intransitive verbs. Other teachers with less positive memories of school grammar try to avoid the subject, but feel guilty about it. Then there are those who adamantly point out that knowledge of grammar (or grammar terms) has little, if any, effect on writing or even language competency.

Yet regardless of a teacher's personal viewpoint in this controversy, she or he rarely makes the decision about what to teach in grammar or how to teach it. At least fifty percent of every language arts or English book focuses on grammar. Most standardized tests have grammar sections and very few schools in the country dare have English midterms or finals which ignore questions on grammar. And much of what is tested is measured by multiple-choice test items which require the student to respond passively rather than actively. If grammar then is so deeply infused into our educational system, why the controversy?

To answer the question, we must first have some understanding of what the term "grammar" means and what the teaching of grammar provides. By having a spoken language, humans are naturally "equipped" with grammatical knowledge. For example, all English speakers know that adjectives precede nouns as in "the bright moon," or that adjectives can follow linking verbs as in "The moon is bright." What the young speaker cannot do is comprehend the terms which describe one's native grammar. The young child does not have the ability to grasp the *metalanguage* which we use to describe our language, or what in school we call grammar.

School grammar, or the "subject" of grammar, provides us with a way of passively describing a language but teaches us very little about actively using that language — a fact well understood by Americans who have studied four years of French verbs only to be lost and tongue-tied in *Le Metro de Paris*. Yet for generations teachers have hoped that by teaching grammar rules and by labelling and diagramming words and sentences their students will emerge as better writers. Unfortunately, they (and their students) have been sorely disappointed. Only by understanding the relationship of grammar to writing and only by appropriately merging these two subjects, squarely placing grammatical knowledge in the service of writing, can we help our students become better writers. Additionally, this is the only way they will internalize grammatical knowledge. Perhaps the following definitions will clarify the distinction between writing and the subject called "grammar."

- *Writing is our spoken language committed to print and adapted or edited to meet specific conventions of form and style; that is, writing is heavily edited speech.*
- *The subject of grammar is a study of the structure of a language as it is used under different social circumstances.*

A brief review of the history of grammar instruction may further clarify the distinction between teaching writing and teaching grammar. Historically, the teaching of grammar meant the teaching of Latin grammar. Beginning in colonial America, every *boy* had to study Latin declensions, moods, and cases. Knowing Latin was considered to be the true test of being educated, since merely knowing English was not considered sufficient to distinguish the schooled from the unschooled.

Nevertheless, even in those early days of American education teachers noticed that knowledge of Latin grammar did not noticeably improve the student's use of "correct" English; nor did it provide *any significant understanding and retention of the rules of English grammar.* They therefore added the study of English grammar to the curriculum. But in many important ways English did not resemble Latin. We came to realize that in many ways English had a greater kinship with German. However, since Latin was assumed to be a "superior" language, the belief was that English might be made more "prestigious" if it could at least share the same grammar terminology. Terms such as predicate, gerund, participle, transitive and intransitive, and other high-sounding Latinate names were used to give English some sense of nobility.

To indicate time (or tense) in English, grammarians spoke of the preterite, the past perfect, the imperfect, and even the future perfect! Some of us may have wondered what was so perfect about "I have eaten" and so imperfect about "I was eating." Certainly the greatest challenge seemed to be figuring out why verbs had to be divided into transitive and intransitive classes. Why did it matter that some verbs took a direct object while others simply refused?

In spite of these historic reasons for teaching grammar, the controversy over whether to teach it, what to teach about it, and when to teach it remains. What should teachers do when the curriculum demands it, the parents expect it, and the students will have to know it for the midterm test? We believe that teaching grammar has a place in the curriculum, but for the following reasons and with a new approach.

First, we must teach the grammar of the English language and not superimpose a Latin system of rules and nomenclature upon a Germanic-based language.

Second, we must use terminology or labels that *clarify,* not *cloud,* meaning. Every school-age English speaker can understand the directive, "Begin your sentence with the *-ing* form of the verb." It may seem more erudite, but is it clearer to say, "Begin with a gerund or a participle?"

Third, we must recognize the *major,* if not the *only,* purpose of teaching grammar is to improve our spoken and written communication. Having students underline the subject once and the predicate twice makes them exercise their hands, not their heads.

We would like to elaborate upon each the above points and then present several examples of how we can effectively teach grammar for writing, for speaking, and for learning about the English language.

We must tell students that the English language, like every language, has its unique rule-governed structure and that every native or fluent speaker of the language knows the rules. Although you may know many Italian words, you cannot speak Italian if you do not know its grammatical rules. Yet every five-year old Italian child knows the rules, routinely applies them, and easily converses with peers and adults.

Rule-governed means that the language has predictable rules; there are virtually no irregularities, only variations. A quick example: for generations teachers have taught regular and irregular verbs, failing to point out that the English verb *system* is highly regular. We have often neglected to tell students that every English verb has

. a **base** form (jump, run, expedite)

. an **-s** form (jumps, runs, expedites)

. a **past tense** form (jumped, ran, expedited)

. an **-ing** form (jumping, running, expediting)

Because every English verb has these four parts, the young child learning to speak automatically "conjugates" according to this arrangement. Parents of three- or four-year-old children are likely to hear, "I buyed a lollipop," "I seed my grandma," or "I runned home." The childen have discovered that English has a past tense. Later, of course, these children will learn that there is more than one way to form the past tense which is not "irregular," but varied.

Rule-governed means that every native or fluent speaker of the language can apply English rules to any foreign word that enters the language. Rarely, if ever, would an American teenager order two *pizzi!* When English-speaking lovers meet, they *rendezvous.* They speak of having "*rendezvous-ed*" yesterday.

Rule-governed means that we never pluralize the adjective; we speak of one *tall* man or three *tall* men; we never add an ending to a verb to mark the future (as in the French *parlerai*). We always understand that when we say, "*Tomorrow we are going home,*" the word "*tomorrow*" implies a future even though the verb phrase "*are going*" is in the present. We always know which types of words can follow different verbs without first asking ourselves whether we need a transitive or intransitive verb.

Rule-governed means that we put our words in a certain order and we learn that order by hearing it over and over again. Here are several words which need to be put in order to make a sentence:

lamps

beautiful   *bought*

three   *hanging*

desk   *I*

Can you form a sentence? How were you able to do it? Did you think about the parts of speech or did you just "figure it out?" You undoubtedly wrote:

I bought three beautiful hanging desk lamps.

After we have impressed upon our students that they already know a great deal about their language, we can provide them with simple, operational labels that all English speakers understand. These labels should be simple enough to explain to a "Martian." For example, when the Martian asks, "*What is a noun?*" the grammar book response is that a noun is the name of a person, place, or thing. The Martian then asks why a *dog* and a *table* are both "things?" What about *beauty?* Is that a thing? And *democracy?* Another thing? Are *six roses* six things, the same as *six tables?* What is *mathematics?* Just one of those things?

When the Martian asks, "*What is a verb?*" we reply that it is a word that expresses action or state of being. The Martian (child, student) wonders why the sentence, "*Sit perfectly still and don't move a muscle,*" contains action. The teacher, of course, insists that there is the "action" of sitting still and the "action" of not moving. "What is the state of being?" asks the bewildered Martian, when it hears the sentence, "*Nothing exists.*" We leave the answer to you.

Finally, we must make grammar functional and meaningful, especially as it relates to the teaching of writing. When teachers teach their students to write, they can bring in those aspects of grammar which apply directly to the writing task at hand. As a teacher of language, you must know what your goals are. Do you want your students merely to *identify* adjectives, or do you want them to *use* adjectives correctly? In grammar programs students merely *identify;* in writing programs students *use,* as in the illustration on the following page:

Learning About Adjectives

THROUGH GRAMMAR	THROUGH WRITING
1. An adjective is a word that describes a noun.	1. We use certain words to stir the reader's imagination.
2. Underline all the words that describe nouns.	2. What words can you use to describe a new-born baby?
3. Make a list of all the adjectives you have found in the story.	3. Write a letter (story, poem) using adjectives to help the reader understand your feelings.

Here is another example of merging writing and grammar. Suppose you notice that some of your students' writing lacks variety and style. Many of their sentences begin with *The, I, He,* or *And then.* With this observation, you can introduce vocabulary and strategies which push the students toward using other sentence starters. One strategy is to ask students to write a paragraph in which every sentence begins with a different letter of the alphabet. Obviously, you will find that no two sentences begin with the same word. Furthermore, you will be amazed to find that even your least verbal students start sentences with the *-ing* form (the old gerund), the *-ed* form (yes, the past participle), and the *-ly* adverb, as in the example below of a fourth grader:

> *Worried about the wolf, the pigs built a fire. Quickly they locked the door. "Burning the wolf will be fun," said the pigs.*

After your students have written this type of piece, you can show them how fluent they are in using different grammatical forms. Then if you wish you can label each starter word, in simple terms and in reference to its grammatical function.

WHAT TO TEACH AND HOW TO TEACH IT

Why might a student learn about English grammar? The answer could be to:
- pass a grammar test in school
- understand what the teacher is talking about when he asks for a list of nouns or verbs or says, "Write a complete declarative sentence with a subordinate clause."
- change one's speech patterns
- improve one's writing style

The following strategies for teaching grammar will fulfill, in varying degrees, some or all of the above reasons for learning or teaching this misunderstood subject. We can begin with the basic vocabulary of school grammar, the "parts of speech," which for generations have been taught as if they were absolutes:

- *How many parts of speech are there? (eight)*
- *What are they? (noun, verb, adjective, adverb, preposition, conjunction, pronoun, interjection)*
- *What is a noun? (a person, place, or thing)*
- *What is a verb? (a word of action or state of being)*
- *etc.*

Obedient students will memorize the answers. If they wonder why the word "anger" is a noun, yet does not seem to be a person, place, or thing, they keep their concerns to themselves. When the teacher says, "A verb shows action," and asks students to find the verbs in the sentence, "*Rigor mortis sets in,*" the obedient students underline "*sets.*" (What should they do about "*in?*") Those who wonder about the "action" in this sentence keep their mouths shut. Or when they write the sentence, "*Everything is dead,*" and try to figure out how such a sentence shows a state of being, they refrain from asking questions. They just obey and hope to pass the test — certainly not an example of active participation or generative learning.

Let's go back to our Martian, a curious visitor who wants clear, unambiguous answers. The Martian has asked, "What is a noun?" Here we can use the technique called **DEFINITION MODE** — a three-part definition system in which three columns are labeled **QUESTION, GENERAL CATEGORY,** and **ATTRIBUTES** — to explain the English "noun" to the Martian.

QUESTION	GENERAL CATEGORY	ATTRIBUTES
What is a noun?		
A *noun* is a	type of word that	a) **names** persons, animals, plants, places, objects, concepts/ideas, emotions, subject areas, or anything else that can be named

In addition, a noun has other attributes which distinguish it from other parts of speech. For example:

A *noun* is a ... word that ...

b)   often has both singular and plural forms

c)   may be classified as common or proper

d)   may be described or modified by other words

e)   may be preceded by *a, the, this,* and similar types of words

> **LIST A**
> These words are **nouns.**
> truck/trucks
> frog/frogs
> kite/kites
> kitten/kittens
> boy/boys
> flower/flowers
> hunter/hunters

Through this procedure we teach students how to explain and define a concept such as a "noun" by using the clearest and most descriptive words available. Students should learn to question how using the word "thing," a word so general as to be practically meaningless, can be included as part of a useful definition. They must be shown how to use more specific words which tell concretely what the concept "noun" means.

We can now tell our Martian about "verbs" by writing a meaningful definition and excluding the *be* verb for the time being from our definition.

QUESTION	GENERAL CATEGORY	ATTRIBUTES

QUESTION
What is a verb?

A *verb* is a ...

word (in English) that ...

> **LIST B**
> These words are verbs.
> drive/drives/drove/driving
> jump/jumps/jumped/jumping
> fly/flies/flew/flying
> wish/wishes/wished/wishing
> look/looks/looked/looking
> grow/grows/grew/growing
> find/finds/found/finding

a)   always has these *four* forms:
  . a *base* form (jump, eat)
  . an *-s* form (jumps, eats)
  . a *past* form (jumped, ate)
  . an *-ing* form (jumping, eating)

b)   may have a *fifth* form, *-en* (eaten)

c)   often expresses action

d)   may express state of being

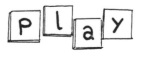

224

PAST TENSE FORMATION OF ENGLISH VERBS

The formation of the past tense in English verbs can be seen as a rule-governed, rather than a regular/irregular system. In schools, however, students are taught that there are *regular* verbs and *irregular* verbs. According to school grammar, regular verbs end in *-ed* and irregular verbs do not end in *-ed*. Such a description is inaccurate since verbs end in "sounds," not in letters. Furthermore, this description fails to show students that there are four distinct ways in which the English past tense is formed. The chart below illustrates these four basic ways.

DENTALIZATION	VOWEL CHANGE	VOWEL CHANGE + DENTALIZATION	NO CHANGE
jumped /t/	ate (eat)	bought (buy)	fit (fit)
pinned /d/	hid (hide)	brought (bring)	hit (hit)
melted / d/	ran (run)	caught (catch)	quit (quit)
	spoke (speak)		
	saw (see)		
	sang, sung (sing)		

There is only one irregular formation — *went* — the past tense of *go*. In addition, there is another group of past tense formations which uses *-n* or *-en* as in *chosen, eaten, given, hidden, risen, seen, spoken,* and several others, all of which are Anglo-Saxon in origin.

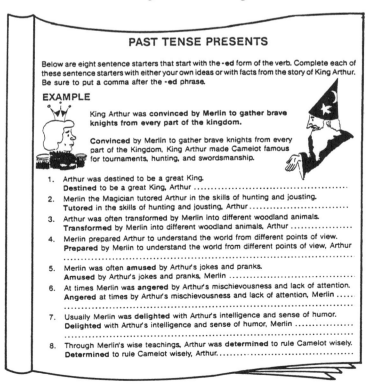

PAST TENSE PRESENTS

Below are eight sentence starters that start with the -ed form of the verb. Complete each of these sentence starters with either your own ideas or with facts from the story of King Arthur. Be sure to put a comma after the -ed phrase.

EXAMPLE

King Arthur was convinced by Merlin to gather brave knights from every part of the kingdom.

Convinced by Merlin to gather brave knights from every part of the Kingdom, King Arthur made Camelot famous for tournaments, hunting, and swordsmanship.

1. Arthur was destined to be a great King.
   Destined to be a great King, Arthur . . . .
2. Merlin the Magician tutored Arthur in the skills of hunting and jousting.
   Tutored in the skills of hunting and jousting, Arthur . . . .
3. Arthur was often transformed by Merlin into different woodland animals.
   Transformed by Merlin into different woodland animals, Arthur . . . .
4. Merlin prepared Arthur to understand the world from different points of view.
   Prepared by Merlin to understand the world from different points of view, Arthur
   . . . .
5. Merlin was often **amused** by Arthur's jokes and pranks.
   Amused by Arthur's jokes and pranks, Merlin . . . .
6. At times Merlin was **angered** by Arthur's mischievousness and lack of attention.
   Angered at times by Arthur's mischievousness and lack of attention, Merlin . . . . . .
   . . . .
7. Usually Merlin was **delighted** with Arthur's intelligence and sense of humor.
   Delighted with Arthur's intelligence and sense of humor, Merlin . . . .
   . . . .
8. Through Merlin's wise teachings, Arthur was **determined** to rule Camelot wisely.
   Determined to rule Camelot wisely, Arthur . . . .

The Martian now asks, "What is the *be* verb?"

QUESTION	GENERAL CATEGORY	ATTRIBUTES
What is the *be* verb? The *be* verb is a	set of words that	a) expresses a state or condition of being b) has a variety of forms: am, is, are, was, were, be, being, been c) provides tense to the *-ing* form of the verb (example: *is* singing, *was* singing) d) links the subject of a sentence (noun or pronoun) with a complement. (example: *I am a happy person.*)

1. The names of my friends are . . . . , ... , and . . . .
2. . . . . is my shortest friend.
3. . . . . is my tallest friend.
4. . . . . is a little taller than . . . .
5. I am . . . .

By now you can follow our organization, which is to define the observable aspects of the parts of speech by using concrete terms and examples. The vague notion of "state of being" can be explained with sentences such as "*I am happy*" (tells the *state* of how I feel) or "*We were in the park*" (tells the *state* of where we were).

Our Martian is becoming increasingly educated and more curious. It is now ready to ask, "What is an adjective?"

QUESTION	GENERAL CATEGORY	ATTRIBUTES
An *adjective* is a	type of word that	a) describes a noun b) answers the questions *what kind of? how many? etc.* c) can be compared with itself, using *more/less, most/least,* or adding *-er* or *-est* d) can be intensified or qualified with words such as *very, quite,* or *rather, etc.*

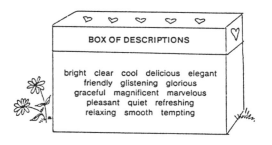

BOX OF DESCRIPTIONS

bright clear cool delicious elegant
friendly glistening glorious
graceful magnificent marvelous
pleasant quiet refreshing
relaxing smooth tempting

By clearly defining the attributes of an adjective, the student will discover that not all words that describe nouns are adjectives. In English, as we shall soon point out to our Martian, nouns, verbs, and "determiners" are among the words which can describe or "modify" nouns. The Martian now asks, "What is a determiner?"

QUESTION	GENERAL CATEGORY	ATTRIBUTES
A *determiner* is a	type of word that	a) determines the singularity or plurality of a noun (example: *each* or *every* book; *both* and *all* books; *few, many,* or *several* books
They sang every **third** day.		
They sang a **half a dozen** songs.		b) may be a number word (example: *one* book, *two* books, etc.)
My great-grandfather celebrated his **ninetieth** birthday. He celebrated for **nine** days.		c) answers the question *how many?*

By this time our Martian is fully determined to understand the remaining parts of English speech, but we will limit our other definitions to adverbs and prepositions since this will be adequate for understanding the process we use for defining. The Martian has asked, "What is an adverb?"

QUESTION	GENERAL CATEGORY	ATTRIBUTES
An *adverb* is a	type of word that	a) often ends in *-ly* and may answer the question *how?* (examples: *angrily, happily*)

ADVERB FILE

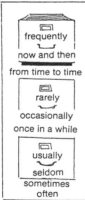

frequently
now and then
from time to time

rarely
occasionally
once in a while

usually
seldom
sometimes
often

b) may answer the question *when?* (examples: *suddenly, immediately*)

c) may serve as a transition from one sentence to the next (examples: *however, nevertheless, therefore*)

d) may be placed at the beginning, middle, or end of a sentence (examples: *Quickly* she entered the room. She *quickly* entered the room. She entered the room *quickly.*)

The curious Martian then asks, "What is a preposition?"

QUESTION	GENERAL CATEGORY	ATTRIBUTES
A *preposition* is a	type of word that	a) expresses relationship or location (example: *The cat is under the bed.*) b) precedes a noun, noun phrase, or pronoun to make a "prepositional phrase"

Notice that you cannot define a preposition merely by listing stand-alone prepositional words, since many of these individual words *(down, up, to, over, around)* may be part of the verb and are not prepositional or locational. In the examples below, the words *down, up, to, over, in,* and *around* are clearly part of the verb, **not** prepositions:

set *up* a program (arrange)   take *in* a show (attend)

turn *on* the oven (light)   take *down* the curtains (remove)

come *to* (revive)   take *up* an issue (consider)

come *around* to my viewpoint (accept)   take *over* the country (control)

By now you will have noticed that, as you are teaching parts of speech using **DEFINITION MODE,** you are teaching your students to write clear explanations and leading them to master a critical *thinking* skill. By writing to the Martian, the student must carefully observe and reflect upon the workings of English and must fully analyze for the reader (the Martian) how each part of speech is distinguished from the others. The student, who is now the explainer, cannot merely repeat rote statements lifted without question from the grammar book, since these would make no sense to the Martian. The teacher, role playing the Martian, can "play dumb" and continue to ask probing questions until the definition is clear and unambiguous.

Furthermore, in writing definitions using this three-part Definition Mode, the student develops a model for all other explanatory writing. She or he a) responds to the reader's question, b) categorizes the information being defined, c) points out appropriate distinctions, and d) provides specific details and examples. Learning that part of grammar which we call "parts of speech" now involves the student in the process of discovering, explaining, and, above all, *thinking.* With this model you can now proceed to have your students define *subject, predicate, subordination,* and whatever other grammatical terms your curriculum stipulates you should teach.

In our student book, *EASY WRITER*, we have included many writing activities which are supported by modern grammar concepts and validated by research on teaching writing. Terms such as **combining, apposition, infinitive** and others are integrated into larger holistic writing activities. We have observed that through this integration students come to recognize and understand why grammar terms need to be learned and how an understanding of one's native grammar is useful in the writing process.

Following this section (pages 232-235) is a sequential approach for relating grammar to writing which includes terminology or *labels* for parts of speech, paragraphs, and mechanics. All of us engaged in the teaching of writing, or in teaching the *whole* of language, have come to realize that students are most motivated and learn best through the *holistic* approach. This means that we do not enter into teaching writing by having students memorize and drill on minuscule pieces of grammar rules in an empty and meaningless way. We must enter with a whole *context* and lead the students to understand the specific conventions of language within the *whole meaningful context.* If you teach your students to write first, *synthesize,* and then *analyze* to improve a whole piece *they* have written, you will achieve your goal of getting your students to write the way "it should be written." Most important, you will engage their interest and active participation so that they see the value of the writing process.

STUDENT ACTIVITY INTEGRATING SPECIFIC GRAMMATICAL FUNCTIONS

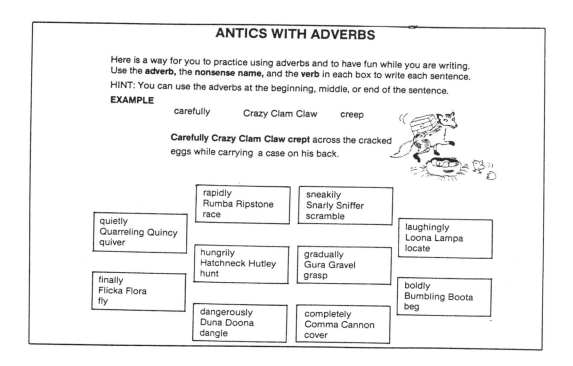

ANTICS WITH ADVERBS

Here is a way for you to practice using adverbs and to have fun while you are writing. Use the **adverb,** the **nonsense name,** and the **verb** in each box to write each sentence.

HINT: You can use the adverbs at the beginning, middle, or end of the sentence.

EXAMPLE

carefully   Crazy Clam Claw   creep

Carefully Crazy Clam Claw crept across the cracked eggs while carrying a case on his back.

quietly
Quarreling Quincy
quiver

rapidly
Rumba Ripstone
race

sneakily
Snarly Sniffer
scramble

laughingly
Loona Lampa
locate

finally
Flicka Flora
fly

hungrily
Hatchneck Hutley
hunt

gradually
Gura Gravel
grasp

boldly
Bumbling Boota
beg

dangerously
Duna Doona
dangle

completely
Comma Cannon
cover

EXAMPLES OF STUDENTS' WRITING   INTEGRATING SPECIFIC GRAMMATICAL FUNCTIONS

Veterinarian
Intelligent, helpful
Helping, caring, thinking
Taking care of animals.
Animal Doctor
Michelle

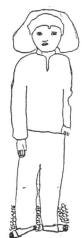

Architect
Creative, intelligent
Building, designing, painting
Carefully planning beautiful buildings
Builder   Nicole

Career Cosmos

I wish I were a friendly
intelligent teacher, having
students working quietly and
creatively.
Dushea

I wish to be the bus
driver of the future.
Driving students to
Dade County Schools-
All wearing seat belts,
safely. Keith

I wish to be a kind teacher
in a brightly colored classroom
Helping students discover and
think   Katrino
positively

SAMPLE EASY WRITER ACTIVITIES FOR GRAMMAR AND WRITING

FRANKENSTEIN'S PART-ING WAYS

Below are eight sentences that start with a **participial** form of the verb. Complete each of these sentence starters with facts from the story of **Frankenstein**. Remember to put a comma after the participial phrase.

EXAMPLE

Dr. Frankenstein pursued his monster through the night.
Pursuing his monster through the night, Dr. Frankenstein discovered a trail of terror and murder.

1. Dr. Victor Frankenstein was determined to create a monster. **Determined** to create a monster, Dr. Victor Frankenstein . . .

2. The mad scientist decided that his creation would be in the likeness of a man. **Deciding** that his creaton would be in the likeness of a man, the mad scientist. . . . .

3. Dr. Frankenstein realized he needed a brain for his monster. **Realizing** he needed a brain for his monster, Dr. Frankenstein . . . .

4. Dr. Frankenstein's assistant disobeyed instructions. **Disobeying** Dr. Frankenstein's instructions, the assistant . . . .

5. The assistant stole the brain of a hardened criminal from the graveyard. **By stealing** the brain of a criminal, the assistant . . . .

6. Dr. Frankenstein unwittingly placed the criminal's brain into the monster's head. **By unwittingly placing** the criminal's brain into the monster's head, Dr. Frankenstein . . . .

7. Dr. Frankenstein discovered that his creation was both powerful and vicious. **Discovering** that his creation was both powerful and vicious, Dr. Frankenstein. . . . .

8. The mad scientist was unable to stop his monster's career of terror and murder. **Unable to stop** his monster's career to terror and murder, the mad scientist . . . .

CHECKLIST FOR PROOFREADING

• Did you complete each sentence with interesting information?

FORGE AHEAD

Use one of the headlines below to write a two or three para

CRIMINAL'S BRAIN PLACED IN ROBOT
TRANSPLANTED BRAIN SAVES YOUNG TEACHER
SUCCESSFUL CAREER ATTRIBUTED TO BRAIN TRANS

Combining and Rearranging
Page 16

MATHEMATICIANS IN APPOSITION

Each pair of sentences below can be combined by using apposition. Follow these steps so that you combine the ten sentences into five.

• Insert the bolded words of one of the sentences after the name of the mathematician.
• Put a comma before and after the bolded words.
• Add the remaining words.

EXAMPLE

A. Albert Einstein developed the equation E equals MC2.
B. Albert Einstein was **an American physicist and mathematician.**

COMBINED:

Albert Einstein, an American physicist and mathematician, developed the equation E equals MC2.

A. More than two thousand years ago, Euclid wrote a textbook on elementary geometry.
B. Euclid was **a Greek mathematician.**

A. Ptolemy was **the founder of plane and spherical trigonometry.**
B. Ptolemy was a Greek mathematician born 400 years after Euclid.

A. Pythagoras was **a Greek mathematician born around 500 B.C.**
B. Pythagoras developed the theorem of the square of the hypotenuse.

A. Rene Descartes was the inventor of analytic geometry.
B. Rene Descartes was **a French philosopher, mathematician, and scientist.**

A. Lise Meitner developed a theory explaining how energy is released from the atom.
B. Lise Meitner wsa **an Austrian physicist and mathematician.**

CHECKLIST FOR EDITING

• Did you put commas before and after the apposition?

FORGE AHEAD

Write a sentence using apposition about one of the scientists below. You may have to use a reference book for information.

Marie Curie   Rosalyn Jablow   Anna Freud

Combining and Rearranging
Page 15

SCOPE AND SEQUENCE
FOR RELATING GRAMMAR TO WRITING

SENTENCE LABELS	PARTS OF SPEECH LABELS	PARAGRAPH LABELS	PUNCTUATION LABELS	WRITING PROCESS LABELS

KINDERGARTEN

SENTENCE LABELS	PARTS OF SPEECH LABELS	PARAGRAPH LABELS	PUNCTUATION LABELS	WRITING PROCESS LABELS
Goal—Development of sentence sense • Teacher uses word "sentence" by asking children to "compose a sentence." • Introduce concept of *telling* and and *asking* sentences.	**Goal**—Development of concept that individual words have different functions. • Have children categorize words which (a) *name* persons, animals, plants, places, and objects; (b) show *action* or doing; (c) *describe* naming words.	————	**Goal**—Obervation of written forms • **Written** sentence as a a group of words that begins with a capital letter ands end with a period or question mark. • Names of people always begin with a capital letter.	**Goal**—To orally compose a sentence.

GRADES 1 AND 2

SENTENCE LABELS	PARTS OF SPEECH LABELS	PARAGRAPH LABELS	PUNCTUATION LABELS	WRITING PROCESS LABELS
Goal—Development of concept that a sentence is a *two-part* arrangement. • One part answers question *who?* or *what?* • Second part answers question *does/did what?* Children begin to distinguish between telling and asking sentences. a) by voice b) by punctuation	**Goal**—Development of concept that words can be labelled. • A word that *names* can be called a *noun*. • A noun is a word that names *one* or *more* than one: boy, boys; friend, friends. • Words that tell "how many" go before nouns: a girl, one hat, many books. • Words that tell "what kind of?" also precede nouns: a *happy* child, six *cute* ducks, lots of *friendly* people. • Note the distinction between these two types of "describing words." One group answers "how many" and are called *determiners*; the second group answers "what kind of" and are *adjectives*.	**Goal**—Obervation (by child) that sentences can be "grouped together." • Written sentences which are grouped together are called *paragraphs*.	**Goal**—To punctuate sentences with a capital and end with a period or a question mark.	**Goal**—To add information to a sentence. • Introduce use of *caret mark* to indicate where words can be added. (∧) • Introduce term *expansion* for adding information to a sentence.

SENTENCE LABELS	PARTS OF SPEECH LABELS	PARAGRAPH LABELS	PUNCTUATION LABELS	WRITING PROCESS LABELS

GRADES 2 AND 3

SENTENCE LABELS	PARTS OF SPEECH LABELS	PARAGRAPH LABELS	PUNCTUATION LABELS	WRITING PROCESS LABELS
Goal—To recognize the two parts of a sentence where the patterns are noun (who/what), verb (does/did what). • Teacher introduces concept of subject/ verb agreement.	**Goal**—Expand list of labels to *verb* and *adjective*. • A word that fits this frame is a verb: *Today I eat.* *Yesterday I ate.* • A word that can add -ing is usually a verb: eating, playing, using, thinking. • A word that tells "what kind of" is an adjective.	**Goal**—Obervation of indentation to begin a paragraph. • Development of concept that sentences which relate are grouped as a paragraph.	**Goal**—Expand punctuation to use of commas in a series. • Awareness of special punctuation in friendly letter, envelope, common abbreviations. • Awareness of apostrophe in contraction.	**Goal**—Develop concept that written sentences may sound different from spoken sentences. • Teach *substitution* as part of above goal. • Develop concept of *simple outline* by asking what happened first, second, last?

SENTENCE LABELS	PARTS OF SPEECH LABELS	PARAGRAPH LABELS	PUNCTUATION LABELS	WRITING PROCESS LABELS

GRADES 3 AND 4

SENTENCE LABELS	PARTS OF SPEECH LABELS	PARAGRAPH LABELS	PUNCTUATION LABELS	WRITING PROCESS LABELS
Goal—To recognize the two parts of a sentence when other "parts"—prepositonal and adverbial phrases—have been added (Example: *This morning* my mother made me clean up my room.)	**Goal**—Expand list of labels: • *common nouns* and *proper nouns.* • *noun markers*— term for words that describe nouns (e.g. the *red* carpet) • *noun phrases*—to indicate the noun and its describers *(the red carpet)* • verb phrase—the verb and the words directly related *(e.g. was sitting on the park bench.)* • *pronoun* to indicate words that replace or "stand for" noun phrases.	**Goal**—Construction of *topic sentence* as a starter for the paragraph: • Introduce construction of topic sentence with words *all, some, most, many, there are* (e.g. *All* children need love.) • Introduce concept of two to three *support sentences* for the topic sentence.	**Goal**—Expand punctuation to: • quotation marks in stories.	**Goal**—Develop concept that *writing is for an audience.* • The writer chooses different words and different punctuation forms for different audiences. Example: a) Hi Tom—any news lately? Things here are O.K. b) Dear Mr. Thomas: I have been looking forward to hearing from you. Expand outlines to *who? what? when? where?* Self-edit for use of capitals and punctuation.

SENTENCE LABELS	PARTS OF SPEECH LABELS	PARAGRAPH LABELS	PUNCTUATION LABELS	WRITING PROCESS LABELS

GRADES 4 AND 5

Goal—Development of coordinate and complex sentence structures.
- Student oberves that *sentences of varying lengths* contain a basic two-part system.
- Two-part system can be labelled *the complete subject,* and the *complete predicate.*
Example:
Betty Perez/swam.
The Olympic champion Betty Perez/swam twenty lengths in record time.
- Introduce the *-ly* adverb as a *word* that can be used in initial, medial, and final positions in a sentence.
- Compose sentences that use *but, or, if, then, in order to*

Goal—Development of concept that there are "correct" forms for writing:
- *Tense*—a term that refers to the *form* of the verb. In English the *tenses* are present or past.

I jump—present
She jumps—present
We jumped—past
The form *jumping* is unmarked and takes its tense from the "be" verb.
I am jumping-present (time)
I was jumping—past (time)
I will be jumping—future (time)
- *Time*—Time in sentence construction is expressed by: tense (I ate) helpers, auxiliaries, or expanded forms, (I *will* eat; I *am going* to eat); "when" words (If it is nice *tomorrow,* I plan to go to the beach.)**
- *Verb Expanders*—Introduce the verb expanders: *be*—am, is, are, been; *have*—has, had, *do*—does, did; can/could; shall/should; will/would.
- *Pronoun System* as a three-part arrangement:

(1)	(2)	(3)
I	me	my, mine
he/she/it	him/her/it	his/hers/its
you	you	your/yours
we	us	our/ours
they	them	their/theirs

- *Introduce term conjunction*—but, and, or

**Notice how the present tense expresses "future" time by use of a "when" word.

Goal—Further development of paragraph to include:
- Sentences in a paragraph are related to each other.
- Certain words may signal the start of a paragraph—*many times, often, frequently, seldom, once in a while,* etc.

Goal—Use of commas between clauses and phrases in a sentence.

Goal—Improve text by combining short, related sentences.
Expand outlines to: describe a person or object.
- What does he/she/it look like?
- What does he/she/it do?
- What else is needed to make the audience know what is being described?
Self-edit for paragraph indentation.
- *Introduce sentence-combining*
Combine:
- Use *and* in phrases and clauses
- In a series (three noun or verb phrases)
- with adjectives
- with *but, so, so that, in order to*
- with *who, which, that*

SENTENCE LABELS	PARTS OF SPEECH LABELS	PARAGRAPH LABELS	PUNCTUATION LABELS	WRITING PROCESS LABELS

GRADES 5 AND 6

Goal—Continued development of varied sentence lengths and types. • Introduce terms *simple* and *complex* with *independent clause* and *dependent clause*. *Example:* *The child went swimming because it was warm.* *Independent*—stands by itself. *Dependent*—must attach itself to independent clause. • *Define clause*—A group of words with a subject (noun phrase or pronoun) and a predicate (verb or verb phrases). • Introduce concept that *independent sentences* can also be called independent clauses.	**Goal**—Expand understanding of the verb system. • Base form of verb may be called the *infinitive* when the word "to" precedes (to eat). • *-ing* form of the verb is called the present participle. • *-ed* and *-en* forms are called past participles. Add *either ... or* and *neither ... nor* as conjunctions. Develop skills in *sentence combining:* Combine: • clauses with related information. • with *although, in which, whenever* • with *apposition*	**Goal**—Identify and practice different types of paragraphs: • Descriptive • Factual • Anecdotal • Definition • Narrative Write a *summary* using the topic sentences of three or more related paragraphs.	**Goal**—Expand repertory of punctuation forms: • colon for the beginning of a list. • commas, quotation marks, and capitalization in reference forms (e.g. bibliography)	**Goal**—Improve text by sentences that start with participles and infinitives. Develop simple outlines *through questions* for different types of writing (see paragraph labels). Self-edit for topic and support sentences in paragraphs. Develop "style" by sentence variation. Begin sentences with: • *-ing* form • *-ed* form

GRADES 6 AND ABOVE

Goal—Introduce the terminology of sentences. • *Simple Sentences* Subject/verb *The girl sleeps.* • S/V prepositional phrase—*The book fell into the pool.* • S/V/adverb— —*Fred fell down.* • S/V/direct object —*The giraffe ate apples.* • S/be verb predicate noun —*Florence is a teacher.* • S/be verb/adjective —*The teacher is great.* S/V/Indirect object/object —*Bill bought Mother a necklace.* • *Compound and Compex Sentences Subordinators* • where, when, while, after • before, until, till, since, as soon as • as if • because, since, so, so that, in order to • though, although even though • if, unless, whether ... or not • as ...as, than • more than, less than Introduce parallel construction. Introduce passive/active constructions	**Goal**—Develop further understanding and use of the clause and phrase system. • prepositional phrases as starters or enders of sentences (In the middle of the room stood a marble statue.) • adverbial phrases as starters of sentences (Very often, teachers and students see themselves as enemies rather than friends.) • use of *transitionals:* however, nevertheless, consequently. Emphasize *sentence combining* • expand use of apposition	**Goal**—Add paragraph formats of: • Persuasion • Compare and Contrast • Research	**Goal**—Add less common and stylistic forms: • semi-colon • hyphen	**Goal**—Develop formal (Roman numeral) outlines Self-edit by relating sentence and parts of speech termology to text. Self-edit for "logical order of paragraphs. Improve "style" Begin sentences with • infinitives • transitionals

WRITING AND TECHNOLOGY
A "FRIENDLY" PARTNERSHIP

In this section, we would like to show how the classroom can fully integrate writing instruction and technology, particularly the computer and its peripheral systems. New York State's *Long-Range Plan for Technology in Elementary and Secondary Education* points out that a modern technology-based curriculum, appropriately implemented, can enhance the following areas of student learning:

. thinking and reasoning

. studying and remembering

. acquiring new concepts and information

. communicating to wider audiences

. applying technological skills to varied uses

As you may notice, the first four areas are also enhanced through writing, so that by combining writing with technology we offer our students superior opportunities for learning. According to another New York State publication titled *Technology Planning for Improving Schools,* there are three broad types of technology applications — instruction, instructional support, and evaluation — all of which relate to the teaching of writing and are discussed below.

INSTRUCTION

The term *instruction* in this context means teaching the student the use of the two most important aids for writing — the word processor and the student data disk. The use of these two aids is generally taught to students by a school's computer specialist who may or may not be the classroom teacher. In our experience, the functions of the word processor and the student data disk are quickly learned. More important is what the word processor and student data disk can do to improve the teaching and learning of writing.

Welcome to our COMPUTER LAB.

We are writing with MAGIC SLATE.

We don't need PENCILS.

Now we don't have to ERASE when we make MISTAKES.

We like to type on our APPLE COMPUTERS.

The Word Processor

The writer's greatest invention since the pencil is the word processor, the magical computer software that makes the typewriter as obsolete as the icebox. Once your students have access to word-processing software and understand its operations, they will be provided with:

. freedom for drafting, without having to worry about
  conventions of capitalization, punctuation, spelling, etc.
. the ability to fully utilize the four "improvers" — adding, deleting, substituting, and
  moving/rearranging
. an understanding of mechanics and layout — spacing, indenting, capitalization, and
  punctuation
. a clear distinction between draft and revision
. the opportunity to move from "final copy" to publication

If you are not fully familiar with the above "enhancements," we'd like to add some supporting details. First, there is freedom to compose. Many writers no longer feel the need to compose in longhand and then "type" their final copy. Because of this freedom, you may want to have your students "handwrite" some of their work as well as compose directly on the computer. As more and more computers become available in school and in the home, students should practice both approaches to composing and, in essence, discover for themselves which types of writing require drafting by hand and which can go directly on the computer.

Because of "spellcheck" systems, students no longer have to "erase" or moan, "I can't write because I can't spell." The advice to "spell as best as you can" takes on trusted meaning to the students when they know that a silent spelling expert in the machine will highlight spelling errors and the dreaded abbreviation "SP" will no longer appear on their papers.

The glory of the word processor is, of course, the system that allows the writer to add (just make some space and put in the new items) or delete (take out what you don't want) or substitute (write over what you don't want) or move or rearrange words, sentences, paragraphs, or pages through the computer's magical "cut and paste" capabilities.

Finally, students actually publish. With desktop software available in both simple and complex arrangements, students can write commercials, books, labels, signs, and whatever else can be written according to the printing conventions of the genre. Through printing and publishing, students learn a new vocabulary — font, type, point, pitch, Helvetica, and so forth. They learn that indenting and/or block style are courtesies to the reader; they realize that different styles and sizes of prints convey different messages. Above all, they see their scratchy, messy drafts become readable pieces enhanced by print, illustration, and layout. The word processor, to us, is truly one of the writer's best friends.

The Student Data Disk

Like the notebook, every student has his or her own data disk each school year. But unlike the notebook, the data disk does not have to get messy or lose pages; even better, it holds easily accessible information that can be added to and modified. Your students' data disks might contain some or all of the following:

- personal writings
- **FRAMES** for book reports, summary biographies, book characters, science/lab formats, interviews, etc.
- dictionary and/or glossary of subject-related terms (math, science, geography, etc.)
- models of letters and other formal/informal genres
- **Q.A.D.** and other outlines
- **DEFINITION MODE** setups
- **BOOK OF LISTS**

INSTRUCTIONAL SUPPORT

Instructional support for writing as it applies to the computer means having specific materials and equipment readily available for teaching and for student use, such as master disks, overhead projection devices, electronic bulletin boards, desk-top publishing programs, and publishing supplies such as paper and bookbinding items. We offer the following suggestions for using these instructional support materials.

Christine, Christine, what do you see?

"I see a blackboard with chalk, and computers with fun games in front of me."

The Master Disk

The master disk might keep exemplary student writing so that other students are able to:

- have models for their own writing
- work cooperatively for modifying these writings
- illustrate or prepare these writings for publication
- offer recognition and self-esteem to the original author(s)

The master disk can also have examples of previously taught and new strategies such as:

- ABC Listing
- Magic "Who"
- Definition Mode
- Three Reasons Why
- Frames
- Q.A.D. Outlines

Lists can be placed in a Hypercard or any other database lists and can then be added to, sorted, alphabetized, and organized into catergories.

In addition, the disk can contain:

- topics for writing
- specialized vocabulary
- names of pen pals and other audiences
- layout designs, print formats, and graphics
- bulletin board information such as homework assignments, news items, classroom rules and regulations, opportunities for good grades and "extra credit", praises and rewards, and much more

The Computer Projection Device

The commonly-used overhead projector can be a valuable technological tool for extending the efficiency of the "one-computer" classroom. By placing the computer projection device on an overhead projector, you can project the computer monitor display on a screen for large group viewing. With this device you can:

- teach specific strategies
- demonstrate the editing techniques of adding, deleting, substituting, and moving/rearranging
- critique writing with the class and model revision strategies
- help your students create group stories with or without graphic enhancements

The Electronic Bulletin Board

The electronic bulletin board is a technological hook-up system which uses two or more computers and telephones for networking purposes. Through the electronic bulletin board, teachers and students can communicate in a variety of ways both within and outside the classroom. Activities can include:

- writing personal messages
- sharing new ideas or information with classmates or other students on a regular or frequent basis
- writing metacognitive statements through specific open-ended frames (e.g., "I now know something that I didn't know before: a new star is called a Nova.")
- asking **WH- questions** about specific content to classmates, teachers, or others who might have the needed information (e.g., "Pat, I know you know a lot about baseball. Who won the World Series in 1989?")
- asking and answering questions about homework, riddles, and unique problems
- writing to someone in one language and receiving a response in another language (e.g., Spanish to English/English to Spanish)

Desktop Publishing

As we mentioned before, desktop publishing becomes the ultimate reason for writing. Through a simple desktop publishing program and materials such as colored paper and binding equipment, you can:

- develop a class library of student authors
- produce student publications for the school library
- share student writing with parents, senior citizens, community members, and others
- develop in your students an esthetic sense of the world of books and encourage both written and artistic creativity
- teach book design, layout, print modes, graphics, and formats
- give every student pride of authorship

EVALUATING STUDENT WRITING THROUGH THE COMPUTER AND RELATED TECHNOLOGY

Now that you have motivated your students to great authorship, you may feel overwhelmed by the voluminous outpouring of their creativity. Again, the computer and related technology can help you organize and manage your writing program. Here are several suggestions you may wish to consider:

- Conferencing at the Computer — Unlike "collecting and correcting," you can easily prompt a student at the computer with statements such as, "Check your spelling," "Use your thesaurus to get better words," "You need a concluding sentence," or "Why did the woman work so hard?" The student can quickly make the changes and you can check back later for the fulfillment of the task.

- Peer Editing Using a Checklist — A peer editor (student) uses a writing checklist and helps the student writer meet pre-selected criteria: length, keeping to the topic, sentence variety, use of specialized vocabulary, and so forth.

- "Top-Editor" Commentary — If you prefer or need to comment directly on a student's writing, you can place the composition on your master disk, type your remarks, and return it to the student for further revision. We believe you should use this system sparingly: first, because it is extremely time-consuming and, second, because of the obvious delay in feedback both to the student and to you.

- Graded Writing vs. Practice Writing — The student keeps a special disk labeled "graded" writing which is distinguished from "practice" writing. In graded writing, the student may be asked to keep three to five pieces of writing on a disk, such as responses to test prompts developed by school districts or state education departments. During the school year, the student improves and "polishes" these pieces of writing in preparation for standardized writing tests.

If your students are fortunate to have ready access to computers, you undoubtedly know their benefits, especially in writing. If you're just getting started using the computer, you will eventually be delighted with its motivational and teaching/learning potential. We know that good writing has existed for several thousands of years, but only a limited number of people have had the patience or energy required for writing and rewriting. The new technology, particularly the word processor, can now make writing more meaningful and accessible even to those who "think they can't write" or "don't want to write." Dorothy Parker, the writer and humorist, once said, "I hate writing; I just love having written." We believe that now she might add "...and especially with a computer."

Can you find the phrase on which this piece was based, using acrostics?*

WAR IN THE PERSIAN GULF

Neetu   FEBRUARY 22,1991

War broke out January 16, 1991 in Saudi Arabia. **A** request was made for Hussein to withdraw from Kuwait by the deadline of January 15. **R**ed blazing fire shot into the air. **I**srael got ready ,due to a threat from Hussein. **N**ext step was sirens, gas masks, and frightened people in Baghdad, and then in Israel. **T**hrough it all; Israel held their fire, due to the fact that the Allied Forces requested them not to retaliate. **H**ussein still targeted Israel with their scud missiles.

Even though Hussein is in power, many of his soldiers surrender every day. **P**eople here show much patriotism for our troops at war. **E**very person knows Hussein is crazy enough to spill many gallons of oil into the Persian Gulf, killing many animals. **R**ight then and there Hussein made P.O.W.s lie on T.V. and treated them unfairly, which is against the Geneva Convention.

Ships got hit by mines on Monday, the eighteenth of February. **I**n some time the Soviet Union came up with a possible Peace Plan that Bush criticizes, saying that Saddam should withdraw without conditions. People say that the USSR has feed Hussein for many years like a baby. **A** mine field was discovered in the Gulf waters, and on February 19,1991 the cost of the war was six billion dollars! **N**ow in wartime, since Israel has been attacked by Scuds in Tel Aviv, the Israelis put newborn babies in special cribs called incubators. They want to save them.

Ground War could be less than a day away, it's the next step. But now they are holding it up. **U**nited States are sending supplies to our troops in Saudi Arabia. **L**ots of people are curious, and full of questions.

Finally the question is, "WHEN WILL ALL THIS END?"

EXAMPLES OF STUDENTS' PUBLISHING

DIAMANTE

WINTER
Cold, Short
Skating, Skiing, Shoveling
Frost, Snow, / Sun, Rain
Picnicking, Swimming, Biking
Hot, Long
SUMMER

We are doing WORD PROBLEMS using MAGIC SLATE.

3 groups of people watch the clowns.
There are 3 people in each group.
How many people are there together.
3 x 3 = 9 people.

There are 8 clowns.
Each clown has 2 hats.
How many hats are there in all?
8 x 2 = 16 hats.

There are 4 kinds of balloons.
There are 4 of each kind.
How many balloons are there in all?
4 x 4 = 16 balloons.

Below are some sentences that have mistakes. You will correct them by using the "MAGIC SLATE" features that you learned in "COMPUTER LAB".

COMPUTER SMARTS - TEST 1

The sentence below should read, "Two clowns played with six seals."

Two plaed with six seals.

Capitalize the words "magic slate".

Delete the words "ugly" and "slowly" in the sentence below.

The ugly creature walked slowly.

Type this sentence using italics.

Type this sentence using boldfaced type.

Underline this sentence.

Delete this entire sentence.

Give the name of the city and state in which you live.

Today's date is.

My teacher's name is.

My name is.

Center the words below.
WELL DONE !!

PYRAMID

Jack
Jumping Jack
Jumping Jack Juggling
Jumping Jack Juggling Joyfully

Substitute the word *nice* for more interesting words.
Use control-E to insert.
Use control-D, Control-W, and RETURN to delete a word

THE NICE STORY

Once upon a time a *sweet* old man named Charlie lived in the *beautiful* town of Spring Valley. Charlie made *pretty* toys for all the children who were *kind* to each other. All the children loved Charlie because he was so *pleasant.* Even the parents would say, "Aren't we lucky to have such a *generous* person in our town?"

EXAMPLES OF STUDENTS' PUBLISHING

LEARNING
by
Brando

Learning is fun. Elementary school has many fun things. Athletes are learning lots of hard things. Reading is lots of learning in textbooks. Not all kids learn quickly. I always like learning a lot. Not everyone likes learning, but I do. Going to school will help you learn lots of things.

BIKE RIDING
by
Matthew

Bike riding is fun. I like bike riding a lot. Kicking the kick stand up is how I get it moving. Excited is the feeling I get when I'm riding. Riding is fun, but it is hard work. I do lots of things on my bike. Delivering newspapers is fun when you are riding a bike. I know I am getting exercise when I ride. Now I have a new bike. Getting use to it is fun because you have to do a lot of riding.

COCKATIELS

Cockatiels are cute and cuddly. Outstanding, they are at tricks. Cockatiels are good listeners. Kind is what they are to other people. Always they are good. Training them not to fly away is easy. Independence is for them. Even birds like to get their back rubbed. Loving people is fun for them. Super birds to have for a pet.

Aaron

SUMMER

Swimming is fun in the summer. Under the umbrella is where I want to be in the summer. Mostly, I like to be on the beach all day long. Many times I get a sun tan. Each day I ride my bike. Roller skating is another thing I really enjoy doing doing during the summer.

Betsey

WRITING AS A UNIFIER OF THE CURRICULUM
ORGANIZING A SCHOOL FOR WRITING

Through the 1980's educators began to notice the value of teaching writing frequently and systematically. They realized that through writing children learn how their language works. They watched children learn more in math, science, social studies, and other subjects when they wrote about these subjects. They noticed that children who wrote journals, stories, articles, and poems developed greater self-esteem. Because of these positive results, several schools around the country made writing the core of their curriculum or became, in some cases, magnet schools with writing as the major focus.

As consultants in writing, we have had the challenging opportunity to help many schools develop and implement writing as the integrator or unifier of the curriculum. One of these schools in Dade County, Florida became *The Center for Learning Through Writing,* and as consultants we had the unique privilege of sharing in the making of significant changes in both teacher and student behavior.

The Center for Learning Through Writing, formerly known as Crestview Elementary School, is located in the northwest section of Miami in a predominantly black neighborhood. Under the direction of its principal, Jill Witlin, the school had received national recognition for excellence during the 1980s. However, the school was under Federal and state mandate to become integrated through parent choice; to achieve this goal Dade County decided to make it a magnet school. Most important, it would be a magnet school for all children through the basic subject of writing, a subject that every student needs to learn.

In developing The Center for Learning Through Writing, Jill Witlin, the principal, asked us to respond to two questions:

1.   **What is special about a writing magnet school?**
2.   **How do we make writing more than just another basic subject?**

Our answer to the first question was that, with writing as a magnet or unifier, the students would:

- learn **how** to write systematically and developmentally
- develop the "voice" of the writer by frequently writing stories, letters, articles, reports, and other major genres
- learn the craft of writing and the art of writing by drafting, revising, editing, and publishing
- understand the relationship between reading and writing because good writers are, or become, good readers
- develop higher-level thinking processes and skills because writing requires analysis, synthesis, application, decision-making, problem-posing, and problem-solving
- build self-esteem through the on-going production of well crafted, beautifully written products

To address her second question, we built the unified curriculum that would change a "regular" school into a "writing magnet" school.

BUILDING A UNIFIED CURRICULUM THROUGH WRITING

A magnet school is a school unified by a theme or themes — music and art, math and science, gifted and talented, and so forth. At the Center for Learning Through Writing, we developed the concept of **UNIFIERS** — themes and activities that focus on writing and, in effect, unify the entire curriculum. After much discussion with Ms. Witlin and the teaching staff, we developed the following unifiers:

- STRUCTURES AND GENRES for process-to-product strategies
- THE JOURNAL for both affective and cognitive writing
- INTEGRATION WITH THE CONTENT AREAS for writing to learn across the curriculum
- KEEPING TRACK NOTEBOOKS for "keeping track" of new learning and for metacognitive entries
- THE BOOK OF LISTS for building the personal thesaurus
- READ-ALOUD for connecting literature with writing
- SPEAK UP/SPEAK OUT for relating speaking to writing

STRUCTURES AND GENRES

The heart of the program at the Center for Learning Through Writing is the direct and specific teaching of writing, which means that the student learns how to write for every purpose and in every appropriate genre. Since all writing is genre-based, the student learns the organizational formats of fables, fairy tales, legends, personal narratives, descriptions, and so forth. Beginning in September, all the teachers from kindergarten through fifth grade build a writing plan for developing both fluency and organization that includes, but is not limited to:

. LISTING STRATEGIES
. "MAGIC WHO"
. DEFINITION MODE
. THREE REASONS WHY
. Q.A.D. OUTLINING
. ABC STORIES
. INTERACTIVE WRITIN(

> Creatvieur
> can be...
> School for learning through
> writing,
> Children's work under con-
> struction,
> Spelling doesn't count, yet!
> Wyanesta

In addition, the students have specific instruction in "starters" and "improvers" that include:

. Sentence Composing
. Writing from Key Words
. Writing from FRAMES
. WH- QUESTIONING
. Planning and Outlining
. Adding, Deleting, Substituting, and Rearranging

Every month the teachers gather samples of the students' writing products, making sure that they select items from students at all levels of achievement, and then put together a publication representing what has been taught. In the samples at the end of this chapter (page 253), you will see word lists, sentences, and pieces based on specific structures. Every child gets "published." All of these publications go home to parents and are shared in different classes throughout the school.

Self Esteem

> What is self esteem?
> Self Esteem is your self-image or
> how you feel about yourself.
> Your self-esteem is made up of thoughts
> and feelings you have about yourself.
> They may be positive or negative.
>
> Examples: Positive   Negative
>   smart   stupid
>   good   loving
>   fun   afraid
>   effective   failing
>   productive   unloved
>   Brian

THE JOURNAL

Journal writing allows the students a type of freedom that other writing doesn't permit. Students can write short or long pieces; they can write about any topic or idea; they can write informally or formally; they can direct it to an audience or keep it private. The writer fully controls the writing in a journal. Journal writing should be non-competitive. Entries in a journal are not graded, but if read by an outsider are commented upon in personal, interactive statements such as, "Oh, I love extra-cheese pizza too, but not with pepperoni," or, "I'd like to know more about your dog."

From the very first day of school, students are asked to write their journals in a journal notebook. In The Center for Learning Through Writing, journal writing takes place during the first period and everybody writes — students and teachers — for about half an hour. The teacher and the children begin by discussing events and happenings of the previous day, or plans for the present day, or any other topics of interest. During this discussion the teacher lists these ideas on the board so that they are available as ideas for journal writing. The students, of course, are free to write whatever they wish, but the discussion and listing help stimulate topics.

After about fifteen minutes of writing, the children are asked to share (if they wish) what they have written. They may share in pairs, in small groups, or with the whole class. The teacher varies the arrangement frequently. The teacher may also share what she has written since the children are always eager to hear her journal entry. Since showing is better than telling, we have presented at the end of this chapter (pages 253-254) several journal items ranging from kindergarten through grade five and from children of different ability levels.

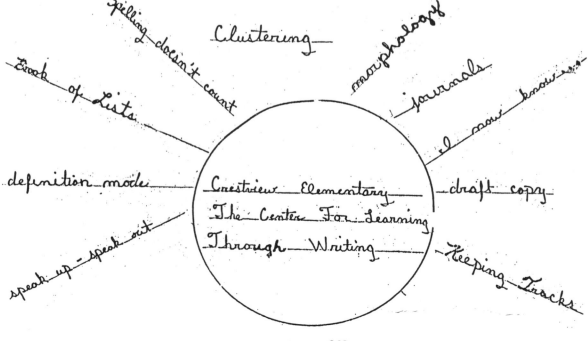

INTEGRATION WITH CONTENT AREAS

Learning to write is obviously learning to write about *something*. Writing in the content areas, therefore, greatly expands the student's knowledge and understanding of the various subjects and provides the student with the opportunity to truly integrate writing strategies with new information as in the example below:

Goal:	To have students write with the "voice" of a scientist.
Fluency:	Students create a cluster of nouns, verbs, and adjectives that are associated with the weather.
Spelling and Grammar:	Students develop a **MORPHOLOGY** chart from selected items in their vocabulary.
Composing:	Students compose sentences about the solar system in which they use in each sentence a noun, a verb, and an adjective from their lists. After they have practiced sentence composing, they write a newspaper article, a letter, or a story about an aspect of the weather.

Every subject area provides an opportunity for writing. We have also included (pages 255-256) what we think are excellent examples of content area writing by students.

KEEPING TRACK NOTEBOOKS

In grades three, four, and five, every student is provided with a **KEEPING TRACK** notebook for each subject area — math, language, science, and social studies. In grade two, each student has a single notebook divided into the different areas, while in kindergarten and grade one the teacher makes a **KEEPING TRACK** book in large print for the whole class.

The students use these notebooks to enter key concepts and to write personal responses to what they are learning. To enhance metacognition, students are encouraged to use response starters such as:

- . I now understand ....
- . I need to know more about ....
- . I would like to know why ....
- . I now know that I know ....
- . I still don't understand (or know) ....
- . If I read more about ...., then I ....

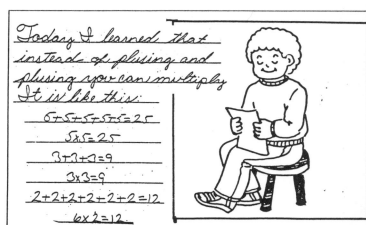

Today I learned that instead of plusing and plusing you can multiply It is like this:

6+5+5+5+5=25
5x5=25
3+3+3=9
3x3=9
2+2+2+2+2+2=12
6x2=12

In the **MATH KEEPING TRACK BOOK,** for example, students write not only math facts, but also enter original story problems, successes, and difficulties with math concepts, as well as metacognitive statements that tell what they need to know. We have included some excellent examples (page 257) from **KEEPING TRACK** books.

THE BOOK OF LISTS

We have already discussed the potential of the **BOOK OF LISTS** and would add only that this small book has given the students at the Center great pleasure and pride. It has become an adjunct to almost every lesson, and the children add to it daily. We thought you'd enjoy looking at the entry we've included (page 258).

READ-ALOUD

To write well, one must have heard **and** read good writing. Being read to, therefore, is essential for every child, especially when the goal is to have each child achieve the highest levels of literary development. At the Center for Learning Through Writing, we instituted **READ-ALOUD,** a planned program in which every teacher reads the best in children's literature to the students every day. With the assistance of the librarian and through extensive staff development sessions, the teachers select books for reading aloud that:

- expose the children to the great themes of literature — family relationships, friendships, interrelationships of humans to animals and nature, ethnic diversity, and themes of love, happiness, sadness, and loss

- expand children's concepts and knowledge — people working around the world, animals and nature, places near and far, working and playing, and going to school and learning

- make children aware of the different genres in the world of literature — poetry, fairy tales, myths, legends, fables, tall tales, fiction, non-fiction, and so forth

- increase children's vocabulary through presentation of literature that is written with respect for the beauty and power of the English language or any other language

. entice children to engage in dramatic presentation — from *The Little Red Hen* to *Charlotte's Web,* from *Mother Goose* to *Hamlet*

. present to children opportunities for composing their own literary structures — original fables, fairy tales, alliterative stories, personal narratives, and all the other genres that are in our world of literature

SPEAK UP/SPEAK OUT

All of us recognize that writing emanates from speech; however, **good** writing must evolve from good speech. According to the eminent linguist Martin Joos, speech has basically five registers which he calls *The Five Clocks* (1962), the word "register" meaning the social nuances which our speech conveys. He has named these registers:

. Intimate — the child's first or "baby" speech
. Casual — the speech of the home and community
. Consultative — the speech of the school and the workplace
. Formal — the speech of presentation
. Frozen — speech "written and edited"

To be fully literate, the student must be able to move through these "clocks" so that he eventually develops the full range of language registers. That is, a literate educated person can converse with equal fluency in the "home language," or what Yiddish calls "Mamaloshen" (Mother speech), and in the language of the external world of professions and literature.

The Center for Learning Through Writing has courageously undertaken to have students become fluent not only in their casual speech but in their consultative and formal speech as well. Children have been taught to distinguish between informal/formal language and to appreciate the appropriate use of each. The public address system is used to demonstrate "frequently used" informal phrases, introductions, idioms, expressions, and sentences followed by "the formal or standard English" version. In each classroom, students enjoy brief discussions of both forms and then identify those that are "formally" correct.

Parent "ambassadors" and PTA leaders are directly involved in assisting the administration and staff in achieving the district's goal of *teaching* standard English without alienating the child from his or her speech community. Gradually, the children collect and list the different ways of saying the same things and soon every class has its own list. We have included some examples that have become part of the **SPEAK UP/SPEAK OUT** unifier (page 259).

A unified curriculum which pivots around writing allows the students to develop their highest levels of literacy. Every classroom and bulletin board is filled with students' writing products and the students know that they themselves are very special in a very special school. Furthermore, in meeting the mandate for integration, The Center for Learning Through Writing has successfully recruited and integrated approximately two-hundred Hispanic, Anglo, and Asian students whose parents have voluntarily enrolled their children in this school because of its reputation for effective teaching and productive learning. This unique school has made "Writing Across the Curriculum" the bridge to literacy and learning.

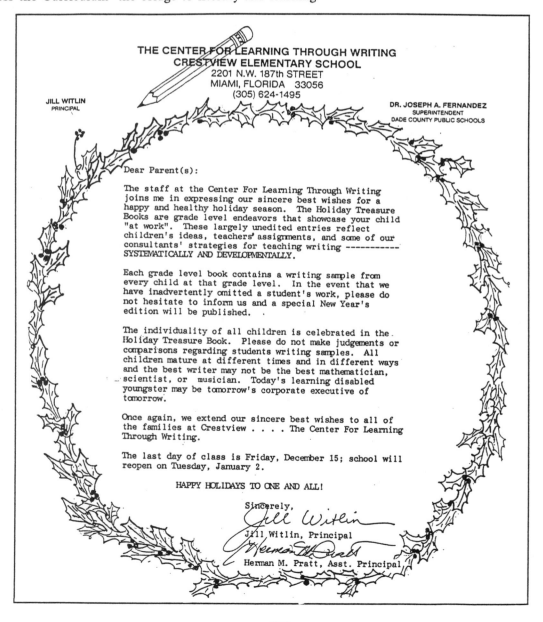

THE CENTER FOR LEARNING THROUGH WRITING
CRESTVIEW ELEMENTARY SCHOOL
2201 N.W. 187th STREET
MIAMI, FLORIDA 33056
(305) 624-1495

JILL WITLIN
PRINCIPAL

DR. JOSEPH A. FERNANDEZ
SUPERINTENDENT
DADE COUNTY PUBLIC SCHOOLS

Dear Parent(s):

The staff at the Center For Learning Through Writing joins me in expressing our sincere best wishes for a happy and healthy holiday season. The Holiday Treasure Books are grade level endeavors that showcase your child "at work". These largely unedited entries reflect children's ideas, teachers' assignments, and some of our consultants' strategies for teaching writing ----------- SYSTEMATICALLY AND DEVELOPMENTALLY.

Each grade level book contains a writing sample from every child at that grade level. In the event that we have inadvertently omitted a student's work, please do not hesitate to inform us and a special New Year's edition will be published. .

The individuality of all children is celebrated in the Holiday Treasure Book. Please do not make judgements or comparisons regarding students writing samples. All children mature at different times and in different ways and the best writer may not be the best mathematician, scientist, or musician. Today's learning disabled youngster may be tomorrow's corporate executive of tomorrow.

Once again, we extend our sincere best wishes to all of the families at Crestview . . . . The Center For Learning Through Writing.

The last day of class is Friday, December 15; school will reopen on Tuesday, January 2.

HAPPY HOLIDAYS TO ONE AND ALL!

Sincerely,

Jill Witlin, Principal

Herman M. Pratt, Asst. Principal

EXAMPLES OF STUDENTS' JOURNAL WRITING

My five wishes are to own a car, a skateboard, an airplane, my own building and a wife.

Frederick

Grade 3

Long long ago in England, the Pilgrims were not happy. The king did not let the Pilgrims go to the church they wanted to go to. So they went on a ship called the Mayflower. The ship landed at Plymouth.

Euneka

Grade 1

My favorite food is shrimp. It's wonderful to have shrimp. Just tasting garlic crabs makes me go wild. Lobster, I can never forget.

Holly

Grade 3

I went to New York by bus because it cost too much money to go on the plane. It took four days and three nights. We went to my aunt's house and played. We went to see the Statue of Liberty and went inside of it.

Tonya

Grade 2

I don't like this class. One day at school, I had a bad day because everyone was playing, kicking and hitting. They were also talking very badly. Lakeisha and I were the best in class. We went home and told our moms and dads.

Nicole

Grade 2

I was angry yesterday because Mrs. Monroe would not let us talk. She made me move because I was talking. I hope we get a new teacher. I wish there wasn't such a thing as school because it's torture.

Bernard

Grade 4

Yesterday, my teacher told me Nakia was hit by a car. Nakia is a good friend of mine. She was taken out of intensive care yesterday. Nakia was in critical condition. She goes to this school. My teacher told me she was going to be in the hospital for while. We made cards for her in class yesterday. Nakia must be very frightened. I hope she will soon get well and come back to school.

Tamieka

Grade 5

This morning I watched the news and found out that George Bush won the presidency. I was disappointed because I wished that Dukakis won as easily in the real world as easily as he did in my school. If he had won, there would be a super duper big smile on my round little face. Well journal, I can't think of anything else to say until tomorrow. Then I will talk to you, not with my mouth, but with my pen. That is what I call feedback with a pen.

Senturon

Grade 4

Today is election day. We are going to vote for the president. I am going to vote for George Bush. Do you want to know why I will vote for George Bush - because he is nice.

Taneisha

Grade 1

I'm glad the whales are safe. I saw them in the news. They made a hole in the ice. When I heard that, I was happy.

Samarah

Grade 2

EXAMPLES OF STUDENTS' JOURNAL WRITING

At 8:45 we wrote in our Journals. I also learned what a Journal is. It is something like a diary, but you share it with your class. The first thing I wrote in my Journal was about Kerry.

Jeanine

WHY? WHY? WHY?

Today Mrs. Berman picked Venson as journal monitor. I haven't been picked for over a week. I want to be journal monitor! I want to be journal monitor! Can't you see the condition I'm in?

Please I'm asking you all: nominate me as journal monitor. For this I thank you.

by LETICIA

Gary

what I liked best about the program Was

the parade And the Soings and the Band and the Sahy oyof Liv and the dnomes and the Baton andthe hons andthe sassafon andthe Bigdnome and Mrs wotlon and Mrs Mat Male

GARY, A KINDERGARTEN STUDENT AT CRESTVIEW,

SUMMARIZES THE BIG DAY ....

"What I liked best about the program was the parade and the songs and the band and the Statue of Liberty and the drums and the baton and the horns and the saxaphone and the big drum and Mrs. Witlin, and Mrs. Maudsley.

David   Journal

I'll never forget the day when I first came to Crestview. I was very excited because I had a chance to learn and write stories as I'm writing now. When I came into this class I was impressed with how the boys and girls were sitting quietly.

Henry

On Sept. 9, 1989 My Mom and My Dad got Maride. They let The Candoles. I was carring The ring. We Went to the resopshen. We had phune chicken Dinnen We had Bread and Butter. We were Dancesing. We were in the lemozine. It had a T.V.

SPELLING DOESN'T COUNT YET

JOURNAL JOTTINGS !!

Journal writing is a good way to express feelings and a good way to get out bad steam.

by Mary Streetzel

When we write in our Journals we are learning about other people's feelings and thoughts. We should listen to the person sitting on the Sharing Chair. When I sit on the Sharing Chair, I feel glad because everybody loves the feelings we share with them.

by Toni Martin

The archeologist found 13 dinosouns fossils. He needed 5 more to finish the Tyrannosour. How many fossils does he need altogether?   13+5=18

Antwan

ON THIS PAPER I GOT THESE EXAMPLES WRONG....

Sheneeka

# + EXAMPLE	I GOT IT WRONG BECAUSE	CORRECTION
412 -94 492	I started on the left side and did everything wrong!	10 12 4 X 2 -94 418
533 -29 51 3	I did not borrow in the one's place	2 13 5 3 3 -29 504
641 - 9 648	I messed up in the one's place again	3 11 6 4 X - 9 632

THE IMPORTANCE OF NUMBERS
Candon

At home, my family and I use numbers to cook with when we measure ingredients for our favorite recipes. We use numbers to play games with and to complete math homework problems. We use numbers when we call someone on the phone, change the channels on the television or radio and to change the speeds on different appliances.

We even use numbers when we talk to each other, by telling our age, birth dates, weight, and so on.

At work my parents use numbers to teach students and to figure out distances. They are sure to check the numbers that appear each week on their paychecks.

We use numbers every day.

CENTER FOR LEARNING THROUGH WRITING
CRESTVIEW ELEMENTARY

WE LEARN THROUGH WRITING IN THE DEFINITION MODE

NAME Lamarri Holliman (Dingle)
GRADE 5

QUESTION	GENERAL CATEGORY	ATTRIBUTES
What are addends? Addends are	numbers that	are part of an addition sentence.
What are sums? Sums are	numbers that	are the answers to addition problems.

My Math Problem
Percy

The Bettels are ordering a tent for $88.99, a lantern for $21.99, and a sleeping bag for $32.89. What is the total cost of the order?

1 2 2
$88.99
32.89
21.99
$143.87

I now understand how to solve story problems.

EXAMPLES OF STUDENTS' WRITING   IN THE CONTENT AREAS

Tyrea   May 2,   Simone Codlen - Books of Lists

Seed Secret

I have leaves and a little
root inside of me. When I
am watered my root grows.
Inside, my leaves grow too, but
you can't see them. The big fat
part of me is seed food so my
new plants can grow.

living things
- plants
- people
- tree
- animals
  fish
  insects

Needs
- water
- air
- shelter
- food
- clothing
  boby-parent

CENTER FOR LEARNING THROUGH WRITING
CRESTVIEW ELEMENTARY

WE LEARN THROUGH WRITING IN THE DEFINITION MODE

NAME Anoushka Cox
GRADE 5

QUESTION	GENERAL CATEGORY	ATTRIBUTES
1. What is a declarative sentence? A declarative sentence is a	statement that	gives information
2. What is an interrogative sentence? An interrogative sentence is a	group of words that	asks a
3. What is an imperative sentence? An imperative sentence is a	statement that	a. gives a command b. makes a request

---

DEFINITION MODE
CENTER FOR LEARNING THROUGH WRITING

QUESTION	CATEGORY	ATTRIBUTES
Ship	large water vessel	Steamboats,
		tugboats,
		cruise ships,
		tankers,
		aircraft carriers,
		cruisers,
		battle ships,
		cargo ships,
		sail boats,
		Mayflower,
		Submarine,
		Royal Carribean,

UNDER CONSTRUCTION

Summer
Ships are large water vessels At the
port there were lots of different ships.

Tavores:
Cluster of ideas

- makes you dizzy
- Stops your brain
- Kill You - bad
- Effects of Drugs
- makes you crazy
- makes you sick
- harmful poison

256

EXAMPLES OF "KEEPING TRACK" ENTRIES

Armind   Keeping Track
In Math we learned
that the question How many
left? Means to Subtract.
The question How
many all together?
Means to Add

Andre
Keeping
                        Track
This week in school I
learned about Christopher
Columbus. He was an
explorer who discovered America.
He sailed three ships.

As a result of reading
Harlequin and the Gift of
Many Colors,
I learned not to feel
bad if you can't
afford things.

Marvin   Reading

Keeping Track Response
Title: Exploring the Mind

Three things I remember from
reading this story are:

1 To think of how each of us
behave when we don't get our
way about something.

2 Why do some of us seem to
get along better with certain
people than with others?

3 It is not easy to say why
we act in so many different
ways.

Monique   Keeping Track Science

If there was No Sun

If there was no sun then the flower Will

not grow.

If there was no Sun then WeWwill not Be able

to go to the Bech.

If there was no Sun then there Wouldn't

Be night and day.

EXAMPLES OF STUDENTS' LISTS AND WRITING

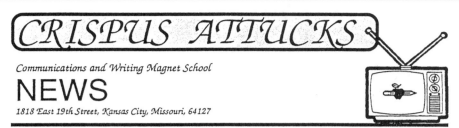

CRISPUS ATTUCKS

Communications and Writing Magnet School

NEWS

1818 East 19th Street, Kansas City, Missouri, 64127

March 8, 1991	Volume 1, Number 24

<u>ABC</u> <u>Listing</u> <u>Of</u> <u>Historical</u> <u>Women</u>

A   Amelia Earhart, Anne Hutchinson, Abigail Adams
B   Barbara Jordan, Betsy Ross
C   Clara Barton, Coretta King, Christa McAuliffe
D   Dorothy Height, Deborah Moody
E   Elizabeth Blackwell, Eleanor Roosevelt, Ella Fitzgerald
F   Florence Nightingale, Frieda Hennock
G   Gold Meir, Gwendolyn Brooks
H   Harriet Tubman, Helen Keller, Harriet Beecher Stowe
I   Ida Wells, Irma Wyman
J   Jackie Kennedy, Jeannette Rankin
K   Katherine Dunham
L   Lucile Bluford, Louisa May Alcott, Leontyne Price
M   Mary Bethune, Margaret Thatcher, Marian Anderson, Madame Curie
N   Nancy Lopez, Nikki Giovanni, Nellie Bly
O   Olga Korbet, Olveta Culp Hobby
P   P cahontas, Pearl Bailey, Phyllis Wheatley
Q   Queen Elizabeth
R   Rosa Parks, Rebecca Felton
S   Sacagawea, Sandra Day O'Conner, Shirley Chisholm, Sojourner Truth, Squanto
T   Tamara Karsavina
U   Urraca
V   Virginia Dare, Victoria Woodhill
W   Wilma Rudolph, Winnie Mandela
X   Xanthippe
Y   Yvonne Burke
Z   Zingha

Mary M. Bethune
(The Magic Who)

I am Mary M. Bethune who worked on a cotton plantation as a youngster, who was the first in her family to learn how to read, who started her own school for blacks, and who won a medal for contributing to education.

George

Marian Anderson
(Three Reasons Why)

There are three reasons why I admire Marian Anderson. First, as a child, Marian Anderson sang in her church choir. Second, the pure quality and wide range of her voice made other people notice her. Third, she won a concert tour that included appearances in New York.

Those are the three reasons why I admire Marian Anderson.

Shanna

258

SPEAK-UP / SPEAK OUT
Informal and Formal Sentences

Informal	Formal
1. Nobody here now.	1. No one is here now.
2. We be good all day.	2. We've been good all day.
3. My mother she help a lot.	3. My mother helps me a lot.
4. This ain't mine.	4. This isn't mine.
5. Why she ain't here?	5. Why isn't she here?
6. That girl stare at me..	6. That girl is staring at me.
7. He not going with us.	7. He's not going with me.
8. If you be going too fast, you get hurt.	8. If you go too fast, you'll get hurt.
9. She real skinny and every time you see her she eating.	9. She's really skinny, but every time you see her, she's eating.

EASY WRITER ACTIVITIES FOR BUILDING FORMAL LANGUAGE

A CHANGE FOR THE BETTER

Combine the six sentences below and write new ones.
In each sentence there is a word or a word ending you will have to change.

EXAMPLE   Al plays cards.
Diane plays cards.
Al and Diane play cards. (Change **plays** to play.)

REMEMBER TO:

1. Sally plays checkers.
   Jim plays checkers.   change plays to play

2. My sister jogs.
   My brother jogs.   change jogs to jog

3. Nora lives on a farm.
   Mike lives on a farm.   change lives to live

4. Mary was eating ice cream.
   Anne was eating ice cream.   change was to were

5. Bill's wagon is in the backyard.
   Bill's bicycle is in the backyard.   change is to are

6. Jill has crayons.
   Jack has crayons.   change has to have

CHECKLIST FOR PROOFREADING
- Did you use the word **AND** to combine your sentences?
- Did you change the bolded verb?

PAST TENSE PRESENTS

Below are eight sentence starters that start with the -ed form of the verb. Complete each of these sentence starters with either your own ideas or with facts from the story of King Arthur. Be sure to put a comma after the -ed phrase.

EXAMPLE

King Arthur was convinced by Merlin to gather brave knights from every part of the kingdom.

Convinced by Merlin to gather brave knights from every part of the Kingdom, King Arthur made Camelot famous for tournaments, hunting, and swordsmanship.

1. Arthur was destined to be a great King.
   Destined to be a great King, Arthur ....

2. Merlin the Magician tutored Arthur in the skills of hunting and jousting.
   Tutored in the skills of hunting and jousting, Arthur ....

3. Arthur was often transformed by Merlin into different woodland animals.
   Transformed by Merlin into different woodland animals, Arthur ....

4. Merlin prepared Arthur to understand the world from different points of view.
   Prepared by Merlin to understand the world from different points of view, Arthur
   ....

5. Merlin was often amused by Arthur's jokes and pranks.
   Amused by Arthur's jokes and pranks, Merlin ....

6. At times Merlin was angered by Arthur's mischievousness and lack of attention.
   Angered at times by Arthur's mischievousness and lack of attention, Merlin ......
   ....

7. Usually Merlin was delighted with Arthur's intelligence and sense of humor.
   Delighted with Arthur's intelligence and sense of humor, Merlin ....

8. Through Merlin's wise teachings, Arthur was determined to rule Camelot wisely.
   Determined to rule Camelot wisely, Arthur ....

CHECKLIST FOR PROOFREADING
- Did you complete each -ed phrase with your own interesting ideas?
- Did you put a comma after the -ed phrase?

EVALUATING THE WRITTEN PRODUCT
FROM DRAFT TO PUBLISHED COPY

Until recently schools placed little emphasis on *teaching* students to write and even less emphasis on the role of *revision* in the writing process. For many teachers writing meant "collecting and correcting," and for students a piece of writing was (and perhaps still is) a one-time draft/final copy activity. Often the emphasis was on "correcting" errors in spelling, capitalization, punctuation, and grammar, with negative comments written in *red*.

The purpose of teaching revision skills is to make students understand that a *first draft* is only a starting point, not a finished product which merely needs to be recopied or typed. Even more important, the student writer must recognize that *revision* extends beyond the correction of mechanical details of spelling and punctuation. While mechanical correctness is essential in the final copy, it is the *redrafting* or *reworking* of the piece that eventually ensures more meaningful communication between writer and reader.

Therefore, before you consider evaluating students' writings, you must teach them what to revise and how to revise. As you have undoubtedly observed in the previous sections of this book, writing and editing are constantly merged so that rarely, if ever, does a student hand in writing which has not first been in draft format and then read aloud by the author to a peer. In addition, if the students have become accustomed to using an editor's checklist, they are likely to improve their editing skills. We recognize, however, that learning to edit requires much practice and a certain maturity on the part of the student. This maturity results when the student writer can fully accept the idea that "*My first writing is not my best,*" and that "*Whatever I have written can be made better.*"

From the inception of your writing program, include the terminology of *self-editor, peer editor,* and "*top*" *editor* as discussed throughout this book. To further develop your students' editing skills, we recommend that you use our books **EDITING WRITES** and **PROOFWRITER.** **EDITING WRITES** contains activities which give the student practice in :

Adding Essential Details	Moving and Rearranging
Deleting Unnecessary Words	Revising for Audience
Substituting Exact Words	Correcting Mechanical Errors

Sample pages from these books are on pages 267 and 268.

PROOFWRITER is designed for the student who has difficulty with the common grammatical constructions (tense, verb agreement, singular/plural, etc.) and needs extensive practice in order to learn the skills of self-editing. Both of these programs provide the editing components necessary for a total writing program. We have included samples of these activities at the end of this chapter (page 267).

INITIATING SELF AND PEER EDITING
Be an editor!

An activity which students enjoy and find useful in improving their writing is playing the role of "editor." The following lesson can be presented to the whole class and will highlight for students the value of editing and revising. Suggested procedures are:

.   Duplicate a story from a workbook or language arts book which has been written at a simple level.

.   Explain to the students that they are to think of themselves as *editors* whose job it is to *improve* the story but not change the ideas.

.   Tell them to improve the story by adding, deleting, substituting, or rearranging words.

.   Have them use appropriate editing marks to indicate their changes —
    .   (to add) caret mark   ∧
    .   (to delete) cross-out line ~~cross-out~~
    .   (to substitute) cross-out line plus write-over   substitute ~~cross-out~~
    .   (to rearrange) circle-and-arrow

.   Have them read edited stories aloud and make any changes they feel will improve the story.

.   Then ask the students to recopy their new, improved versions *for publication.*

261

Peer Editing

After students have become fully aware of the editing and revision techniques through self-editing, they can be introduced to peer editing. Learning to peer edit is a gradual process which requires student understanding of the rules and procedures of editing. One way to begin peer editing is through a **Listening Committee.**

. Begin orally. You or a student read a composition to the class. The class is instructed to listen to a specific aspect of the writing (for example: *organization*) and then make suggestions for improvement. Their oral comments are shared. You may wish to begin with an anonymous selection and move to the students' own writings later.

. Teach the students how to be critics in a positive atmosphere. Appropriate positive comments are, "Do you think you need more details?" "Your ideas are great, but do you need some stronger and more interesting words?"

. You, the teacher, write notes on the board from students' oral comments.

. Give "author's privilege." The student author has the right to accept or reject advice relating to style or other aspects of his writing.

. Plan for publication. The writer decides what format to use for publishing the writing.

EVALUATING WRITING

At our workshops, we have asked teachers to express their feelings about grading student writing. Inevitably they say that red-pencil markings bring virtually no change in a student's subsequent writing. Yet teachers have felt obligated to meticulously correct student work, a practice which may improve the teacher's proofreading skills, but often leaves the student's composing skills unaffected. Evaluating writing, therefore, must have as its goal the *improvement* of the writing product through the *growing insight of the writer* — not the teacher. The writer has to be an active participant in the evaluation process and must be able to observe his/her growth and development. Consistent with the idea of *student as editor,* we suggest the following procedures for evaluation.

Keep a Writing Folder For Each Student

Every student should have a writing folder which contains *selected* pieces of the student's writing over a period of time. The folder should contain a variety of writing products which have been chosen jointly by the student and teacher. The pieces selected should also indicate changes or growth in the student's writing.

Take Specific Samples of Writing

In addition to having samples of student writing which have grown out of classroom activities, you may want writing samples which indicate how a student writes independently or in situations where there has been little direction. For this purpose, we recommend that you get at least three samples of independent writing during the school year, preferably in October, January, and May, using the following procedures:

. Discuss with the students topics of general interest and appropriateness.
. Elicit ideas, concepts, and vocabulary from the students and list them on the board or chart.
. Ask each student to write a first draft on a selected topic.
. Collect the drafts and return them several days later completely *uncorrected.*
. Ask the students to reread their compositions and identify ways to improve them.
. Have the students rewrite their draft copy.
. Collect both the original drafts and the second copies and review them for revision.
. Conference either individually or with small groups to discuss the necessary revisions.
. Ask each student to make revisions, edit, and make a final copy.

Analyzing the Writing Samples

Because analyzing student writing is often a lengthy process, grade only selected pieces of each student's writing. Use a combination of *holistic assessment, primary traits,* and *detailed analysis,* and compare the student's growth only against his or her own previously written products, rather than against other students' writings. Unlike giving a grade in spelling or math, you cannot unequivocally state that a student's paper is 100, 87, or 63. Even the grading system of A, B, or C strains your powers of decision-making. Because of the subjectivity of grading papers, we would like to offer these suggestions.

First, you should be familiar with the following terms which are currently used in evaluating writing:

Holistic Assessment refers to grading a paper based upon first impressions of organization, keeping to the topic, elaboration of details, and general fulfillment of the paper's purpose. Mechanics and spelling are considered secondary to the evaluation of ideas and content. In *holistic assessment,* you judge the total quality of the student's writing without specific attention to details of grammar and spelling. If possible, you can seek confirmation of your assessment by having one or two colleagues read the composition and give their reactions. After you have determined your assessment holistically, you might want to rate it on a scale of 1 (poor) to 5 (excellent). Then analyze it for specific content using the writing checklist forms at the end of this chapter.

Primary Traits serve as a basis for evaluation on the specific requirements of the assignment, such as attention to genre, length, paragraph organization, style, and format. As in holistic assessment, evaluation by primary traits does not focus on mechanics or spelling, but places emphasis upon clarity of ideas and organization.

Analytic Assessment is used when you need a thorough diagnosis of a student's writing. You begin by looking at the writing for primary traits and then for correct usage, spelling, punctuation, and other aspects that prepare a piece of writing for "publication" or viewing by others. Use of appropriate mechanics becomes a criterion.

Decide on your purpose for evaluation. If you need to quickly evaluate the range of your students' writing abilities, or if you need to know broadly what types of writing your students know how to do, use holistic assessment. However, when you begin to teach your students specific genres, look for the primary traits. For example, when you evaluate a **THREE REASONS WHY** essay, look for three significantly different reasons with clearly stated supporting sentences. If you have asked for a character study and have *provided* the students with exact and clear requirements, look for the fulfillment of those requirements. Use analytic assessment when you need to analyze a student's strengths and weaknesses. As we mentioned, fully assess a piece of writing only when the student has to prepare it for others to read. For total analytic assessment, we recommend that you use the Writing Checklists at the end of this chapter.

Evaluate only those aspects of the writing which contain elements that students have been taught and have *practiced.* To grade a student's paper on "What I Did Last Summer" is unfair to both you and the student unless you have taught the format for such a paper and the student has practiced several types of writing which can be used for this purpose.

Finally, grade only those papers which have met the basic criteria or "primary traits." In our workshops, we have strongly urged teachers to guide their students through a piece of writing so that even the draft copy can be graded "Very Good," or **VG.** This means that you provide your students, *in advance,* with the criteria for the grade. Then check their organizing schemes or outlines for **VG** before you permit them to proceed with the full-length piece. We believe you will find that this procedure, while time-consuming initially, saves you many hours of grading badly-written papers and returning these papers with comments which your students may not always appreciate. We strongly urge your sitting down with each student individually to discuss his/her actual writings as frequently as possible, using selected items on the Student Writing Checklists on pages 269 and 270 as a guide for your conferences.

GIVING A GRADE

At the elementary school level teachers may feel quite comfortable in not giving grades for specific pieces of writing. Young students are often satisfied with comments such as, "I loved your story," or "This article certainly belongs on the outside bulletin board." However, by junior high school and through college, students assume that they get either number or letter grades for their writing. Yet as we have already mentioned, such grades are difficult to determine objectively. Perhaps the following concepts on grading will help:

. Think of every paper as potentially rating an "A" on the assumption that the student has unlimited time or motivation to continually revise the draft until it meets your criteria or specifications.

. Then use the Writing Checklists (page 271 or 272) and mark each aspect of the writing that needs to be improved or revised; for example, the checklist might note that the student has done everything to meet the pre-established criteria except write a sufficient amount for the assignment or use varied sentence structure. If the student appropriately *adds* to the writing and *substitutes* repetitive starters with varied and more precise starters, the student's grade is an "A" since all criteria were fulfilled.

When teachers have pointed out to us that the above system might result in almost everyone getting an "A," we had to respond (perhaps chidingly), "Then get a bigger box of 'A's!"

A final word on this rather difficult subject. Please do not resort to the terribly misused system of grading separately for "content" and "grammar." If you have a piece of writing that has excellent or good content, say to the student, "Your writing is so well done that it is a shame to let it remain with so many grammatical (or spelling) mistakes." On the other hand, if a piece of writing is grammatically perfect, but does not address the purpose of the writing, then we suggest that you politely and gently tell the student to "try again," "do it over," or even "put it away."

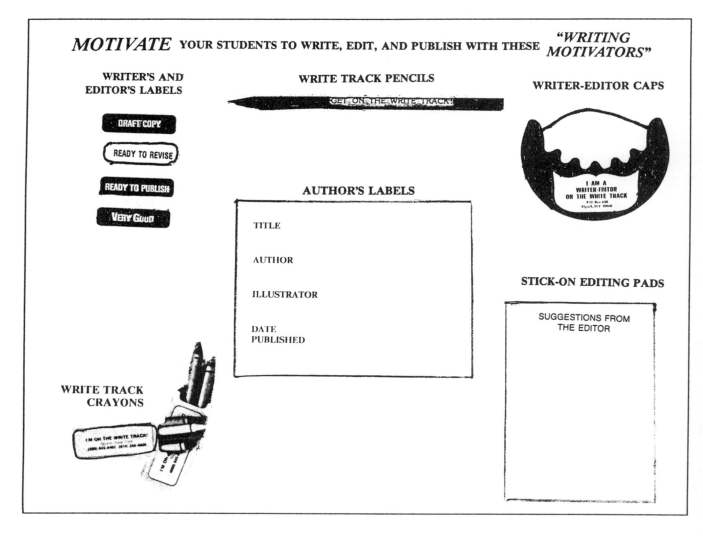

REVISE BY ADDING, SUBSTITUTING, DELETING, AND COMBINING

Use the skills you have learned to improve the story below:

> Add details to sentences where there are caret marks.
> Substitute better, more interesting words for the bolded words.
> Remove any unnecessary words and phrases.
> Combine short, choppy sentences.

You may also make any other changes that will improve this story.

SPACE STORY

My space adventure in outer space was **very nice**. The rocket took off .

. . . . .∧. . . . . and zoomed . . . . . .∧. . . . . We traveled for three months. We

finally landed on a **planet**. Tiny little creatures with three eyes . . . . .∧. . . .

welcomed us. They had . . . . . .∧. . . . arms. They had . . . . .∧. . . . . legs.

These creatures didn't talk. Instead, they mad[e]

hands which we didn't understand. They wer[e]

homes where they lived. After **a while**, they [took us]

spaceship. Then we headed back to Earth wh[ere]

always remember this **really good** adventure [in space]

CHECK YOURSELF
- Did you add important details to your story?
- Did you replace the bolded words with better, [more interesting words?]
- Did you remove unnecessary words?
- Did you combine short, choppy sentences?

WORK WITH A CLASSMATE
- Compare the sentences you combined with thos[e of a classmate]
- Are there any other changes you can make to im[prove your story?]

PUBLISH YOUR STORY
If you can, type your revised story on a computer. [Share it with]
your friends and family.

REVISE BY ADDING, SUBSTITUTING, DELETING, AND COMBINING

Compare your editing with the editing below. Your version will be different.

SPACE STORY

My space adventure ~~in outer space~~ was ~~very nice~~. **incredible.** The rocket took off~~.~~ ~~e~~

without a problem . . . . .∧. . . . . and zoomed . . . . . .∧. . . . . **into space at eight hundred miles an hour.** We traveled for three months. We

finally landed on ~~a planet.~~ **Jupiter.** Tiny little creatures with three eyes . . . . .∧. . . . **on the top of their head**

welcomed us. They had . . . . . .∧. . . . **ten different sized .** arms. They had . . . . . .∧. . . . . **short, stubby** legs.

These creatures didn't talk. Instead, they made . . . . . .∧. . . **strange** signs with their

hands~~,~~ ~~which we didn't understand.~~ **However,** ~~They were friends.~~ ~~They~~ **they** **friendly and** took us to their

homes ~~,~~ ~~where they lived.~~ After ~~a while,~~ **three weeks** they took us ~~right~~ back to our

spaceship. ~~Then~~ we ~~headed~~ **were heading** **Within minutes** back to Earth ~~where we came from.~~ ~~I know~~ I'll

always remember this ~~really good~~ **thrilling** adventure ~~in space~~.

SAMPLE EDITING ACTIVITIES FROM ProofWriter*

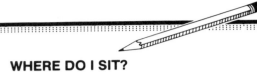

WHERE DO I SIT?

DIRECTIONS: Correct the errors. The hints below each sentence are given in order. Use the Peer Checklist. Compare your corrected sentences with those on the next page. Then rewrite the sentences correctly on another piece of paper.

1) i wonder were i should sit at are thanksgiving diner.
   capital spelling spelling capital spelling

2) it doesnt seem rite to sit with the younger childern
   capital contraction homonym spelling period

3) Thay yells end play swords with the drumstiks
   spelling noun/verb agreement spelling spelling period

4) Wouldnt you be embarrass by the sillyness of the childs.
   contraction noun/verb agreement spelling plural question mark

5) the adults talk about monee and people they no
   capital spelling homonym period

6) Have the time I cant figure out wat they are says
   spelling contraction spelling noun/verb agreement period

7) Wen I due try to tak, Know one lisens to me.
   spelling homonym spelling homonym spelling

8) I might says loudly, I have thos problems wit
   noun/verb agreement quotation spelling hor

9) i hate this I think families shud have have kids
   capital period spelling omit spelling spelling

10) then they're would bee people I could talk twc
   capital homonym homonym homonym peri

PEER CHECKLIST:
Compare your corrections with those of a cla
Take turns reading your sentences aloud to ε

UNIT V

SPRING FEVER

DIRECTIONS: Correct the underlined errors. The hints below each sentence tell you what corrections to make. Use the Peer Checklist. Compare your corrected sentences with those on the next page. Then rewrite the sentences correctly on another piece of paper.

1) most day   school are fine, but during The Spring I gets restless.
   capital plural noun/verb agreement capital noun/verb agreement

2) The whether is grate and i want to be outside geting a suntan_
   homonym homonym capital spelling period

3) you sweat and sticks to the school_s plastic chairs__
   capital spelling noun/verb agreement possessive period

4) You're brane doesn_t work very well wen its hot.
   contraction spelling contraction spelling contraction

5) i yawn and and sometimes fall aslep at My desk__
   capital omit spelling capital period

6) Won day my Math teacher call_ on me to anser __ question.
   homonym capital noun/verb agreement spelling add

7) Unfortuneately, I ____ fallen asleep and didnt here her__
   spelling add contraction homonym period

8) The hole class laugh_ at me__   i felt dum.
   homonym noun/verb agreement period capital spelling

9) my parent's still expect me to study_ butt I don't want too.
   capital plural comma homonym homonym

10) I thinks shool should end buy march 15th__
   plural spelling homonym capital period

PEER CHECKLIST:
Compare your corrections with those of a classmate's.
Take turns reading your sentences aloud to each other.

UNIT II

*AVAILABLE FROM ERA/CCR CORP.

WRITING CHECKLIST
Primary Grades

Scale of 1 to 5 (high)
N.O. Not Observed

Name of child _____

Grade _____

School _____

Holistic Assessment

	Oct.	Jan.	May
Superior	—	—	—
Very Good	—	—	—
Good	—	—	—
Poor	—	—	—
Very Poor	—	—	—

Comments
List Titles of Writing Products
& Dates Completed

	Oct.	Jan.	May
UNDERSTANDING OF TASK			
1. Uses draft format			
2. Writes on topic			
SEMANTIC ORGANIZATION			
3. Organizes logically			
4. Uses a topic sentence			
5. Uses a support sentence			
6. Writes conclusions			
SENTENCE STRUCTURE			
7. Writes complete sentences			
8. Uses varied sentence structure			
9. Uses pronouns appropriately			
10. Uses tenses appropriately			
VOCABULARY & LANGUAGE			
11. Uses varied nouns and verbs			
12. Uses various adjectives			
MECHANICS			
13. Uses end punctuation			
14. Uses beginning capitals			
15. Uses proper name capitals			
16. Spells correctly			
PROOFREADING & IMPROVING (Teacher directed)			
17. Slots for adjectives			
18. Replaces with synonyms			
19. Combines into series or other forms			
20. Finds errors in capitalization			
21. Finds errors in end punctuation			
22. Finds errors in spelling			
FLUENCY			
23. Writes sufficient amount for the assignment			

WRITING CHECKLIST
GRADES 4 - 12

Scale of 1 to 5 (high)
N.O.—Not Observed

Name of Student _____

Grade _____

School _____

Holistic Assessment

	Oct.	Jan.	May
Superior	—	—	—
Very Good	—	—	—
Good	—	—	—
Poor	—	—	—
Very Poor	—	—	—

Comments
(List Titles of Writing Products & Dates Completed)

	Oct.	Jan.	May
UNDERSTANDING OF TASK			
1. Uses draft format			
2. Writes on topic			
3. Has consistent point of view			
4. Indicates sense of audience			
SEMANTIC ORGANIZATION			
5. Organizes logically			
6. Paragraphs correctly			
7. Uses topic sentences			
8. Uses support sentences			
9. Writes conclusions			
SENTENCE STRUCTURE			
10. Writes complete sentences			
11. Uses varied sentence structure			
12. Uses pronouns appropriately			
13. Uses appropriate transitional words ("however", "therefore", etc.)			
14. Uses tenses appropriately			
VOCABULARY & LANGUAGE			
15. Distinguishes between spoken and written language			
16. Uses varied nouns and verbs			
17. Uses varied adjectives			
18. Uses adverbs and adverbial phrases			
MECHANICS			
19. Uses end punctuation			
20. Uses internal punctuation			
21. Uses beginning capitals			
22. Uses proper name capitals			
23. Spells correctly			
PROOFREADING & IMPROVING			
24. Slots for adjectives			
25. Replaces with synonyms			
26. Combines into series or other forms			
27. Shifts adverbs			
28. Shifts sentences or phrases			
29. Combines sentences with words other than "and"			
30. Uses apposition			
31. Finds errors in mechanics			
32. Finds error in syntax			
33. Finds errors in organization			
34. Finds errors in spelling			
FLUENCY			
35. Writes sufficient amount for the assignment			

STUDENT'S WRITING CHECKLIST
Steps in Reviewing My Draft

My Name_____ School_____

DATES

1. I understood the task. I
   a. used a draft format
   b. wrote on the topic
   c. thought about whom I was writing to
   d. wrote as much as I was supposed to

2. My writing is organized. I
   a. wrote logically
   b. used topic sentences
   c. used support sentences
   d. wrote a conclusion

3. I have good sentences. I
   a. wrote complete sentences
   b. used different kinds of sentences
   c. used pronouns correctly
   d. used the right forms of the verbs

4. My vocabulary and language are interesting. I
   a. used different nouns and verbs
   b. used many different adjectives and adverbs

5. I revised my writing. I
   a. added adjectives and other interesting words
   b. substituted repeated and "boring" words
   c. took away extra or unnecessary words
   d. combined short, choppy sentences
   e. moved words and sentences that were in the
      wrong place

6. I proofread my writing. I
   a. checked for capital letters
   b. checked for punctuation
   c. checked my spelling

FORM I

STUDENT'S WRITING CHECKLIST
Steps in Reviewing My Draft

My Name_____ School_____

DATES

1. I understood the assignment. I
   a. used a draft format
   b. wrote on the topic
   c. kept a consistent point of view
   d. addressed my audience appropriately
   e. wrote a sufficient amount for the topic

2. My writing is organized. I
   a. wrote logically
   b. used topic sentences
   c. used support sentences
   d. wrote a conclusion
   e. paragraphed correctly

3. I used good sentence structure. I
   a. wrote complete sentences
   b. used varied types of sentences
   c. used pronouns appropriately
   d. used appropriate transitional words
   e. used tenses correctly
   f. used apposition

4. My vocabulary and language are appropriate for my audience. I
   a. distinguished between spoken and written language
   b. used varied nouns and verbs
   c. used a variety of adjectives and describers
   d. used adverbs and adverbial phrases to improve my writing style

5. I revised my writing. I
   a. added adjectives and other interesting words
   b. substituted repeated and "boring" words
   c. deleted unnecessary words
   d. combined short, choppy sentences
   e. shifted words, phrases, and sentences to improve my style
   f. used transitional words to link ideas

6. I proofread my writing. I
   a. checked for final and internal punctuation
   b. checked for beginning and proper name capital letters
   c. corrected my spelling errors

Form II

SCOPE AND SEQUENCE FOR DEVELOPING AND EVALUATING WRITING SKILLS
K — 12

EMPHASIS	ORAL SKILLS	WRITING SKILLS	EDITING SKILLS
		KINDERGARTEN	
• Developing oral skills to serve as a basis for written expression	• contributes to group discussion	• has rudiments of "invented spelling"	• can suggest words to add or subtract in a group composition
	• tells a story from a sequence of pictures	• begins many words with correct or nearly correct consonant	
	• tells a story in sequential form	• scribble "writes" notes and brief messages	
	• can dictate a story		
	• can supply titles for group composition and captions for pictures		
	• can use a word in a sentence with correct meaning		

EMPHASIS	ORAL SKILLS	WRITING SKILLS	EDITING SKILLS
		FIRST GRADE	
• Exploring writing as a means of commun-ication to different audiences	• all previous pre-writing skills are reinforced	• expands invented spelling to include vowels	• can read original written stories aloud to teacher and group for editing purposes
	• can present one or two ideas in sentence form	• can begin to use *two* words in one sentence	• develops understand-ing of draft copy
	• can indicate meaning or usage of a word in a complete sentence	• can write an idea in a simple sentence	
		• can write at least two original sent-ences on a topic	
		• can begin to write simple captions and story titles	

EMPHASIS	ORAL SKILLS	WRITING SKILLS	EDITING SKILLS
		SECOND GRADE	
• Developing writing as means of communic-ation to to varied audiences	• all previous pre-writing skills are reinforced	• can select a topic of interest to self and others	• begins to understand words proofreading and editing
	• can contribute to the development of word lists through group brainstorming	• can expand a simple sentence by answering wh- questions	• can proofread for sentence sense
	• can brainstorm an individual list on a familiar topic of three to five words	• can list events and directions in sequence	• can proofread for capitals at beginning of sentences and end punctuation
	• participates in writing conferences	• can write a paragraph of at least 3 sentences on a topic	• can suggest improvements in peer editing situations
		• can write a story with beginning, middle, and end	• can use caret mark (ʌ) for expanding and cross-out _kind_ ~~nice~~ for substitution
		• can write invitations, thank you notes, and a friendly letter	
		• can address an envelope	
		• can write a simple report using a framed outline	
		• can write simple poetry forms	

EMPHASIS	ORAL SKILLS	WRITING SKILLS	EDITING SKILLS
		THIRD GRADE	
• Expanding types of writing (genre): personal expression directions events poetry simple narrative	• all previous pre-writing skills are reinforced	• can write a friendly letter	• begins to understand concept of revise
	• can brainstorm individ-ually and in a small group	• can write a set of directions or "how to"	• can revise sentences by expansion or substitution
	• can explain or "rehearse" a story before writing	• can write a topic sentence and three or four supporting details to form a paragraph	• can revise story for paragraph division
		• can begin to write in response to content areas	

EMPHASIS	ORAL SKILLS	WRITING SKILLS	EDITING SKILLS
		FOURTH GRADE	
• Further expanding and refining of students' writing: writes simple social studies reports, describes animals, persons, and objects	• all previous writing skills are reinforced • enlarges "rehearsal" techniques for planing full-length piece	• can write a business letter • can write a simple autobiography using framed outline • can write a fable, myth, tall tale using framed outline • can write 2 or more paragraphs about a person, event, or topic related to science or social studies • can write a one-page story or report • can write a **biography** using a framed outline • can develop simple plots and use narrative and dialogue	• continues use of proof-reading symbols: adds move sign ↜ to moving and rearranging

EMPHASIS	ORAL SKILLS	WRITING SKILLS	EDITING SKILLS
		FIFTH GRADE	
• Developing a "style" in writing by improvement in clarity, sentence variety, and imagery	• all previous writing skills are reinforced • participates in peer writing conferences • critiques peer writing based on teacher direction	• can write a three-reason essay for personal expression • can write a specialized story: ghost, mystery, humor, etc. • can write news articles and titles • can write a personal observation of an event • can write at least three related paragraphs • can prepare interview questions • can write dialogue and prepare an outline • can write a two-page story or report • can write a bibliography for books and encyclopedias	• uses writing checklist to revise compositions • revises for varied vocabulary • uses thesaurus, dictionary, etc. • revises for correct punctuation • revises for sequential organization

EMPHASIS	ORAL SKILLS	WRITING SKILLS	EDITING SKILLS
		SIXTH GRADE	
• Exploring the different types of writing: fiction, journalism, research, biography	• all previous writing skills are reinforced	• uses three-reason format to write a persuasive essay	• revises for style using peer-editing
		• can write a short biography	• revises for correct form and punctuation
		• can write a short story	
		• can write up an experiment	
		• can write a short play or dialogue story	
		• can write an opinion article	
		• can write several styles of poetry	
		• can write a business letter requesting inform-ation of material	
		• can write three or more related paragraphs	
		• can complete a simple application form	
		• can prepare at least 2 or 3 page research paper using simple notetaking, outline, table of contents, bibliography	

EMPHASIS	WRITING SKILLS	EDITING SKILLS
	SEVENTH AND EIGHTH GRADES	
• Planning and generating full-length composings	• all previous writing skills are reinforced	• evaluates own and peer writing for: organization topic development appropriate usage intended audience
	• uses three-reason format to write explanatory and informative essays	
	• can write multiple paragraph piece	• proofreads for sentence fragments, run-ons, non-agreements
	• can use a combination of dialogue and narrative	• distinguishes between formal and informal language
	• can use direct quotations from oral and written sources	
	• practices a variety of genres	

EMPHASIS	WRITING SKILLS	EDITING SKILLS
	GRADES NINE THROUGH TWELVE	
• writing with unity, clarity and coherence	• can write several forms of genre: fiction, non-fiction, research	• writes more than one draft revises fully and appropriately
	• can support opinion and fact with documentation	• uses mature references unabridged dictionaries, thesauruses, original sources
	• can write analytically on ideas and concepts	• evaluates own and peer writing
	• can write for a variety of audiences: young, peer, adult	

We would like to call your attention to the organization of the scope and sequence. It consists of oral (pre-writing) skills, writing skills, proofreading, instructional techniques, and terminolgy. Each of these areas are utilized at every grade level, except kindergarten which does not have "writing." All skills taught at one level are reinforced at the next level, with new skills added on. You will also find that the writing techniques taught at one grade are not expected to be independently applied by the student until the following year. On the scope and sequence, therefore, you will note that "instructional techniques" do not get incorporated into "editing skills" until a year later.

WRITE TRACK GLOSSARY

ABC Listing — A procedure for having students list or brainstorm items on a topic and place them alphabetically

Acrostic — A device in which the writer uses a different letter of the alphabet to begin each sentence or phrase

Active Participation — Each student personally responds in writing to the teacher's questions or requests

Advance Organizers — The gathering and listing of items on a topic which come from prior knowledge, but which will be used to acquire new knowledge

Analytic Scoring — An evaluation system in which the reader judges a piece of writing based on all aspects of "final copy": length, voice, style, mechanics, grammar, layout

Attributes — The qualities or characteristics of a particular concept, person, or character

Book of Lists — A student's personal thesaurus, arranged alphabetically in a small notebook, containing words and phrases related to subject areas and items of personal interest

"Bought" Words — All the subject area vocabulary which students are expected to learn in their school years; examples: *subtraction, peninsula, acids* and *bases, mammals,* etc.

Brainstorm — A free association of words and phrases related to a given topic, the purpose of which is to acquire a variety of ideas

Cluster — Words associated with and organized around a key word or phrase

Collaborate — The sharing or exchanging of words and phrases (ideas) by two or several people in a group

Combining — An editing strategy in which of two or more sentences are joined through deleting and/or expanding

Content Areas — Subject areas such as Social Studies, Math, Health, Science, etc.

Cooperate — A small group of students who search for and share information on a given topic (similar to collaborate)

Cross-Pollinate — Gathering and sharing ideas from "outside" groups or from other seemingly unrelated topics. For example, words from a social studies topic may suggest ideas in math

Definition Mode — A three-part procedure for defining a word, consisting of QUESTION, GENERAL CATEGORY, and ATTRIBUTES

Deleting — An editing procedure for removing redundant or unnecessary words

Draft Copy — The first or unedited copy in which details such as spelling, punctuation, indentation, and overall format are minimized

Eagle Eyes — The editor (peer or "top") who reviews a paper for spelling, punctuation, capitalization, and minor word errors

Editing — The total process of moving a draft copy through revision, proofreading, and final copy production

Editor — One of several people who help move a piece to final copy, including self-editors (the writers), peer editors (classmates, colleagues), and "top" editors (teacher, writing expert)

Etymology — The study of the origin of words; example: *impedimenta* meaning baggage in Latin

Expanding — Adding words, phrases, or sentences to provide more information to the audience or to make a piece of writing more interesting

Final Copy — The reworked draft ready for the audience or publication

Fluency — The ability to evoke (call forth) and use specific words on a given topic both orally and in writing

Frame — A writing "starter" that provides the structural format for a genre. For example, a frame for a fairy tale might start, "Once upon a time there was a .... who ...."

General Category — The segment in the Definition Mode that defines the category to which an item belongs; example: A dinosaur belongs to the category of *reptiles*

Genre — A specific form of writing such as fairy tale, myth, essay, narration, and so forth

Good/Better/Best — The terms used to evaluate any three pieces of writing of a particular student

Grammar — 1. The total system of rules that govern language or a particular language 2. The school subject which deals with labeling different words and constructions of a specific language

Holistic Scoring — An evaluation system in which the reader judges a piece of writing based on its totality rather than on specific details

Improvers — The four basic ways to revise or improve a piece of writing: add, delete, substitute, move, or rearrange

Interactive Writing — A term to describe the imagined writings of fictional character to fictional character or of historic character to historic character

Invented Spelling — The spelling used by young children prior to formal spelling instruction

Journals — A genre for free, unedited, personal, expression

Keeping Track — A system (of notebooks) for students to enter newly-learned concepts or to "keep track" of writing procedures

Listing — A "starting" procedure for collecting words (ideas) related to a given topic

Metacognition — The consciously-aware knowledge carried by an individual, summarized as "What do I know that I know?" and "What do I know that I don't know?"

Magic "Who" —An organizational frame for writing 1) about oneself, 2) about a famous person, 3) about literary characters

Martian — A "distant" audience who needs exceptionally clear written statements or directions

Morphology — The study of the different grammatical forms of words, also known as prefixes and suffixes (or affixes)

Moving and Rearranging — An editing procedure which results in improved organization or style of a piece of writing

Organization — The aspect of writing that permits a reader to follow the thinking of the writer

Primary Traits — An evaluation system in which the reader or editor judges a piece of writing based on the aspects of the assignment or "traits"; for example, length, number of paragraphs, specialized vocabulary, etc.

Proofreading — An editing procedure mainly to find grammatical and punctuation errors

Publishing — Bringing a piece to final copy and sharing it through display or distribution

Q.A.D. — An outlining or planning procedure in which the writer asks QUESTIONS, responds first with a general ANSWER, and then adds related DETAILS

Read-Aloud — A planned, scheduled reading aloud program which presents to students carefully chosen literature that meets specific literary criteria

Revised Copy — The reworked draft copy which has been improved with appropriate expansions, deletions, substitutions, and rearrangements

Sentence Composing (Synthesis) — A "starter" procedure in which the writer selects key words from a brainstormed list to begin a piece of writing

Starters — The basic ways to start a piece of writing: Words, Sentences, WH-Questions, Frames, Outlines

Substituting — An editing procedure in which a word, phrase, sentence, or punctuation mark is substituted to improve the writing

Three Reasons Why — An outlining procedure for writing personal, persuasive, and explanatory essays

"Top" Editor — In school, the teacher or editing "expert" who decides when the draft is in final copy

Unifiers — Those aspects of a curriculum that are related to a school's theme. For example, with writing as a core or theme, unifiers might be the Book of Lists, Read-Aloud, Journals, Structures and Genres, Speak-Up/Speak Out, Keeping Track, and others

Very Good — An initial evaluation indicating that the student has followed all the directions related to the written assignment

Whole Sentence — A grammatical construction that contains both a subject (noun, noun phrase, or pronoun) and a verb form known as the predicate; in contrast to Half Sentence which contains either the subject or the predicate

Writer's Questions — The basic questions a writer needs to ask to satisfactorily complete a written assignment: How long? What should I say? How do I start? What counts?

Writing from Key Words — Using a collection of words or phrases to write on a given topic

Writing Implement — Any writing instrument: pencil, pen, marker, chalk

Writing Surface — Any area which can be written on: paper, chalkboard, tablet, slate

Words Are Free — A slogan that indicates to the student that words and phrases can be shared and used by anyone who has access to them, in contrast to the statement "Sentences are not ....[free]."

Whole Language — A term used to indicate the interrelatedness of listening, speaking, writing, and reading as the basis for becoming fully literate

WH-Questions — The questions starters WHO, WHAT, WHERE, WHEN, WHY, HOW

BIBLIOGRAPHY

Atwell, Nancie
 IN THE MIDDLE. Portsmouth, NH: Heinemann, 1987.

Bell, James K. and Adrian A. Cahn
 HANDBOOK OF GRAMMAR, STYLE, AND USAGE (second edition).
 Beverly Hills: Benziger Bruce & Glencoe, Inc. 1976.

Berlitz, Charles
 NATIVE TONGUES. New York: Grosset & Dunlap, 1982.

Bernardt, Bill
 JUST WRITING. New York: Teachers and Writers Collaborative,
 1977.

Berthoff, Ann E.
 FORMING, THINKING, WRITING. Rochelle Park, N.J.: Hayden
 Book Company, Inc., 1978.

Bramer, Mary
 THE DESPERATION OF DAY TWO. New York: Scholastic Book
 Services, 1980.

Britton, James, et al.
 THE DEVELOPMENT OF WRITING ABILITIES (11-18). London:
 Macmillan Education Ltd., 1977.

Bruner, Jerome S.
 THE PROCESS OF EDUCATION. Cambridge, MA: Harvard
 University Press, 1960.

Bruner, Jerome S., et al.
 A STUDY OF THINKING. New York: Wiley, 1977.

Bryson, Bill
 THE MOTHER TONGUE — ENGLISH AND HOW IT GOT THAT WAY.
 New York: William Morrow and Company, 1990.

Bruce, Bertram, Sara Michaels, Karen Watson-Gageo.
 How Computers Can Change the Writing Process.
 LANGUAGE ARTS, Vol. 62 (2) February, 1985, pp. 143-149.

Calkins, Lucy M.
 LESSONS FROM A CHILD. Exeter, New Hampshire: Heinemann
 Educational Books, 1983.

Cassedy, Sylvia
 IN YOUR OWN WORDS. Garden City, N.Y.: Doubleday & Company,
 1979.

Church, Susan M.
Blossoming in the Writing Community. LANGUAGE ARTS,
Vol. 62 (2), February, 1985, pp. 175-179.

Clay, Marie M.
WHAT DID I WRITE? London: Heinemann Educational Books, Ltd.,
1975.

Collins, John
THE EFFECTIVE WRITING TEACHER. Andover, Mass.: The Network,
Inc., 1985.

Cooper, Charles R. and Lee Odell
EVALUATING WRITING. Buffalo: State University of New York,
1985.

Costa, Arthur L., Editor
DEVELOPING MINDS. Alexandria, Va.: Association for Supervision
and Curriculum Development, 1985.

Intelligent Human Behavior and How to Develop It.
Workshop presented at Texas ASCD Convention, Galveston, Texas, 1988.

Donovan, Timothy R. and Ben McClelland (editors)
EIGHT APPROACHES TO TEACHING COMPOSITION. Urbana, Ill.:
National Council of Teachers of English, 1980.

Dowhower, Sarah, et al
Improving Writing Instruction Through Staff Development.
JOURNAL OF STAFF DEVELOPMENT, Vol. 2, Summer, 1990.

Duckworth, Eleanor
**THE HAVING OF WONDERFUL IDEAS AND OTHER ESSAYS ON TEACHING AND
LEARNING.** New York: Teachers College Press, 1987.

Elbow, Peter
WRITING WITHOUT TEACHERS. New York: Oxford University Press,
1973.
WRITING WITH POWER. New York: Oxford University Press, 1981.

Emig, Janet
THE WEB OF MEANING. Upper Montclair, N.J.: Boynton/Cook
Publishers, Inc. 1983.

Foster, David
A PRIMER FOR WRITING TEACHERS. Upper Montclair, N.J.: Boynton/
Cook Publishers, Inc. 1983.

Frank, Marjorie
**IF YOU'RE TRYING TO TEACH KIDS HOW TO WRITE, YOU'VE
GOTTA HAVE THIS BOOK.**
Nashville: Incentive Programs, 1979.

Goodman, Kenneth
WHAT'S WHOLE IN WHOLE LANGUAGE? Portsmouth, NH:
Heinemann, 1986.

Goodman, Kenneth., and Yetta M. Goodman
THE WHOLE LANGUAGE EVALUATION BOOK.
Portsmouth, NH: Heinemann, 1988

Graves, Donald H.
WRITING: TEACHERS & CHILDREN AT WORK. London: Heinemann Educational
Books, 1983.

Gretton, Francis and Ann Gewing
WRITE! WRITE! WRITE!. New York: College Skills Center, 1982.

Geuder, Patricia, et al. (editors)
THEY REALLY TAUGHT US HOW TO WRITE. Urbana, Ill.: National
Council of Teachers of English, 1974.

Guilford, J.P.
Traits of Creativity. In H. Anderson (Ed.) CREATIVITY AND
ITS CULTIVATION. New York: Harper and Row, 1958.

Hailey, Jack
TEACHING WRITING K-8. Berkeley: The Instructional Laboratory,
University of California, 1978.

Haley-James, Shirley
PERSPECTIVES ON WRITING IN GRADES 1-8. Urbana, Ill.: National
Council of Teachers of English, 1981.

Hall, Janice K.
EVALUATING AND IMPROVING WRITTEN EXPRESSION. Boston: Allyn &
Bacon, Inc., 1981.

Hasenstab, M. Suzanne and Joan Laughton
READING, WRITING, AND THE EXCEPTIONAL CHILD. Rockville, Md.:
Aspen Systems Corporation, 1982.

Hawley, Robert C. and Isabel L. Hawley
WRITING FOR THE FUN OF IT. Amherst, Mass.: Education Research
Associates, 1974.

Hennings, Dorothy Grant and Barbara Moll Grant
WRITTEN EXPRESSION IN THE LANGUAGE ARTS. New York: Teachers
College, Columbia University, 1981.

Hillerich, Robert L.
SPELLING: AN ELEMENT IN WRITTEN EXPRESSION. Columbus: Charles
E. Merrill Publishing Company, 1976.

Hipple, Marjorie L.
Journal Writing in Kindergarten. LANGUAGE ARTS, Vo. 62, (3)
March, 1985, pp. 225-261.

Hirsch, E.D. Jr.
CULTURAL LITERACY. Boston: Houghton Mifflin, 1987.

Hollingsworth, Helen and Susan Eastman
TEACHING WRITING IN EVERY CLASS: A GUIDE FOR GRADES
6 TO 12. Boston: Allyn and Bacon, 1988.

Hubbard, Ruth
Second Graders Answer the Question "Why Publish?". THE
READING TEACHER, Vol. 38, (7), March, 1985, pp. 658-662.

Hunt, Cecil
WORD ORIGINS: THE ROMANCE OF LANGUAGE. New York: Philosophical Library,
1949.

Hunt, Kellogg W.
GRAMMATICAL STRUCTURES WRITTEN AT THREE GRADE LEVELS. Urbana,
Ill.: National Council of Teachers of English, 1965.

Johnson, Roger and David
COOPERATION IN THE CLASSROOM. Edina, MN: Interaction
Book Company, 1988.

LEARNING TOGETHER AND ALONE. 2nd Edition, Englewood Cliffs,
NJ: Prentice Hall, Inc. 1987.

Joos, Martin
THE FIVE CLOCKS. New York: Harcourt Brace Jovanovich,
1967.

Judy, Susan and Stephen
GIFTS OF WRITING: CREATIVE PROJECTS WITH WORDS AND ART. New
York: Charles Scribner's Sons, 1980.

Kahn, Elizabeth, et al.
WRITING ABOUT LITERATURE. Urbana, Ill.: ERIC/NCTE, 1984.

Kasdan, Lawrence N. and Daniel R. Hoebner (Editors)
BASIC WRITING: ESSAYS FOR TEACHERS, RESEARCHERS,
ADMINISTRATORS. Urbana, Ill.: National Council of Teachers
of English, 1976.

Malmstrom, Jean
   UNDERSTANDING LANGUAGE. New York: St. Martin's Press, 1977.

McCrum, Robert, et al.
   THE STORY OF ENGLISH. New York: Elisabeth Sifton Books.
   1986.

Mellon, John
   TRANSFORMATIONAL SENTENCE-COMBINING: A METHOD FOR ENHANCING
   THE DEVELOPMENT OF SYNTACTIC FLUENCY IN ENGLISH COMPOSITION.
   Urbana, Ill.: National Council of Teachers of English, 1969.

Moberg, Goran
   WRITING IN GROUPS. New York: The Writing Consultant, 1984.

Murray, Donald M.
   A TEACHER TEACHES WRITING. Boston: Houghton Mifflin
   Company, 1968.

   WRITE TO LEARN. New York: Holt, Rinehart and Winston, 1984.

Myers, Miles
   A PROCEDURE FOR WRITING ASSESSMENT AND HOLISTIC SCORING.
   Urbana, Ill.: National Council of Teachers of English, 1980.

Newman, Judith M., Editor
   WHOLE LANGUAGE: THEORY IN USE. Portsmouth, NH: Heinemann,
   1985.

O'Hare, Frank
   SENTENCE COMBINING: IMPROVING STUDENT WRITING WITHOUT FORMAL
   GRAMMAR INSTRUCTION. Urbana, Ill.: National Council of Teachers
   of English, 1973.

Olson, Carol Booth
   PRACTICAL IDEAS FOR TEACHING WRITING. California State
   Department of Education, 1986.

Piazza, Carolyn L. and Carl M. Tomlinson
   A Concert of Writers. LANGUAGE ARTS, Vol. 72 (2),
   February, 1985, pp. 150-158.

Pisano, Anita and Marilyn Tallerico
   Improving Writing Instruction Through Staff Development
   THE JOURNAL OF STAFF DEVELOPMENT, Vol. 11, Summer, 1990, pp. 139-148.

Potter, Robert
   WRITING SENSE. New York: Globe Book Company, Inc., 1975.

Shipley, Joseph T.
   PLAYING WITH WORDS. Englewood Cliffs, N.J.: Prentice-Hall,
   Inc., 1975.

Simon, Sidney B., Robert C. Hawley, David D. Britton
    VALUES CLARIFICATION THROUGH WRITING. New York: Hart
    Publishing Company, 1973.

Slavin, Robert
    STUDENT TEAM LEARNING. Baltimore: Johns Hopkins University. 1988.

Smith, Frank
    ESSAYS INTO LITERACY. Portsmouth, NH: Heinemann, 1983.

    WRITING AND THE WRITER. New York: Holt, Rinehart and Winston,
    1982.

Traiger, Arthur and Leon Gersten
    SOLUTIONS TO YOUR WRITING PROBLEMS. Woodbury, N.Y.: Barron's
    Educational Series, Inc., 1980.

Tway, Eileen
    TIME FOR WRITING IN THE ELEMENTARY SCHOOL. Urbana, Ill.,
    National Council of Teachers of English, 1985.

Weaver, Constance E.
    GRAMMAR FOR TEACHERS. Urbana, Ill.: National Council of
    Teachers of English, 1981.

Weiss, M. Jerry (Editor)
    FROM WRITERS TO STUDENTS. Newark, Delaware: International
    Reading Association, 1979.

White, E.B.
    THE ELEMENTS OF STYLE. New York: The MacMillan Company, 1959.

Zavatskty, Bill and Ron Padgett
    THE WHOLE WORD CATALOGUE 2. New York: Teachers and Writers
    Collaborative, 1985.

Ziegler, Alan
    THE WRITING WORKSHOP. New York: Teachers and Writers
    Collaborative, 1981.

Zinsser, William
    ON WRITING WELL (second edition). New York: Harper Row, 1980.

Write Track™ Consulting Services
Diane Gess, Ed.D., Senior Consultant

I   The Concept of THE WRITE TRACK - A Developmental, Systematic Approach to Teaching Writing

   A. Genre-Specific
       All writing has defined structure - e.g. essay, fable, persuasive, descriptive--and must be taught/learned.
   B. Strategy-Based
       To become a writer, the student must have techniques for starting, continuing, and improving a piece of writing.
   C. Sequentially-Organized
       A successful writing program has a defined scope and sequence.
   D. Process-Oriented
       The writer must systematically move through defined steps to produce a well-written product.

II   Teaching Writing vs. Assigning Writing -- WRITE TRACK Sequences

   A. Where Do We Begin?
       September, October, November -- Specific lesson plans for writing - composing and beginning editing strategies.
   B. Where Are We Heading?
       More specific plans -- framing, combining and rearranging, outlining and blueprinting.
   C. What Has Been Taught and What Has Been Learned?
       After 35 weeks of instruction, students can draft, revise, and publish numerous genres -- Magic "Who", Three Reasons Why, Q.A.D.'s, Definition Mode, ABC Stories, Morphology, and more.

III   Writing as Unifier and Integrator

   A. Learning to Write Across the Curriculum
       Every subject can be written about and students must be taught the writing structures of each area.
   B. Writing to Learn About the Curriculum
       As we write about a subject, we learn more deeply about that subject.
   C. Writing for Thinking/Thinking for Writing
       Through the teaching of writing, students learn the higher level thinking skills of classifying, observing, hypothesizing, synthesizing, deciding, inferring, imagining, and more.

IV   Writing to Meet Curriculum Objectives -- WRITE TRACK Materials Provide Skills

   A. Writing and Reading -- A Merged Process
       Writers are readers. Writing helps students to comprehend and to use new vocabulary in a functional manner.
   B. Writing and Editing -- Revision, Not Correction
       Writers learn when and how to improve their writing; through writing, they learn layout, organizing, and the appropriate mechanical conventions.
   C. Grammar for Grammar or Grammar for Writing?
       Grammar for grammar means underlining and labeling; grammar for writing means transferring one's spoken language into one's written language.
   D. And What About Spelling?
       Writers spell and spell better than those who do not write.

V   Implementing and Assessing -- WRITE TRACK Training and Consulting

   A. Supporting the Teachers
       Successful implementation means building a cadre of experts within a district to mentor colleagues
   B. Supporting the Students
       Successful implementation means teaching students from kindergarten through high school using a combination of expert instruction and well-designed student materials.
   C. Raising Expectations/Building Self-Esteem
       The student who learns to write well has tangible evidence of her/his ability to communicate. Good writing brings praise to the writer -- "You must be smart -- you write so well".
   D. Implementing Authentic Performance Assessment
       Teachers and students learn to identify, create, and communicate appropriate exhibitions of learning.
   E. Providing Instruction to Students With a Wide Range of Learning Abilities and Styles
       A multi-strategy approach provides classroom management structures for the heterogeneous class.